62353   PR
                         6001
Replogle   U4Z78

Auden's poetry

Date Due

FE 9'71		
FE 5'73		
DEC 15 '75		
JUN 15 '78		
JUN 19 '86		

CHABOT
COLLEGE
LIBRARY

25555 Hesperian Boulevard
Hayward, California 94545

 PRINTED IN U.S.A.

Auden's Poetry

Auden's Poetry

by
Justin Replogle

University of Washington Press
Seattle and London

Grateful acknowledgment is extended to Random House, Inc.,
for use of quotations from W. H. Auden volumes of poetry
and prose. Copyright © 1934 through 1962 by W. H. Auden.

Acknowledgments

MY THANKS are due to the University of Wisconsin Graduate School for financial aid on several occasions, and to the following journals in which some of my ideas originally appeared: *Criticism, Bucknell Review, The Journal of English and Germanic Philology, PMLA,* and *Wisconsin Studies in Contemporary Literature.* I am greatly obliged to Auden's British publisher, Faber and Faber Ltd., for permission to quote from all the works published by them.

Preface

IF, AS Auden sometimes says, poetry is a kind of game, then criticism is talk about the game. Though the literary commentator who thinks of life as morally earnest may prefer more sober definitions, whether he favors aesthetic or ethical terminology, the critic's most perilous leap comes right at the beginning, at that first moment of choice when he decides what to talk *about*. The scrupulous reader will notice with guilty dismay that all his responses are somehow tied to those forbidden irrelevancies, his own peculiar past and singular temperament. Whatever guilty fondness he may secretly have for these, such personal reactions must be diligently disguised, somehow, in publicly acceptable discourse. Worse yet, the pleasant visceral flame kindled by all good poems, that is most of his "poetic experience," he must glumly admit. Again this is awkward. Somehow these untranslatable nonverbal responses must be wrestled into words, and the wide world of sensibility narrowed to the dimensions of language. Anything this reader says will be a compromise. As everybody knows, literary historians (and most writers with other titles) compromise by taking out of the poem something vaguely called its "subject," or "idea," its "theme," "content," or "intellectual matter." This is then treated as though it were The Poem. Properly manipulated this "content" can be turned into patterns of all sorts, giving ideological shape to an author's career, uncovering his intellectual paternity, his cultural affinities, and perhaps dozens of other things. This "thing taken out," critics agree, is not really the poem, but having said so almost all take it out anyway. I do this too.

But for the critic to stop talking after he takes this "content" out is probably worse than not talking at all. With the poem's "idea" sprawling naked before him, the reader is about as far from the poetic artifact as he will ever get. Still, a reader can learn something from this part taken out, both about the poem and about himself. If he responds similarly to both poem and extracted idea, for instance, he will know either that the idea plays an extraordinarily important role in the poem, or else that he is not reacting to the poem but only to some concept partly visible in it. For myself, comparisons of this sort suggest that in most English poetry the extractable idea plays only a small—often negligible—part in creating the total poetic effect. Then the trouble starts. What things *are* causing the effects? And if these are not "ideas" in some sense, how can they be talked about? Faced even with this elementary dilemma, any critic may understandably decide to look ingenuous and stick to the customary topics of conversation.

The more I read Auden, the more I believe that what his speakers *are* is more important than what they talk about, that what they show about themselves is more important than what they say. The two can be separated (for examination at least) since the personalities of Auden's speakers are determined less by what they talk *about* than by *how* they talk. To use less anthropomorphic terms, the message of Auden's *style* is more important than the message of his *content.* But how does one talk about the message of a poet's style? The thing conventionally known as "style" can, of course, be directly analyzed: the author's rhetorical devices, syntax, diction, and so forth. But the result will not be a statement about his "message." A better way is to assume that the poem is spoken by someone. If what the speaker talks *about* and *how* he talks create his personality, by describing this personality the critic will be saying something about the "meaning" of both style and subject matter. Once we know what kind of person he is, we can extract from the speaker's temperament whatever values, world visions, and philosophical systems we are interested in, if those are what we *are* interested in.

Since Auden's manner seems to me at least as important as his matter, I was tempted to write a book exclusively about his personae and style. But that seemed one-sided. His speakers do talk about ideas, and in any case the whole intellectual content of his poetry cannot be called entirely negligible—or even as negligible as that of many other poets. "Ideas" *are* more important in Auden's poetry (in the first twenty years of it at least) than they are in the poetry of, say, Yeats, Eliot, Pound, or Dylan Thomas. For one thing Auden is a highly conceptual poet by any standard of comparison. Whatever effects they produce, his poems are always made out of conceptual diction—out of "idea" words—even when the speaker's subject itself may not be an idea, and even when the poem's total message is not what the speaker talks *about*. And even that total message can often be described—if only roughly—in terms of some idea. In the end, then, I concluded that Auden's ideas could not be left out—even if they had been the things most talked about by other Auden commentators. Yet ideas could not be allowed to parade all by themselves. So I decided to write about Auden's poetry in three different ways, by describing it as a storehouse of ideas, as the dwelling place of speakers, and (in Auden's neat phrase) as a verbal contraption. Whatever the relative importance of each, none of these makes a satisfactory description by itself. But together they begin to describe the kind of thing the poetry is—and that I take to be the critic's job. Furthermore, they all help trace a pattern of development or growth, and this is something that should come out in any large-scale examination of a man's art. Any writer's total output can be considered a static object, the *oeuvre*—some sort of "whole" that exists without beginning, end, or movement—and there are times when such a consideration is useful. But of course the work will really have a history, and the most useful description usually is an account of it as a thing moving through time, in a state of Becoming rather than Being. Auden's poetry shows all the growth and change one would expect, and I try to show how his ideas, personae, and style move forward toward what I take to be his greatest achievement, the late comic poetry. The last chapter is devoted to that. In the comic poems, where Auden's ideas, personae, and style fit harmoniously together, I can treat his art as a whole thing.

Auden's texts create minor problems. I examine the poetry chronologically in the first two chapters, and would prefer to use his individual volumes, since *The Collected Poetry* appeared in mid-career for one thing, and furthermore displays a notorious organization designed to put as many obstacles as possible in the way of chronological readers such as I. Yet citing the earlier volumes would undoubtedly be an empty formality. Readers will be much more likely to have *The Collected Poetry*, and so wherever possible I refer to it. But I identify originally untitled poems by first lines, not by the often whimsical titles Auden stuck on later. First lines are less ephemeral than titles, and they are much more likely to show up in later collections. The volumes listed below are cited in the text (where I do not use first editions, the original publication date is in brackets).

P 1928	*Poems* (hand printed by Stephen Spender, 1928); Micro-film-Xerography reprint by University Microfilms, Ann Arbor, Michigan, 1965)
P	*Poems* (London: Faber and Faber, 1933 [revised from 1930 ed.])
O	*The Orators* (London: Faber and Faber, 1946 [revised from 1932 ed.])
DBS	*The Dog Beneath the Skin* (London: Faber and Faber, 1954 [1935])
F6 } *OF* }	*The Ascent of F.6* and *On the Frontier* (with Christopher Isherwood. London: Faber and Faber, 1958 [1936, 1938])
LS	*Look, Stranger!* (London: Faber and Faber, 1936)
LLB	"Letter to Lord Byron," in *Letters From Iceland* (with Louis MacNeice. London: Faber and Faber, 1937)
AT	*Another Time* (London: Faber and Faber, 1940)
CP	*The Collected Poetry of W. H. Auden* (New York: Random House, 1945)
AA	*The Age of Anxiety* (New York: Random House, 1947)
N	*Nones* (London: Faber and Faber, 1952 [1951])
SA	*The Shield of Achilles* (New York: Random House, 1955)
HC	*Homage to Clio* (New York: Random House, 1960)
DH	*The Dyer's Hand* (New York: Random House, 1962)
AH	*About the House* (New York: Random House, 1965)

Contents

Auden's Poetry

ONE

The Pattern of Ideas

I

THE PATTERN of Auden's ideas, though often talked about, has never been very clear. His earliest poetry was vigorous, energetic, and on the surface at least original, untraditional, and obscure. Readers could sense vast energies pouring forth without quite knowing what the commotion was about. Yet at first the energy itself seemed meaningful. To a young generation at odds with society, energy suggests rebellion. Coupled with gestures of random defiance, however indefinite, and disapproving speeches, however vague, it can become an identifying badge of the rebellious spirit. Exact ideological credentials need not be presented. Largely on the basis of such unspecific behavior, Auden began to emerge early in the 1930's as a spokesman for a dissatisfied generation. Just what he spoke for and against—or even about—was not always clear. The ideas in the earliest poetry were at best general, nearly always vague, and sometimes entirely incomprehensible. But the more blurred the poetry, the more easily could hopeful admirers see in it the message of their own desires, and one clear poetic certainty made this even easier. Nobody could fail to notice in the early poems that some sort of good and bad forces battled each other across the ruins of an unhealthy landscape. If these too were vague and general, the reader could the more easily find his own cause embattled there.

One of Auden's early admirers, Michael Roberts, thought Auden's cause was Communism. As early as 1933 he put the Marxist label on Auden and on a number of other young writers he had brought together in an anthology called *New Country*.[1] A year later Dylys Powell, in the

[1] Michael Roberts (comp.), *New Country* (London: The Hogarth Press, 1933).

3

first short study of these new authors, remarked that Auden's Marxism, whatever its substance, seemed generously intermixed with Freudian ingredients.[2] During the next twenty years this Freud-Marx mixture became a "truth" so firmly established by mere repetition that no one until Richard Hoggart bothered to examine its ingredients.[3] Today it is sometimes hard to reconstruct what Auden's earliest readers saw in his pages. In any case, since the thing perceived changes with the perceiver, Auden's *Poems* (1930) on publication day undoubtedly contained some things never to be seen again. But looking back from a different world, more than thirty-five years later, Auden readers will suspect that his early audience saw their own wishful image as much as anything. Today's reader will find no Marxism (however the word may be defined) in Auden's work before 1933, not even proletarian sympathies, aside from two ambiguous poems—both partial burlesques and one certainly more parody than anything else.[4] And the reader will have to search hard to find much more than a tincture of political Marxism any place in his poetry. The "Freudian" material is easier to identify, though it is almost always vague, nonsectarian, and often embedded in obscurities that can numb the hardiest source hunter. Still, if any intellectual climate contributes its airs to the bloom of Auden's earliest poetry (and such airs should not be overemphasized), that climate is psychological in some sense rather than political. Yet early readers can be excused for confusing the two, because in some ways they are very similar.

The good and bad forces in the early poetic landscape (1928–33) might be described as roughly equivalent to Freud's id and superego, or to analogous forces in other psychological theories. The forces themselves, of course, vary considerably in the level of their abstraction. The "bad" in one poem may be the nearly naked superego itself, or the whole middle- and upper-class British culture, or merely a personal enemy of Auden's,

[2] Dylys Powell, *Descent from Parnassus* (New York: Macmillan, 1934).

[3] Richard Hoggart, *Auden: An Introductory Essay* (London: Chatto and Windus, 1951). Hoggart first identified the nature of Auden's "Freudian" ingredients, an identification I agree with and am indebted to, though our paths lead in different directions from the common facts. About "Marxism" Hoggart said almost nothing.

[4] "Get there if you can and see the land you once were proud to own . . ." (*P*, p. 73) and "Brothers, who when the sirens roar . . ." (*LS*, p. 34). The latter was first printed as "A Communist to Others," *Twentieth Century*, IV (September, 1932), 7–8. Both are discussed later.

some sort of schoolmaster, or boys who bite their fingernails. Whatever their nature, these "enemies" became part of the allegorical texture of the early poems, so that even the vaguest concept could march living and breathing across a furnished plain to attack his opposite number from the other side. The virtue of allegory, of course, is to turn concepts into people and tangible objects. In allegory, for instance, the superego, that repository of conservative restrictions, will look like a man defending the cultural status quo. The id, a collection of explosive, unwashed, shaggy-headed energy, will gesticulate wildly like some social rebel threatening to blow up the Establishment. In short, put in the same allegory, id and superego will resemble middle-class men threatened by rough proletarian belligerents. The more vague and general the thinking, the more nonspecific the action and landscape, the more Freudian and Marxist allegory will look identical. The thinking in Auden's early poems is usually both vague and intermittent, and so is the allegory. As a result, while Auden's mind played over the dialectial drama of psychology, hopeful Marxist readers could see in his allegorical landscapes something similar to their own beliefs. And of course this similarity is not just an accident. In some ways Freud and Marx really are genuinely much alike, and this likeness reveals something important about the whole pattern of Auden's intellectual development.

Freud and Marx look alike only if the viewer stands off at a suitable distance. Up close they look very unlike, even like enemies, and in the 1930's many intellectuals looked at them from a very short distance. The names Freud and Marx became rallying cries for members of two warring camps engaged in intellectual battle. The Freudians held, roughly, that social change and individual health should start with the individual. Marxists favored starting with the environment.[5] Change of heart versus change of environment became one of the fierce ideological issues of the decade, and writers lined up behind one or the other slogan, or worried over how to reconcile the two. But, observed from two steps backward, these "opposites" begin to blur, and Freud and Marx come to resemble each other. Both habitually apprehend the world in much the same fashion—as a struggle between large, powerful, basically hostile and unlike forces. From this distance Marx's proletariat and bourgeoisie really

[5] See, for instance, Christopher Caudwell, *Studies in A Dying Culture* (London: John Lane, 1938) and C. Day Lewis, *A Hope for Poetry* (Oxford: Basil Blackwell, 1947), first published in 1934 and discussed later on.

do resemble Freud's id and superego. Marx seems to be describing, in society at large, something very like the forces Freud discovers in the individual. What we can see at this distance is the tradition of post-Hegelian Germanic thought showing through the individual features of two great practitioners. The battle between Freud and Marx (though based on genuine and perhaps important differences) is an internal battle between intellectual cousins, whose family resemblance—observed from a modest distance—looks more striking than anything else. Readers may have been mistaken in believing Auden's Freudian allegory was Marxist, but their mistake is understandable. And the reason for it helps explain Auden's later behavior, when he drifted from psychological to Marxist poetry, and still later wrote Christian works indebted to Kierkegaard. Freud, Marx, and Kierkegaard all belong to the same philosophical tradition, and Auden's entire intellectual development, in a general way, takes place within it—within the tradition of post-Hegelian Germanic thought. When he began fitfully to make poems under the influence of vague Germanic psychology, Auden entered an intellectual stream he would drift down always. Along its banks camped all those feuding Germanic cousins. The feuds themselves are complex, and if the viewer moves a bit old enemies seem friends, alliances shift, and issues differ. At one point Marx, Engels and Kierkegaard appear to stand together in battle against Hegel, their intellectual father. But looked at from another angle, the grouping changes. Marx and Engels join Freud and Nietzsche to attack their Christian relatives, while in another action Marx and Freud part in the quarrel between the community-minded advocates and their cousins who stay home to explore the individual psyche.

For the partisans at hand-to-hand combat in the field, these feuds seem the whole world, their nature clear, their issues important, and their leaders truth bearers worth defending. But as the observer moves farther off, and hostile contestants begin to look identical, their wars seem nothing more than a family quarrel. And at some distance all those family brawlers appear to stand shoulder to shoulder against other large enemy clans spread out across the intellectual landscape. As Auden floated down the Germanic intellectual stream, he stopped for varying periods of time at the encampments of feuding cousins. To battling partisans, his each move seemed irrational, even treasonous. Sometimes, outraged, they attacked him and set to work to uncover the baffling reasons for such capricious and unintelligible behavior. His move from

"Freud" to "Marx," though upsetting, was the most understandable, since many intellectuals, attracted to both, had gone back and forth from one to the other, and had even tried to effect a merger between the two. But Auden's sudden religious leap about 1940—condemned by both "Freudians" and "Marxists"—seemed incredible. Even his friend Stephen Spender thought this an incomprehensible switch and puzzled over it in several articles.[6] Admirers became ex-admirers, and one of these, Randall Jarrell, believing such behavior impossible for a man governed by rational faculties, sought an explanation for it down among the recesses of Auden's irrational unconscious.[7] And certainly to those in the middle of the family feud Auden's intellectual changes did appear genuinely large, even abrupt and contradictory. But what looks up close like a series of gaps and abysses, from a short distance back appears to be a smooth unbroken line. In this chapter I try to move back far enough to see that line and yet close enough to see some of the gaps and abysses too—and what is between them.

At the beginning two precautions must be mentioned. First, to trace such an intellectual pattern will initially overemphasize it, simply because other poetic matters will be ignored even when they are more important. Poems with little ideological interest will be skipped over, and much that is only implicit will swell to undue importance merely by being made explicit. Second, and vastly complicating everything, the early Auden is highly inconsistent. Sometimes he even reverses himself completely by mocking and burlesquing his own message. To ignore all these things entirely would create a false picture of his work. Yet in this section they will be mostly ignored. Succeeding chapters, each with the limitations of its own methods, must be relied on to correct the distortions of this one, and all of them finally to coalesce into a single more accurate description.

II

The year 1928 might be called the birth date of Auden's intellectual self, a year heralded by signs of what was to come. That year Auden left Oxford for Germany. In 1965, looking back on the pattern of his life, he recalled, "The first personal choice I can remember making was my

[6] See, for instance, Stephen Spender, "W. H. Auden and His Poetry," *Atlantic Monthly* (July, 1953), pp. 74–79.

[7] Randall Jarrell, "Freud to Paul: The Stages of Auden's Ideology," *Partisan Review* (Fall, 1945), pp. 437–57.

decision, when my father offered me a year abroad after I had gone down from Oxford, to spend it in Berlin." [8] Isherwood and others report that Auden's clinical interest in human behavior owed something to early adolescent—and salacious—glances into his father's medical books.[9] But Berlin clearly started his genuine psychological thinking. He met there among others, Isherwood tells us, "loony Layard," a follower of the controversial educator Homer Lane, and soon afterward became a some-what extravagant and unbearable amateur diagnostician.[10] Persuaded that all illness had psychological origins, he declared that lying had caused Isherwood's tonsilitis, that stifling creativity produced cancer, and that obstinacy might bring on rheumatism.[11] Just how much of this was intentional burlesque, horseplay, and parody is not entirely clear—some obviously was. Still, Auden put the very same psychosomatic stuff into an exceedingly solemn poem:

> Sir, no man's enemy, forgiving all
> But will its negative inversion, be prodigal:
> Send to us power and light, a sovereign touch
> Curing the intolerable neural itch,
> The exhaustion of weaning, the liar's quinsy,
> And the distortions of ingrown virginity.
>
> (*CP*, p. 110)

Homer Lane and Layard taught Auden (so Isherwood reports) that man's greatest sin was "disobedience to the inner law of our own nature." "Crime" and "disease" followed such sinful behavior. Both men stressed the evil of letting the mind repress the body. Instincts were natively "healthy," they believed, and in the "pure in heart" they flourished more or less untrammeled by crippling interference from intellect or society. By

---

[8] W. H. Auden, "As It Seemed to Us," *The New Yorker* (April 3, 1965), p. 190.

[9] See Christopher Isherwood, *Lions and Shadows* (London: The Hogarth Press, 1938), pp. 181–82.

[10] *Ibid.*, pp. 299–306. "Loony Layard" is Auden's epithet (*O*, p. 84). Isherwood calls him "Barnard." He is John Layard, described as an English disciple of Jung by J. A. C. Brown, *Freud and the Post-Freudians* (Baltimore: Penguin Books, 1961), p. 50. See also Monroe K. Spears, *The Poetry of W. H. Auden* (New York: Oxford University Press, 1963), p. 62. Auden mentions Layard in several places: "I met a chap called Layard and he fed / New doctrines into my receptive head" (*LLB*, p. 210).

[11] Isherwood, *Lions and Shadows*, pp. 302–3.

implication the mind seemed almost a sinister force, polluting the holy wells of the body and turning joyous natural man into an inhibited creature with tics. Born free, the instincts lay everywhere in chains in modern society, and illness, both cultural and personal, followed, with all such malignant symptoms lumped collectively under the heading of death wish.[12]

The Lane-Layard ideas sound much like those of D. H. Lawrence ("Part came from Lane, and part from D. H. Lawrence," *LLB,* p. 210) —at least of Lawrence the theoretician and preacher—and Lawrence too had an important place in Auden's early pantheon of healers ("Lawrence, Blake and Homer Lane, once healers in our English land," *P,* p. 75). Among Auden's images of gaiters, gamekeepers, mines, mountains, crowing cocks, wheel chairs, and so on, one can suspect a ready borrowing even of Lawrence's almost symbolic stage properties. But it was Lawrentian theory that apparently impressed Auden most (he has remained all his life uninterested in Lawrence's major artistic achievements).[13] Lines from *Psychoanalysis and the Unconscious,* for instance, appear in one early poem, and punning references to *Fantasia of the Unconscious* in another.[14] Like Lane, Lawrence believed in the psychosomatic nature of most illness, and taught (part of the time, at least) that in our perversely mental culture, modern man's instincts had atrophied. Since the mind dominated everything, death and sickness spread everywhere. The cure for all this lay within the individual. He must restore the balance between mind and body by freeing the impounded instincts, especially those most severely curbed, the sexual instincts, and live once more from solar plexus and lumbar ganglion as well as from the head. If such statements come

---

[12] *Ibid.,* pp. 300–7.

[13] In *The Dyer's Hand* Auden says explicitly what the poems show implicitly —that as a young man he read Lawrence for his message, and found it particularly in "his 'think' books like *Fantasia on {sic} the Unconscious,*" p. 278.

[14] In *Psychoanalysis and the Unconscious* (New York: Compass Books, 1960), Lawrence wrote, "The mind is the dead end of life" (p. 47). Ideas are "thrown off from life, as leaves are shed . . . , as feathers fall from a bird. Ideas are the dry, unliving insentient plumage . . ." (p. 46). Auden compressed this: "What's in your mind, my dove, my coney; / Do thoughts grow like feathers, the dead end of life . . ." (*CP,* p. 239). "It's no use raising a shout . . ." plays with Lawrence's notion of the lumbar ganglion and related matters from *Fantasia of the Unconscious:* "In my spine there was a base; / . . . But they've severed all the wires . . ." (*P,* p. 52).

close to a caricature of Lawrence the novelist, a marvelously complex, endlessly inconsistent, and very great artist, he did at times nevertheless preach just such simplistic doctrines, particularly in expository writings. At any rate these are the ideas that most interested the early Auden.

But on the matter of psychosomatic illness neither Lane-Layard nor Lawrence could match Georg Groddeck, the fantastic Teutonic psychologist understandably fascinating to the writer whose childhood brain had been "laden, / With deeds of Thor and Loki" (*LLB,* p. 205). Groddeck's sick patients convinced him not just that physical illness had a psychological source, but that trauma and disease were in effect the acts of some evolutionary world spirit groping for greater self-realization. This teleological force, called the It, "lived" through individuals, and their somatic anomalies were the It's experimental efforts to spiral upward to self-fulfillment. "Illness has a purpose," Groddeck claimed, "to resolve the conflict [in the individual], to repress it, or to prevent what is already repressed from entering consciousness." So from Groddeck too Auden could learn the habit of attributing physical symptoms to nonphysical sources. "Whoever breaks an arm," Groddeck said, "has either sinned or wished to commit a sin with that arm. . . ." [15] Blind as it is, Groddeck's It bumbles along making preposterous blunders—some of them quite disastrous for the individual inhabited by this eager but confused force. The healer's job, then, is to help the It give birth to evolutionary progress by diverting its experimental gropings into fruitful channels. Though a basically healthful force, the It, floundering in darkness, can destroy individual or even species, by accident. Something of a Don Quixote, the It benefits from the services of a harried but indispensible psychological Sancho Panza, who can help save it from itself. These comic overtones occurred to Groddeck too, and he anticipates jocular critics by being the first to laugh at his own theoretical construction. In *The Book of the It* his mixture of medicine and familiar Germanic philosophy appears in a series of comic letters, whose author mocks himself and jokes in a manner that surely must have appealed to Auden. Groddeck's self-mocking discourse, in fact, is somewhat like Kierkegaard's, and the comedy of these two Germanic dialecticians surely plays its part in attracting a poet addicted throughout his life to horseplay and burlesque, who would ultimately

[15] Georg Groddeck, *The Book of the It* (New York and Washington: Nervous and Mental Disease Publishing Co., 1928), p. 91.

make comic self-mockery his habitual manner. Even in the solemn 1930's Auden could not help but joke about Groddeck: "I can't think what my It had on It's mind, / To give me flat feet and a big behind" (*LLB*, p. 202). But Groddeck's dialectical psychology went into his sober poetic landscapes nevertheless.

Freud borrowed Groddeck's term "It" for his own theories, turning It into id, just as he borrowed much from other German predecessors.[16] And of course, in a general way all the psychological theories described so far resemble Freud's. In each, human behavior arises from a dialectical struggle between some primordial unstructured energy and an opposing force that restricts, orders, channels, or represses it. Whether different theories call this energy It, id, or instinct makes little difference. The energy is much the same in each, and so are its enemies, whether identified as superego, rational mind, or the conservative forces of the cultural status quo. Each theory also argues that in modern times this dialectical contest has been one-sided, that the once rampant might of instinctive energy now staggers beneath the growing strength of its opponent. And each theory further agrees on the cultural effect of this. When native human drives are repressed, sickness and decadence follow—various in form and so widespread in society they might well be called, after Freud, symptoms of a general death wish. In Freud's original formulation, the term was "death instinct," a force seeking to reduce life once more to the inorganic state from which it had emerged. The death instinct, Freud said, asserts itself when the id—a wild and destructive force—is turned from its natural outward direction by various inhibitions. Turning inward it destroys the self.[17]

Students of Freud and Lawrence may object that I have blurred important distinctions by oversimplifying, and no doubt I have. There are family feuds among all these psychologists. Lawrence wrote *Psychoanalysis and the Unconscious,* for instance, explicitly to attack Freud. But his quarrel was over details: over the definition and source of the unconscious. Both men agreed on its existence, importance, and (in part) function. Again, if the theorists are all observed from a few paces back, they appear more similar than dissimilar. And this is not an arbitrary vantage point, because in his poetry Auden looked at them from this distance too. He ignored the

[16] The borrowing is reported in Brown, *Freud and the Post-Freudians*, p. 28.
[17] See Sigmund Freud, *New Introductory Lectures on Psycho-analysis* (New York: W. W. Norton, 1933), pp. 144–47.

differences and the details of each man's position.[18] What shows in the poetry is simply a general habit of psychological thinking going on. The way speakers talk, the things they say, the allegorical framework they often exist in—all have a psychological cast that comes from an artist who at the moment of writing tended to apprehend the world psychologically. Not that a psychological message is always explicit, or even intentionally implicit. Much is vague, chaotic, obscure, inconsistent. Auden is learning to write poetry, and in the process any message is often secondary to other matters, to problems of persona, diction, and voice, for instance. But the maker of these early poems is a "psychological maker," immersed in a psychological way of looking at things that can be described as an amalgam of the similarities in those sources mentioned so far. Society and individuals are sick because men and their culture have repressed vital human forces. The superego has nearly defeated the id. Cure demands a change of heart, a change in the individual. The power of the superego must be overthrown and the languishing id released from its fetters. This is the most obvious message of Auden's early poetry—insofar as it has any. This is the "Freudian" climate of the work from about 1928 to 1933. If examined in detail, the sources cited are obviously not all "Freudian," or even German. But German psychology is the unacknowledged spiritual home of Lawrence the psychological analyst, and the acknowledged intellectual home of everyone else. From a distance they all resemble Freud, and we see them from this distance in Auden's poetry.

Hegel's progeny, rebellious or otherwise, sucked in teleology with their first breath, and once it lodged in their systems few could get it out. The idea that history moves purposefully upward in a continuous spiral of dialectical thesis and antithesis can be detected not only in the perceptual apparatus of writers like Marx, Engels, and Groddeck, but in many other intellectuals perhaps unaware of their philosophical ancestry. According to Isherwood, the teleological view of history Auden heard about from Lane and Layard taught that human life was a record of dialectical opposition between mind and body. First one would get the upper hand, then the other. Since in general the mind was bad and the body good,

---

[18] There are obviously others who contributed to Auden's psychological thinking, but these seem most important—or at least most characteristic. Auden mentions Klages and Prinzhorn in "The Good Life," *Christianity and the Social Revolution,* ed. John Lewis *et al.* (New York: Charles Scribner's Sons, 1936), pp. 37, 45–46.

evolution displayed a series of leaps from bad to good. When the usurping intellect gained nearly universal power, like Marx's capitalists it would destroy itself by internal contradiction, in this case with physical and psychological illness. "If the conscious mind were really the controlling factor [in man] . . . the world would become bedlam in a few generations, and the race automatically die out. So diseases and neurosis come to kill off the offenders or bring them to their senses." [19] In this scheme the death wish is nothing more than a teleological life force seen at close range. For the sick individual trapped in a sick culture, evolution appears destructive. It demands his death, and he will experience it as a death wish. But seen from afar, evolution can be properly identified as a life force, restoring social health by destroying decadence. Lawrence described history in just this way: in its beginning every culture draws strength from the instinctual sources of somatic energy, but eventually each declines as society retreats from these wellsprings of life. Each time this happens, he wrote, "this Life that we have shut out from our living, must in the end turn against us and rend us." At this point "there is only one thing left to do. We have to struggle down to the heart of things, where the everlasting flame is, and kindle ourselves another beam of light. . . . We have to germinate inside us . . . a new germ. . . ." Each germ of "Life-knowledge will . . . in the end die again. . . . It is the cycle of all things created. . . ." [20]

Just such a notion of dialectical evolution lies behind many early Auden poems. In each, the speaker clearly lives somewhere near the end of a declining cycle. With their healthy instincts everywhere stifled, men wallow in sickness of all sorts. For them, the life force, busy cleansing and purging, is a death force. The speaker in "Look there! The sunk road winding . . ." compares the present with a healthier past and wonders at what point on the curve of evolutionary decline he now stands:

> Along what crooked route
> By hedgehog's gradual foot
> Or fish's fathom.
> (*CP*, p. 78)

[19] Isherwood *Lions and Shadows*, pp. 300–1.
[20] D. H. Lawrence, *Assorted Articles* (London: Martin Secker, 1930), pp. 214–15. In the novels this evolutionary idea shows most clearly in *The Plumed Serpent* and *Women in Love*.

In the healthy past, the speaker explains in "On Sunday walks . . . ," men feared only genuine threats from an unsubdued external environment ("fever and bad-luck"). Now fears are internal and neurotic, symptoms of the prevailing death wish:

> A need for charms
> For certain words
> At certain fords.
> (*CP,* p. 93)

Ingenious at disguises, the death force appears in numerous and often deceptive forms. As master of selective breeding, it kills (metaphorically at least) in "Under boughs between our tentative endearments how should we hear . . ." by proliferating recessive genes, passed from one generation to the next. The sick recipients, bewildered, can only

> . . . wonder at the well-shaped heads
> Conforming every day more closely to the best in albums:
> > Fathers in sons may track
> > Their voices trick.
> > (*CP,* p. 148)

Sometimes the teleological force shows itself almost directly, as it does in "Consider this and in our time. . . ." The sick know it as a "supreme Antagonist," a killer of unhealthy cultures: "Your comments on the highborn mining-captains, / Found they no answer, made them wish to die . . ." (*CP,* p. 27). The fate of these early English mining captains turned, apparently, on their response to some question put to them by the life force. The poem never explains what this was, but it shows up again in "Taller today, we remember similar evenings. . . ." Another captain ("Captain Ferguson") disappears amid imagery of collapse and decline, brought on by "the Adversary" who "put too easy questions / On lonely roads" (*CP,* p. 113).

These vague allusions to fateful questions and answers become clearer in "To ask the hard question is simple . . . ," where the Adversary and the Antagonist lose their personification and become merely evolution. Confused though it is, this poem shows clearly enough that evolution poses a "question" to which modern men have forgotten the answer ("But the answer / Is hard and hard to remember," *CP,* p. 141). Having forgotten how to live enriched by human instincts ("What has been dark and rich and warm all over"), men turn sick and seek neurotic escapes in idealism ("windy skies"), self-destruction (the "water" of an earlier evolutionary stage), and fawning surrender to authority ("Obedience for a master," *CP*, p. 142). "It was Easter as I walked in the public gardens . . ." shows just how this large historical drama looks up close, at the level of individual psychology. Born into a culture already dominated by superego, each child is plagued by desires he must repress and beset by conflicts whose existence is everywhere denied. In such an unhealthy environment, outgoing instincts become inverted in the manner Freud described. What should have been love for another becomes love of death:

> Body reminds in him to loving,
>
> . . . .
> But takes no part and is unloving
> But loving death.
>   (*CP*, p. 65)

In short, having got a wrong answer to the question it poses, the evolutionary force will destroy this mistaken culture with sickness. On the next dialectical leap forward it will create a society whose members can "remember / The question and the answer" and "recover / What has been dark and rich and warm all over" (*CP*, p. 142). Both destroyer and creator, the teleological force plays a dual role, and on one occasion it speaks directly about its job and reminisces about past efforts. Like "Lizards" who "Could not control the temperature of blood," today's equally unsatisfactory invention, repressed modern men, those "Holders of one position, wrong for years," must die. "Do not imagine you can abdicate," the life force warns a fleeing neurotic, "Before you reach the frontier you are caught; / Others have tried it and will try again" (*CP*, pp. 109, 110).

History marches dialectically forward guided by a psychological life force. This idea shows through these early poems, but less clearly than my description would suggest. Much of Auden's psychological musing is going on behind or outside the poems and drifts into them in varying amounts, often in enigmatic fragments or obscure allusions. Terse commands ("Leave for Cape Wrath tonight," *CP*, p. 44) and curious bits of information ("His favourite colour as blue / Colour of distant bells / And boys' overalls," *CP*, p. 178) have the authority of meaning without much of its substance. Delivered by the grave knowing voice of one of Auden's clinical speakers, lines often have the certainty only of his solemn tone. Since such assured speech ordinarily accompanies clear meanings, readers may nod their heads affirmatively, scarcely noticing that certainty of tone and of meaning often part company here. The voice most high, filled with diagnostic precision and epigrammatic assurance, suggests that here is a man who knows what he is talking about. In this golden haze the youthful Auden sometimes strode among his early public like a splendid oracle, disapproving of what he saw, diagnosing illness, commanding a change—and all with such an authoritative voice that his public could often hear in it the certainty of a leader and believe the voice spoke about their own beliefs and programs. What the voice actually said, though, was far from clear. Ideas were often vague, allusions private, references mysterious; and both ideas and meaning itself slip in and out of poems as though Auden's attention were often on something else. In fact, it often was. While his early public longed to turn him into a prophet and political leader, he struggled with other problems: of diction, usage levels, rhythm, and related matters. In short, he struggled to find a suitable poetic voice. The strangest thing of all is that his early audience, so eager to make him into an orphic counselor, seldom noticed that the commanding exterior of their pontifical soothsayer sometimes hid a clown, pulling the strings and laughing at his performance.

III

Auden wrote in 1965,

Between the ages of six and twelve, I spent a great many of my waking hours in the construction and elaboration of a private sacred world, the basic elements of which were a landscape, northern and limestone, and an industry, lead mining. In constructing it, fantasy had to submit to two rules. In deciding what objects were to be included, I was free to select this and reject that, on condition that both were real objects. . . . It is no doubt psychologically significant that my sacred world contained no human beings.[21]

At about the same time two slightly older boys, Christopher Isherwood and his closest friend, Edward Upward, whiled away odd hours at Gresham's School, Holt, fashioning a different sort of private myth. Theirs (later called Mortmere) had some literary pretensions. Part was written down, but most remained oral, a protective aura of shared meaning and private fantasy encircling two schoolboys. Outside it were the "others."

[21] Auden, "As It Seemed to Us," pp. 169–70.

Inside was home. Auden came up to Gresham's School a few years later but merited scarcely a glance from the older Mortmere plotters, who knew him only as a precocious pasty faced boy with an unusual knowledge of psychological matters and sex, gleaned from his father's medical library. When Isherwood and Upward moved to Cambridge, Mortmere went too and flourished. Its world had now hardened allegorically into two sides—their side and the "enemy side," a mixture of ideas, habits, people, gestures, and whatever seemed hostile to their schoolboy conception of the good life. The written Mortmere grew into something that might have been invented by a dialectical Ronald Firbank. The two sides plotted against each other in a detailed landscape of joking and odd melodrama.[22] In its daily unwritten form the myth still carried over into the private language of these long-time friends. "Our conversation," Isherwood reports, "would have been hardly intelligible to anyone who had happened to overhear it; it was a rigmarole of private slang, deliberate misquotation, bad puns, bits of parody and preparatory school smut. . . ." All this was delivered in a "semi-telepathic" manner. Elaborate jokes could be conveyed by the "faintest hint." [23]

Auden went up to Oxford in 1925 as a science exhibitioner but switched almost immediately to literature. Enthralled by the voice of J. R. R. Tolkien declaiming *Beowulf*, enhanced by the resonance of his own Icelandic ancestry, he began reading Old English poetry and Norse sagas.[24] Then at Christmas of the first year, he met by chance his old schoolmate Isherwood, by this time expelled from Cambridge for writing Mortmere-like answers on his final examinations. The two congenital mythmakers, now both aspiring writers, became close friends. In the summer of 1926, vacationing together on the Isle of Wight, they fashioned a joint myth in the midst of much private joking, horseplay, and general hilarity. Onto their common schoolboy root, Auden grafted a strange spur from his new interest, northern heroic literature. The two

[22] Upward's novel, *Journey to the Border* (London: The Hogarth Press, 1938), shows much of this, but his story "The Railway Accident," *New Directions 11* (New York, 1946), may be its purest flowering. (Upward published this under the pseudonym Allen Chalmers, the name Isherwood used for him in *Lions and Shadows.*) *Lions and Shadows* gives examples of the original invention itself. See pp. 103–14.

[23] Isherwood, *Lions and Shadows*, p. 65.

[24] Mentioned in "Making, Knowing and Judging" (*DH*, pp. 41–42) and other places. Auden has been a lifelong admirer of Tolkien.

traditions had something in common, both writers noticed: a fondness for practical jokes, riddles, puns, understatement, and—obviously—melodrama. But the comic incongruity of putting bare-kneed British schoolboys in the land of *Beowulf* probably appealed most to these literary pranksters. "In time the school-saga world became for us a kind of Mortmere," Isherwood wrote, "a Mortmere founded upon our preparatory-school lives. . . ." [25] Auden refers to the myth and that first Isle of Wight vacation in a 1935 poem to Isherwood:

> Our hopes were set still on the spies' career,
> Prizing the glasses and the old felt hat,
>
> . . . .
>
> . . . many wore wigs,
> The coastguard signalled messages of love,
> The enemy were sighted from the norman tower.
>
> (*LS*, p. 64)

Meanwhile Upward had not disappeared entirely from the Mortmere scene. Temporarily tutoring in Cornwall, he kept in close touch with Isherwood. Soon another writer entered the circle, C. Day Lewis, who had come up to Oxford in 1923. Auden first met Day Lewis in the fall or winter of 1926. By the next summer they had become close friends, and they continued to see each other often during the following year when Day Lewis taught at Summer Fields School in Oxford.[26] Day Lewis' closest friend at Oxford was Rex Warner, then a beginning writer at work on his first novel. When Stephen Spender arrived in 1927 and timidly approached Auden in his forbidding Oxford rooms, he found that all these writers had been dubbed "The Gang" by Auden, who had apparently half-transformed them into allegorical figures in his private myth.[27] This Gang, with Spender a timorous latecomer, became the "Auden group," what journalists and editors later tried to make into a coherent "movement," representing the literary and political hopes of the 1930's generation.

All six writers certainly knew about the private Mortmere world that

[25] Isherwood, *Lions and Shadows,* pp. 192–93.

[26] See C. Day Lewis, *The Buried Day* (London: Chatto and Windus, 1960), pp. 176–80.

[27] See Stephen Spender, *World Within World* (London: Hamish Hamilton, 1951), pp. 51–63.

Auden, Isherwood, and Upward created around their personal relationship. There is good evidence that all except possibly Spender became part of it, and there is no doubt that the original Mortmere trio grew even closer during the next few years. Isherwood had followed Auden to Berlin, and shortly afterward Auden and Upward shared teaching duties at a Scottish school in Helensburgh. Warner was not so closely involved with these three, apparently, but he was certainly a friend, and in a long joking poem to him Auden casually refers to Reynard Moxon, a Mortmere character (*O,* p. 100).[28] Warner apparently knew the Mortmere saga well. But whatever their exact relationship to Mortmere and to one another, during the next few years Auden, Day Lewis, Warner, and Upward wrote stories, poems, novels, and plays whose common mythical contents resembled a Mortmere turned respectable. Whether Warner and Day Lewis helped fashion this myth or simply borrowed it from Auden and the rest is of no concern here. (Auden's first myth work, "Paid on Both Sides," is dedicated to Day Lewis.) The point is that the myth's appearance in the work of one author sheds some light on what the others make of it. And though the light falling among the obscurities of Auden's early poetry may be feeble it is welcome—even if we can never see very far in the dimness.

The extent of Auden's early psychological theme cannot be understood without recognizing how much of it appears fully or partly embedded in this myth. When Auden's mind pored over his psychological matter, his congenital mythmaking self habitually turned it into allegorical drama. The psychological matter scarcely resisted such treatment, of course, since by itself dialectical psychology came equipped with good and bad forces perpetually struggling for control of a somatic kingdom—or even for society at large. The whole psychological dialectic could easily be combined with the ready-made dialectical world of Mortmere or the Gang myth, with its spies, shootings, deserted mines, and so on. Auden simply added the superego to the pet peeves, obnoxious schoolboys, eccentric masters, dying saga heroes, and intellectual anathema that made up the "enemy" in the Auden-Isherwood private world. The id went to the good side, where it joined a gallant band of Auden's personal friends, approved ideas, psychological healers, and a few right-thinking intellectuals and special eccentrics. "Some say that handsome raider still at large, / A terror

---

[28] See Isherwood, *Lions and Shadows,* p. 104 and elsewhere.

to the Marches, in truth is love . . . ," Auden wrote in a very early poem
(*P 1928,* p. 35).

Much of Auden's earliest poetry, then, resembles a psychological Mortmere made unusually somber by the sonorous pronouncements and solemn high tones of his grave speakers. But just as the psychology floats in
and out of the poetry, half-formed and obscure, so does the mythmaking.
The best way to describe the presence of both is to say that the early
poems look like the product of a man who had, *outside* the poetry, both a
ready-made myth and a collection of psychological ideas. Poems do not
show us either one whole. Many do not contain within themselves even
enough information to make either ideas or myth intelligible or self-sus-
taining. If we know about doctrine and myth beforehand, these poems
become fairly meaningful. If we do not, many remain obscure or baffling,
or contain meaning that is indiscriminately general. Auden's friends knew
about both psychological doctrine and myth, and the often repeated guess
may be true—that at first Auden wrote mainly for them. At least this
would explain quite a bit about why the poetry looks as it does. Friends
needed no further explanations. They knew what lay outside the poetry.
Yet knowledge about friends and myth is not the secret key to all the
doors. It does not explain all the peculiar comedy and burlesque, for
instance, though it may have helped it along. When Auden draped his
speakers with the sober robes of pontifical language, he undoubtedly laid
an oddly solemn veneer over a myth made out of a good many private
jokes. Sometimes the jokes show through, and the pontifical language
keeps turning into burlesque. Yet the myth is certainly not responsible for
all the comedy. Part of the time Auden is genuinely laughing at himself.
But analysis of these extraordinary happenings must be left for a later
chapter.

The Gang myth takes literary form mainly in Auden's *Poems* (printed
with overlapping but different contents in 1928, 1930, and 1933),
The Orators (1932), and *The Dance of Death* (1933); in Day Lewis'
The Magnetic Mountain (and a few short poems); in Rex Warner's *The
Wild Goose Chase;* and in Edward Upward's *Journey to the Border.* If
the literary archaeologist set out to reconstruct it from bits and pieces dug
out of this literature, it would go something like this: In the world of the
Gang myth, a border or frontier separates the healthy from the sick.
Conflict between these enemies gives the myth nearly all its action and
subject matter for characters to talk about. The main figures most often

live on the wrong side of the frontier, where they struggle externally with the enemy, or internally with the attractions of both sides, or suffer the baffling multiplicity of torments allotted to the sick. Some hope to make it across the border to health. These travelers are always members of the younger generation, sometimes a youngest or third son (Auden, like the winner of many a fairy tale quest, is both a third and youngest son). In Auden's work a band of right-thinking disciples generally accompanies the young quester towards the healthy land. During and after the trip, temptations and importunities from the sick culture assail everybody. If he gets to the border, the traveler may still collapse, too frightened to take the leap, or he may finally succumb to the sweet decay of his familiar home soil. Even if he jumps across, he may still turn unaccountably sick beyond the border, incompletely cured of his native maladies. In Auden's work whole bands of pilgrims languish and sink in exile, surprised and bewildered by the absence of miraculous cures they expected to find beyond the frontier. Types of travel play their part in the myth too. Auden's heroes often go by rail, as do those in Day Lewis' *The Magnetic Mountain.* Sometimes travelers sail to the border by ship. The three questers in Warner's *The Wild Goose Chase* ride motorbikes, and bicycles also appear in *The Magnetic Mountain.* Special significance also rubs off on other features of travel. Ships, engines, railheads, junctions, harbors, coastguardsmen—all show up in the literature carrying some kind of allegorical import because of their connection with borders and the journey to them. Once across the border the exiled gang prefer to settle in mountains. From this height they plan attacks on the unregenerate, who generally live in valleys. But their spartan surroundings guarantee nothing. Auden's mountain bands generally fall apart before long, as they notice with surprised horror the reappearance of old diseases. There are heights other than mountains too. Airmen figure importantly in Auden and Warner, and most flying creatures—especially geese, hawks, kestrels, and gulls—have some special significance. And there is a good deal of additional allegorical furniture. Woods, gamekeepers, gaiters, farms, flowers, tunnels, mines, borings, glaciers, islands, power lines, boots, overalls, comic names—all have some sort of special associations, not always very clear, and appear not only in Auden but in Warner, Day Lewis, and Upward as well.

All these fixtures provided each author with a very general ready-made dialectical landscape of warring good and bad forces and provided a generous amount of detail that carried special, if rather loose, meaning from their private world of intellectual interests, prejudices, private jokes, and so on. By the time Upward had reworked Mortmere material into his first novel, *Journey to the Border,* he had turned Communist, and across his mythical landscape a hero journeys from bourgeois hallucination to the frontier of Marxist reality.[29] Warner's *The Wild Goose Chase* (by far the most detailed rendering of the myth) and Day Lewis' *The Magnetic Mountain* combine Marx with Freud—or, more accurately, political with psychological dialectics. (In *The Wild Goose Chase* three sons cross the border, and after detailed allegorical adventures the third and youngest achieves success.) [30] Auden and Warner are both named in Day Lewis' allegorical work. Along with others they journey by rail toward the generative mountains beyond the border.

Auden put a good share of his poetic message into this myth, and since his myth work appears earlier than that of his friends, its message is psychological, Freudian rather than Marxist. By the time they and he turned their thoughts to political matters, Auden had almost completely dropped the myth from his work, and along with it most of his early diction, rhythms, and poetic voice as well. (His plays are major exceptions. Apparently Auden and Isherwood could never work together without revitalizing some of the old schoolboy material.) There is nothing particularly systematic or uniform about Auden's use of myth material. The grand design of its structure never appears in a single work where the reader can survey the whole landscape and get his bearings (except possibly in *The Ascent of F.6,* but there, where the myth structure is most clear, its meaning has changed.) But it is not essential for the reader to know about the myth at all. He can make some sense out of most poems without ever having heard of such a thing, though he can make more sense out of many if he does know about it.

Auden uses the myth in several ways—or rather the myth floats in and out of the poetry in several ways. Sometimes entire poems are set inside the world of the myth itself. Others simply draw on it for illustrations or

[29] According to Spender, Upward joined the Communist party in 1932. See *World Within World,* p. 132. Isherwood remarked in 1938 that Upward could not seem to free his adult imagination from the early Mortmere fascination (*Lions and Shadows,* p. 274).

[30] Portions of Warner's later novels, *The Professor* and *The Aeorodrome,* show traces of the old myth too, even though Warner's ideology changes.

incidental imagery. "Paid on Both Sides" is of course the obvious example of a work set within the myth world, though this rather clumsy first effort is as much straight Mortmere as psychological allegory. Other works, if shorter, have more psychological content. "Control of the passes was, he saw, the key . . ." (*CP*, p. 29) is one of these; "Who will endure . . ." (*CP*, p. 176) another; and there are others: "O what is that sound which so thrills the ear . . ." (*CP*, p. 222) and large sections of *The Orators*. In these we are inside the myth world, looking around. No commentator from outside tells us what we are looking at—or its significance. In all, at least seven poems in the 1933 edition of *Poems* are the utterances of sick men, while at least twelve others are spoken by a healthy or neutral commentator. Still other poems are not speeches or scenes from within the myth at all, yet they too may draw on it for parts of their poetic language: images, allusions, allegorical meanings. Altogether, despite its fragmentary quality, the myth pervades a good deal. Of the thirty-one selections in *Poems* (1933), I find only three that appear to contain no myth material. Very little, if any, of *The Orators* exists totally apart from the myth, and *The Dance of Death, The Dog Beneath the Skin, The Ascent of F.6,* and a few poems in *Look, Stranger!* show signs of it too, as does *On the Frontier*. But after 1933, when Auden's ideas and style change, the myth becomes of negligible importance and changes meaning.

Amid the myth's shifting point of view the unwary reader can go completely astray, since he must decide what to believe from speakers who may or may not be reliable. He must know that if the speaker is sick the ugly-looking enemies in the poem are probably really the healthy good, but unfortunately the unhealthy bad enemies in speeches given by healthy speakers look much the same. To complicate matters further, the allegory operates at various levels of abstraction. The enemy may be people—on either side of the border—or personified ideas, or some personified psychological problem within an individual psyche. Yet while all this is certainly confusing, it is less bewildering than it might be. Luckily, in allegory people, personified ideas, and personified problems not only act and look alike but also mean about the same thing. If readers cannot distinguish one from the other, not much is lost. To make matters much worse, though, in addition to creating this complex dramatic landscape with reliable and unreliable speakers, Auden never decided just how he felt about it. Sometimes, changing his mind in mid-poem, he reversed his message in the second half—or several times in the course of the poem.

Since the early poems are anything but clear it is probably worthwhile to give a few illustrations of just how and where the myth appears in them. The border frequently remains off stage in Auden's drama, but it is nearly always implicitly there, and often enough explicitly. The sick escapist in "Since you are going to begin today . . ." flees toward it, though too late to avoid destruction: "Before you reach the frontier you are caught" (*CP*, p. 110). In a complex and elaborate myth poem ("Though aware of our rank and alert to obey orders . . .") the sick speaker reports at length about rumors from the other side: "They speak of things done on the frontier we were never told" (*CP*, p. 139). Many travelers depart for this border. Dick sails for it in "Paid on Both Sides" (*P*, p. 27), while the chorus tells of throwing "away the key" and crossing a mountain frontier (*P*, p. 28). Whole generations in "Hearing of harvests rotting in the valleys . . ." cross their various mountain frontiers seeking health (*CP*, p. 47), while in "Again in conversations . . ." a frightened neurotic cannot work up courage to step across, "for fear / Is over there . . ." (*CP*, p. 5). The exile in "Doom is dark and deeper than any sea-dingle . . ." makes it across, despite the tempting memories of waving from window and "Kissing of wife under single sheet" (*CP*, p. 34). And there are many other border examples. In fact Auden seldom wrote a poem in this period without having in the back of his mind, at least, this allegorical line separating the healthy good from the unhealthy bad.

Less consistently, but still frequently, he imagined the mode of travel questers might use. He particularly favored railroads, and so railroads became associated with potential health, and could be depended upon to carry that meaning even in small isolated images. Rex Warner's son John, en route to fight the sick, crosses the border by train (*O*, p. 100), while a less stalwart traveler gives up in fright before reaching it, "stopped by heart failure at a branch line station" (*O*, p. 55). These branch lines are nothing more than subtle temptations luring weak-hearted travelers off the main route to the border. "Under boughs between our tentative endearments how should we hear . . ." warns against them, against the attractions of pastoral rustication offered by a "station's chance delay" where the "Lines branch to peace, iron up valleys to a hidden village" (*CP*, p. 148). In other poems, shattered health can be indicated by mere unexplained references to unused "Snatches of tramline running to the wood" (*CP*, p. 175) or to a deathly country where "no one goes / Further than railhead or the ends of piers" (*CP*, p. 177). Mention of piers indicates that Auden sometimes associated the journey toward health with the more traditional water travel. This appears in "Paid on Both Sides," where Dick sails across the border to health (*P*, p. 27), in "Doom is dark and deeper than any sea-dingle . . ." (*CP*, p. 34), and elsewhere. ". . . leaders must migrate: / 'Leave for Cape Wrath tonight,' " the speaker says in "From scars where kestrels hover . . ." (*CP*, p. 44). Elsewhere the sick sit placidly "Within a stone's throw of the sunlit water" but never embark (*CP*, p. 28).

Once across the border, migrants generally live in mountains, as they do in a number of places in *Poems* and nearly everywhere in *The Orators*. But Auden's mountain dwellers seldom find the promise they expected. Escape from sickness does not ensure health, he implies. Many Auden exiles "escape" sickness in the bad sense of the word: simply turn away from it, withdraw, deny its reality. While mountains provide something like the hawk's view and the airman's perspective, they can also represent the unreality of self-deception, a retreat from the valleys where life must be lived (even if corrupt) to the arid heights. Harvests may be "rotting in the valleys," but men can "gush, flush" them back to health, and trips up the mountains can become mere escapes from a world that needs rebuilding (*CP*, p. 48). This meaning, explicit in "Hearing of harvests rotting in the valleys . . . ," is implicit many other places too. Long sections of *The Orators* report on mountain gangs gone sick, decadent, and defunct after a hopefully regenerative escape across the border. One of these sick mountain men tells his story in "Control of the passes was, he saw, the key . . . ," where we can see the death wish strong in him (*CP*, p. 29), and in "From scars where kestrels hover . . ." we hear of a leader of "doomed companions" who "died beyond the border" in the mountains (*CP*, p. 43). Here as in various other places Auden clearly associates mountains with a form of escapism: intellectual idealism, intellectualism in general, or even religion, a special form of idealism. In a world made sick by mind dominating body, various forms of hyperintellectuality show up as symptoms of culture's final decadence. Then when evolution moves forward, religion appears as a symptom of the culture's terminal illness. Escape "into the wilderness to pray, / Means that I wish to leave and to pass on," the life force tells a doomed neurotic (*CP*, p. 110), and this final decadent escapism is often indicated by height imagery. One class of escapists are labelled "stork-legged heaven-reachers" (*CP*, p. 177). In "From scars where kestrels hover . . ." the speaker tells us that "bravery is now" in "resisting the temptations / To skyline operations" (*CP*, p. 43). Unable to resist this very temptation, many in "Hearing of harvests rotting in the valleys . . ." "perished in the mountains, / Climbing up crags to get a view of [paradisal] islands" (*CP*, p. 48). The mountain itself, apparently a legacy from the Gang myth (it is very important in *The Wild Goose Chase* and *The Magnetic Mountain*), could obviously be both a blessing and a curse. As a suitable habitat for all those who flee sickness, it is a place where they are "above" illness, where they can see their world against a larger perspective, and from whose ascetic peaks they can swoop down on the decadents below. Sometimes Auden uses it this way. At other times he is more interested in the many self-deceptions that afflict those who reject their sick culture. Not all rejections are healthy. Some are a subtler symptom of the prevailing illness itself. For self-deceived exiles, the mountain itself will be a mistake, and Auden shows them going sick and dying up in the craggy fastness.

Without searching further into the particulars of other allegorical features, what I want to suggest is that the psychological climate of Auden's early poetry is not created merely by the few poems where speakers talk openly about psychology. The poems themselves are often part of a large, incomplete, psychological allegory. And most of his psychological message comes from this allegory—not from direct statements. For Auden nearly everything in the early poetry exists on one or another side of that psychological border. On the sick side are all those "stork-legged heaven-reachers" (religious idealists) and "compulsory touchers" (the sexually perverse) (*CP*, p. 177), who support the old and fear the health of evolutionary change. These are defenders of the status quo: "Perfect pater. Marvellous mater. Knock the critic down who dares" (*P*, p. 74). In the middle and upper classes, naturally, the superego burns brightest, and we see them, sickened by it, throughout the poems, distinguished by their class trappings, at the "first garden party of the year" or "Dangerous, easy, in furs . . . at reserved tables" (*CP*, p. 27). The early work presents a vast portrait of this group, with their death wish symptoms specially inflated for emphasis: the financier with his typist; the dons "Who are born nurses, who live in shorts" (*P*, p. 88); "bird watchers" and those who "prefer as a rule the big cities, living voluntarily in a top room" (*O*, p. 13). In places *The Orators* is little more than a notebook listing the odd characteristics Auden used to identify those people who live on the wrong side of the border. When "chairs are being brought in from the garden," when children play "by the flooded football ground," these images tell us we are looking at the wrong side of the border, where public schools and garden parties are enemy institutions (*CP*, p. 67). Individuals described as handsome, tall, well-dressed, good at games, participants in most social functions, living in big houses, going to public schools—all are being specially identified. These are the insidiously attractive elements in a sick culture. Partly they are middle- and upper-class humans, partly personified psychological concepts, and partly just private enemies of the Mortmere Auden, whose schoolboy self liked to abuse the older generation at large and exaggerated prep-school enthusiasts both young and old. Usually if characters have any strange traits (and Auden delighted in imagining dozens)—collecting habits; a fondness for overalls, boots, bootlaces; any kind of cough or telltale ailment, however minor; an interest in games, and so on—they are the sick, living on the wrong side of the border. And the physical landscape mirrors their sickness—"Power-stations locked, deserted," "Pylons fallen" (*P*, p. 73); "silted harbours, derelict works, / In strangled orchards" (*CP*, pp. 27–28)—all the familiar crumbling machines and broken stage props of his allegorical world.

Some of these special enemy traits can be assigned more than just general meaning. "Collecting" is a familiar neurotic practice of anal-retentive types, a socially respectable channel for their special perverse pleasure, and Auden delights in identifying these enemies. Collecting is listed in *The Orators* as one of "Three enemy occupations" (*O*, p. 52), and we see a variety of examples. Defective lovers, we are told, collect "Old tracts, brackets . . . powders, pieces of wood" (*O*, pp. 14–15). Other defective types accumulate "bus tickets . . . pocket mirrors, foreign envelopes etc." (*O*, p. 33), and "a unique collection of indigenous insects" (*O*, p. 30). When a mountain gang carries along "labelled specimens in japanned boxes" (*O*, p. 20), we expect these hopeful exiles soon to turn up sick, and they do. The Airman's case is even more serious. An indiscriminate kleptomaniac, he collects everything. So does his pathological counterpart, Gunn, in *The Ascent of F.6*, who makes off with "bits of indiarubber . . . watches, pencils"—anything (*F6*, p. 48). This sick mountain gang in *The Ascent of F.6* also includes an additional

compulsive collector. Lamp, a botanist, dies trying to find a new addition
to his collection of flowers (all of them surely indigenous to Mortmere
—Stagnium Meningitis, Polus Naufrangia, Frustrax Abominium, *F6,* p.
50). Another mountain-climbing flower collector appears in *Look,
Stranger!*

> . . . the tall
> Professor in the mountains with his large
> Tweed pockets full of plants . . .
> (*CP,* p. 72)

Botanical collectors are doubly sick, since flowers themselves are special-
purpose stage props of some sort. "Rose-lovers" are included among types
of neurotics listed in *The Orators* (p. 99), and in *The Dog Beneath the
Skin* the Vicar explains that "flowers in a vase" express "some unsavoury
double entendre" (*CP,* p. 244). What all this means is not completely
clear, but in "Paid on Both Sides" the sexuality of flowers is associated
with masturbation (*P,* pp. 23–24), and we can assume that Auden and
his friends thought of flowers in connection with some kind of sexual
pathology.[31]

Woods and gamekeepers have special psychological meaning too, presumably borrowed from Lawrence. In two poems the frontier is the edge
of a woods, across which the sick may not pass. Gamekeepers turn back
ineligible questers in both (*CP,* pp. 84, 177). To Auden's young friends,
apparently, "woods" meant that place behind Clifford Chatterley's house,
and "gaiters" what his wife's lover wore. Both could then be put, without

---

[31] Flowers seem clearly to be a Gang myth feature. Rex Warner's hero in *The
Wild Goose Chase* also collects flowers—with a girl who busies herself with
natural history when he tries to kiss her. This seemingly trivial detail apparently
is Warner's dramatization of Lawrence's belief that science destroys man's capacity
for healthful sexual relations (the novel owes much to Lawrence). The same idea
turns up in Upward's *Journey to the Border.* Mavors (modeled on Lawrence and
his famous fictional gamekeeper, Mellors) claims that science begins by "observing a few harmless 'facts' about starfish or flowers or domestic animals," moves to
examining the body, and ends by poisoning the observer so that he becomes
"shifty and timid." When "the disease of reason will have run its course . . . you
will sink into a final coma," he says (pp. 144–45). Auden's friends apparently
thought of science as "collecting things," and of the things collected (flowers, for
instance) as symptoms of an inadequate ("scientific") approach to life. (Upward,
though, as a Marxist, uses the same ideas to attack Lawrence through his Mavors
invention.)

further explanation, into allegorical landscapes. "Woods" stand for health, the release of the id from the strangling grasp of the superego, and they obviously flourish on the good side of the border, where the thoroughly corrupt counsel their young never to go. "But whatever you do don't go to the wood," a sick speaker warns in an early sestina (*CP*, p. 155). But even if they wish to, the unhealthy cannot get across that border, even in dreams, where

> Pursued by eaters
> They clutch at gaiters
> That straddle and deny
> Escape that way. . . .
> (*CP*, p. 92)

A glance at these cited poems will show how much Auden relies on a meaning that lies outside the poetry. The psychological meaning in the woods-gaiters passages is exceedingly vague, and the last example especially obscure. Like so many of Auden's early psychological landscapes, the allegorical significance apparently draws on a meaning established outside the poem, in the private myth.

My purpose in discussing all this is to show the psychological climate of the early poetry, not to search for the sources of meaning in all the myth features. Yet the more features one can attach meaning to, the more one can see just how widespread and pervasive that early allegory was. Such incidental items as rugs and bath chairs and islands, of course, are clear enough. And the reappearing imagery of boots and bootlaces surely owes something to the psychopathology made plain in a couplet from *The Dog Beneath the Skin:* "Or does the thought of a thorough whipping / By ladies in boots set your pulses skipping" (*DBS*, p. 57). Recurring tunnels, mines, and borings lead in a general way down to the dark underground id, just as Africa becomes the "dark" id-releasing continent ("the spinster in love with Africa," *O*, p. 24). All of these features appear, similarly used, in the myth creations of other Gang members as well. But many things remain dim. What significance did they all attach to overalls or blue ("His favourite colour as blue / Colour . . . of boys' overalls" *CP*, p. 178)? And what of coast guard towers and men (especially prominent in Day Lewis' first novel) [32] and of farms, important in *The Wild Goose Chase?* Much of the action in *The Wild Goose Chase*

---

[32] C. Day Lewis, *The Friendly Tree* (London: Jonathan Cape, 1936).

radiates from a farmhouse, in which hero and friends hear, on the radio, news of the city. Day Lewis' "Moving In" is similar—the hero this time connected to the city by cable.[33] In the later work of Auden's friends these may have something to do with the Marxist notion of country-city opposition, but they all had an earlier non-Marxist existence in the myth. Auden has a farm connected by radio to the sick culture (*CP,* p. 27), and several images suggesting (but just barely) that the "farm" is a dwelling place of the strong and healthy, perhaps deriving ultimately from the fortified farms of saga heroes. Though just what each of these items means is vague, the peculiar knowing tone speakers use for each, the faint emphasis given to each by its verbal context, and the unusual reappearance of each in other special situations suggests that all of them are stage props brought in from the private world encircling Auden's friends. The outsider cannot hope to understand everything about that buried world simply by digging up fragments and piecing them together.

IV

Obviously psychological allegory could easily be converted to Marxist allegory. Both have common philosophical roots, and both psychological and political traditions provide, in their dialectical structure, a built-in drama of opposing groups. Even more important, the picture of human life in each looks very similar, if the observer stands off from it a short distance. I have mentioned already that the Germanic psychologist and his cousin the Marxist political economist portray life as a power struggle between opposing forces. While the psychologist watches the struggle in the individual, the political economist observes the group. The struggle itself is described in similar terms by both. They agree that modern men, whether in groups or alone, suffer from repressive forces emanating from the cultural status quo. In the individual psyche such forces (perhaps collectively called the superego) stifle the vital, if unruly, energy essential to health (perhaps called the id). In society at large, repressive forces inhere in the entrenched powers of the state, primarily in its economic machinery. These repressive forces, both would agree, whether external or internal, grow deepest roots in the middle and upper classes, those stal-

---

[33] *Collected Poems of C. Day Lewis* (London: Jonathan Cape and the Hogarth Press, 1954), p. 126. Originally published in *A Time to Dance* (London: The Hogarth Press, 1935).

wart defenders of the political, economic, moral, emotional, and sexual status quo. Their power needs to be overthrown, and whether the rebellion is political or psychological, it will be violent. Power-holders must perish.

The Wild Goose Chase and *The Magnetic Mountain* mix together psychology and politics in just this way, and something similar appears in Auden's *The Dog Beneath the Skin* and much more feebly in *The Ascent of F.6.* But when Auden began to move out of his psychological climate he did not simply convert his old psychological landscape into a political one. Instead, he stopped relying on the Gang myth and its attendant allegorical features about the time they flowered, or were about to flower, in his friends Day Lewis, Warner, and Upward. He did not simply slip from Freudian myth into Marxist myth. Yet some sort of intellectual change began about 1933, and soon afterward Auden became in the eyes of his public a leader of the literary Left. If he had any "Marxist" years, then, they lie somewhere between 1933 and the publication of *New Year Letter* (1941), when his new religious conversion showed up to astonish his political public. Yet now that we can look back on Auden's work, apart from partisan fervor of the 1930's, his poetry scarcely looks "political" at all. It certainly shows almost nothing that rabid leftists could rally around, and very little Marxism of the sort that enflames men's souls.

Several peripheral matters help explain what intellectual changes the poetry shows. At Oxford, Auden recalled in 1965, "we imagined that the world was essentially the same as it had been in 1913, and we were far too insular and preoccupied with ourselves to know or care what was going on across the Channel. Revolution in Russia, inflation in Germany and Austria, Fascism in Italy . . . went unnoticed by us. Before 1930, I never opened a newspaper." [34] In the context of mellow reminiscence here, Auden's statements need not be taken too literally, of course. Nearly forty years afterward, many details had no doubt dissolved in his happy recollections. We can guess that by age twenty-three he had probably glanced inside a newspaper at least a time or two. And during his 1928–29 winter in Berlin with Isherwood, he had probably not missed seeing *all* the European events his friend later set down so graphically in his Berlin stories. Still, Auden's recollection probably accurately reflects

[34] Auden, "As It Seemed to Us," p. 180.

his general mood during the late 1920's. Spender remembers the Oxford Auden saying that "above all poets must in no way be concerned with politics," [35] and the poetry before 1933 shows that in fact he was not. But even Auden must have noticed "what was going on across the Channel" when Hitler came to power in March, 1933, an event that soon drove Isherwood from Berlin. He surely knew, as well, that the year before, after a trip to Russia, Upward had joined the Communist party. This act seemed "extraordinary" and shocking to Upward's friends, Spender reports,[36] but some of the reasons for it must have been obvious to Auden, who had been teaching with Upward at Helensburgh. As the decade moved forward, the depression worsened, unemployment rose, and bread lines lengthened, yet the British government did little. Labour had nearly disappeared in the 1931 general elections, while the subsequent coalition national government had alienated both Left and Right. Soon after the election Oswald Mosley had founded the British Union of Fascists. In short, the familiar world of the 1930's had begun. Even Auden, in 1932, published a poem about the proletariat, whom he addressed as "Comrades" (though the performance burlesqued itself almost immediately),[37] and the next year he put Marx himself on stage in *The Dance of Death,* though here too the situation looked suspiciously farcical. But at any rate the years of Oxford isolation had gone forever, whatever the truth about their innocence. Like nearly everyone else, Auden found himself in a world that could hardly be ignored by even the most firmly nonpolitical temperament. Nineteen thirty-three seems to be a dividing year. Upward had already joined the Communist party; Spender had begun to put Marxist ideas in his poems. In that year Day Lewis published his first political work, *The Magnetic Mountain,* Marx appeared in Auden's *The Dance of Death,* and, most important, Hitler came to power. Soon Europe of the "external disorders, and extravagant lies, / The baroque frontiers, the surrealist police" began to look more fantastic than Auden's allegorical myth itself.[38] At the end of 1933 most writers were taking political

---

[35] Stephen Spender, "W. H. Auden and His Poetry," *Atlantic Monthly* (July, 1953), p. 74.

[36] Spender, *World Within World,* p. 132.

[37] Called "A Communist to Others," the poem first appeared in *Twentieth Century,* in September, 1932. With "Comrades" changed to "Brothers" and a number of omissions it became XIV in *Look, Stranger!* (p. 34).

[38] Dedicatory lines to Erika Mann in *Look, Stranger!*

sides, Spender wrote in *Bookman:* Pound, Shaw, and Wyndham Lewis on the Right; Upward, Auden, and himself on the Left.[39]

But the intellectual content of Auden's poetry does not change abruptly after 1933 (Spender in fact probably overdramatized matters). The first thing noticeable is that its psychological atmosphere begins to thin out. Men and society still appear sick, but their illness is not so psychological as before, and unchaining the instincts no longer appears to be an attractive cure. The dialectical life force and its accompanying view of history nearly disappear. Whatever the immediate cause of all this, it is part of the larger pattern of the time. Western society seemed to be collapsing, and democratic governments, bewildered and ineffectual, apparently could not stop the decline. Intellectuals, habitually inclined to cherish individual man above everything, began to reexamine their assumptions. Individual dignity existed, they began to realize, only because a certain kind of political system made such human valuation possible. Now that political system appeared to be dying. Abroad it was already dead. Fascism, the maggot on the corpse, grew fat. Intellectuals who before had shunned political affairs and national culture began now to take a look at these. Many believed Russia alone had escaped the general corruption, though very few writers knew much about what was happening there. If the complex intellectual situation of the early 1930's were reduced to a few simple sentences, Day Lewis' might serve to describe it. "It is a truism that a sound society makes for sound individuals," he wrote in 1934 in *A Hope for Poetry,* and "society [is] undeniably sick. . . ." He felt certain there were only two alternative cures, both revolutionary. One, following "D. H. Lawrence" and "current psychological doctrines," wanted to begin by changing the individual. The other, backed by "Communism," wanted to start with the environment. "So there arises in [intellectuals] a conflict," he said, "between the idea of a change of heart that should change society and the idea of a new society making a new man. . . ." [40] The Marxist recommendation, Day Lewis reluctantly felt, seemed the more promising. The dilemma Day Lewis defines here appears in some form or other in other writers of his generation as well. *The Magnetic Mountain* and *The Wild Goose Chase* try to resolve the same conflict by combining Marx and "current psychological doctrines."

[39] Stephen Spender, "This Age in Poetry," *Bookman* (October, 1932), p. 10.
[40] Lewis, *A Hope for Poetry,* p. 47.

Spender wavered back and forth, deciding for Marxism as early as *Vienna* (1934), but clearly unable to accept his choice as late as 1938 in *Trial of a Judge*. These writers, of course, are not Auden, and it is true that he stands apart from them by virtue of the fact that nothing he ever wrote (with the possible exception of *On the Frontier*) shows him supporting Communism or Marxism as an activist political program. Nor does his work show any unhappy wavering between Marxism and something else. But he was not totally outside the contemporary intellectual climate either, and we can find important symptoms of it in his work. In fact, if he escaped nearly all the frenzied doubts and conflicting anxieties of his neo-Marxist, middle-class friends, in the end the philosophical tenets of Marx and related thinkers probably had a more lasting effect on him than on the others.

The earliest poem showing an important change is "Here on the cropped grass of the narrow ridge I stand . . ." (first published in 1933). Among its psychological images, economic reports emerge from the real world: "Gross Hunger took on more hands every month . . . / Combines tottered, credits froze" (*LS,* pp. 42–43). All this cultural decadence is no longer blamed on a tyrannizing superego. Both language and thought have changed. Men have let industrialism get out of hand, Auden's speaker says. Instead of controlling machines, "we assumed their power to be our own, / Believed machines to be our hearts' spontaneous fruit." Not that industrialism itself is bad. On the contrary, modern men should be the "rejoicing heirs" of "vital advantages" provided by a technology that makes matter submissive to "the unbounded vigours of the instrument[s]." If rejoicing is scarce in the modern world, the trouble can be traced to a faulty intellectual assumption, the notion that the universe itself contains some benevolent design. Let alone, according to this mistaken view, life would automatically spiral upward to shower men with increasing benefits. So industrialism has been left to its own devices, "While the disciplined love which alone could have employed these engines / Seemed far too difficult and dull" (*LS,* p. 45).

Just beneath the surface here is a crucial philosophical issue that can be described by a pair of opposing statements about man's place in nature. One notion has it that the universe is benevolently purposeful—or, one might say, contains original goodness. Left alone, it will flourish beneficially. Evil comes from thwarting its design and intentions. If men, born free, are everywhere in chains, throwing off the chains will automatically make them free. Into this philosophical camp go Lawrence, Homer Lane, Groddeck, and at times Freud (the therapist if not the Hebraic pessimist) —in general much of European psychology. Writers in this tradition assume that spontaneous man, nature's unspoiled progeny, would be fine and healthy if he could only escape interfering society, inhibiting customs, and his macrocephalic superego. The opposing view holds that the indifferent universe contains no discernible design beneficent or otherwise, and its organic offspring do not harbor goodness in their untrammeled id, lumbar ganglion, or anywhere else. Since these two camps are so general, they probably exhaust nearly all the philosophical possibilities (except for diabolists of various sorts, who agree that through all existence one increasing evil purpose runs ever more successfully). It may not be saying a great deal, then, to note that within the feuding family of post-Hegelians, Kierkegaard and Marx join forces in the second camp against their psychological cousins in the first. Still, it is a more profound philosophical leap to change philosophical camps entirely than to shift allegiance among members of a single one, and Auden is in the midst of just such a leap in "Here on the cropped grass of the narrow ridge I stand. . . ." However general and vague his original faith in the innate goodness and healthiness of man, this faith is disappearing now. Goodness and health are no longer things to be simply gathered in from a proffering universe, but things to be won from an indifferent one. Or, more accurately, things to be *made,* from the ethically neutral raw material at hand. "Spontaneity," no longer the password to health, becomes at best an excuse for irresponsibility and at worst a menace. "Control," formerly the slogan of the superego and all its evil henchmen, now becomes the banner for the healthy to march under. Auden's Kierkegaardian years are still a long way off, yet his philosophy in the 1940's and after is based on a conception of human nature much like the one in this 1933 poem. Even this early, Auden had begun to move toward a philosophical camp occupied by both Marx and Kierkegaard, but not by Lawrence and the secular psychologists.

When Auden's thinking started to drift in this direction, his poems began to show a number of differences. For one thing the old change-of-heart cure for ailments of society and self naturally began to disappear. If some enchained native energy in the self could no longer be blamed for culture-wide sickness, the cure obviously could not be effected by simply releasing the prisoner. Something was wrong outside the self, in the social machinery itself, and this could not be remedied merely by tinkering with individual psychology. The environment, rather than the heart, needed changing. This called for action, real action in a world outside the landscape of psychological allegory. Auden writes all this to Isherwood in a 1935 poem. He recalls how in 1931, watching "The Baltic from a balcony," both had believed spontaneous love, freed from the machinations of a superego dominated society, capable of curing everything:

> . . . the word is love.
> Surely one fearless kiss would cure
> The million fevers, a stroking brush
> The insensitive refuse from the burning core.
> Was there a dragon who had closed the works
> While the starved city fed it with the Jews?
> Then love would tame it with his trainer's look.

Now this doctrine is rejected, and along with it the "private joking" and personal eccentricities of their Mortmere imagery. Auden asks

> Pardon for these and every flabby fancy.
> For now the moulding images of growth
> That made our interest and us, are gone.
>   (*LS*, pp. 64–65)

Under the tutelage of Isherwood's "strict and adult pen," he expects to do something in the outer world of "crisis and dismay." Isherwood will guide, making "action urgent and its nature clear" against the "expanding fear" and "savaging disaster" (*LS*, pp. 65–66). Not that Auden entirely lived up to this sober conversion, of course. Private joking still went on, especially when he and Isherwood wrote plays together, but the wish is symptomatic of important changes taking place. Now that spontaneous love, rushing forth from a released id, no longer seemed an effective panacea for cultural ills, he sometimes began to look suspiciously even at private love itself and to condemn those who favored its spontaneity above rational control. Love might be only a pernicious escape from reality, he wrote, a private pleasure blotting out the need for social action. Love cannot, after all, change anything significant. "Before the evil and the good / How insufficient is / The endearment and the look," the speaker says in a 1935 poem (*CP*, p. 215). Another speaker talks about love's ability to turn "lands of terrifying mottoes" into "worlds as innocent as Beatrix Potter's." With this enormous power love can easily obscure the existence of genuine evil. Worse yet, love itself can become an evil, an instrument of unscrupulous oppressors ("Hitler and Mussolini in their wooing poses," *CP,* p. 37), a charismatic weapon for manipulating the masses. These lines, from two poems in the mid-1930's, show how far Auden had come from his early doctrines. Men, no longer good at birth and turned bad by inhibiting society, are now, at best, born amoral. Thus they must be made good, a job that cannot be left to the caprices of native instincts, as likely as not to serve an evil cause as a good. Instincts must be guided by reason. Men must control their world, in effect *make* their world. It cannot be left to grow in its own disorderly way. Unless he can control it, man is a slave to its every whim. Freedom means control of self and nature, and control demands action, not the passive attendance upon some flowering of innate goodness. Most important, action demands choice. At every point in their existence men must choose to act, choose to control, choose between good and evil—in love as in everything else:

> "Yours is the choice to whom the gods awarded
> The language of learning and the language of love,
> Crooked to move as a moneybag or a cancer,
>   Or straight as a dove."
>   (*CP,* p. 38)

Brought together, translated into philosophical terms, and neatly labeled, these thoughts form the basis of an empirical epistemology. All empirical philosophies begin with the notion that action produces knowledge. Knowledge arises when men, acting upon their environment, discover (or make) connections between objects and events. These connections exist as hypotheses, to be tested by further action that either verifies or changes them. Knowledge is a hypothesis about something acted upon. Hypotheses enable men to control themselves and their world, and control is freedom. In any empirical epistemology, then, action produces knowledge, knowledge produces control, and control enlarges human freedom.

What has all this to do with Marxism? The whole philosophy of Marx and Engels rests on just this epistemology. Marx began his career, in fact, by rejecting Hegel's idealist method (not his insights) in favor of the empirical methods of natural science. Properly used, "natural science . . . will become the basis of *human* science," he wrote in 1844 (at the age of twenty-six) and in time "the science of man will subsume under itself natural science: there will be *one* science." [41] Two years later, now joined by Engels, Marx insisted that their own research follow this rigorous empirical method. Facts must be "verified in a purely empirical way," both demand. "Empirical observation must in each separate instance bring out empirically, and without any mystification and speculation, the connection" between cause and effect.[42] For nearly half a century, with equal vigor, both Marx and Engels insisted on this same empirical discipline. The famous Marxian dialectic itself, Engels declared late in life, was nothing more than the scientific method: "Dialectics . . . [are simply] the science of the general laws of motion, both of the external world and of human thought. . . ." [43] Whether or not Hegel's idealism remained to taint this empiricism, as some claim,[44] Marx and Engels *thought* they were empiricists and described their epistemology in empirical terms. Knowledge arises from action, from the interaction of men and environment, they taught, and by its nature is nothing more than a hypothesis. "The question whether objective truth is an attribute of human thought—is not a theoretical but a *practical* question," Marx wrote. "Man must prove the truth . . . in practice." [45] Forty years later Engels rephrased this often repeated description of truth. "The proof of the pudding is in the eating," he said. "From the moment we turn to our own *use*" our notions about the nature of things, "we put to an infallible test the correctness or otherwise of our sense-perceptions." [46] Acting in their environment, then, men gain knowledge, and knowledge enables them to change and control the environment. Just such a process lies at the heart of the Marx-Engels view of human nature and history. One such interaction, in fact, *created* human nature. Men evolved from animals when some nonhuman beast began to *use* his environment as a tool. Men

[41] Karl Marx, *Economic and Philosophic Manuscripts of 1844,* trans. by Martin Milligan (Moscow: Foreign Languages Publishing House, 1961), p. 111.

[42] Karl Marx, *The German Ideology,* ed. R. Pascal (New York: International Publishers, 1947), pp. 7, 13.

[43] "Ludwig Feuerbach and the End of Classical German Idealism," Karl Marx and Frederick Engels, *Selected Works* (Moscow: Foreign Languages Publishing House, 1955), II, 386. Hereafter *SW.*

[44] See, for instance, John Dewey, *Freedom and Culture* (New York: G. P. Putnam's Sons, 1939), for an extreme case.

[45] Marx, "Theses on Feuerbach," *The German Ideology,* p. 197.

[46] "1892 English Introduction to 'Socialism: Utopian and Scientific,' " *SW,* II, 100. My italics.

began "to distinguish themselves from animals as soon as they [began] to *produce* their means of subsistence. . . ." [47] Acting on their environment, organisms change themselves (perhaps into men) and in turn change their environment. This transformed environment, acted upon again, further modifies them, they it, and so on—the Marxian dialectic in its most basic philosophical form.

Such a philosophy puts squarely on man the responsibility for choosing what to do. Far from denying man the free will to make choices, the Marx-Engels philosophy (and all empirical philosophy) rests on the notion that men must choose if they are to rise above the slavery of spontaneous animal behavior. ". . . the more that human beings . . . make their history themselves, consciously, the less becomes the influence of unforeseen effects and uncontrolled forces on this history," said Engels in his "Introduction to Dialectics of Nature." [48] All this is summed up admirably in what Auden calls Engels' "famous definition," "Freedom is consciousness of necessity." [49] The phrase appears in an equally famous passage in his *Anti-Dühring:*

"Necessity is *blind* only *in so far as it is not understood*" [Hegel]. Freedom does not consist in the dream of independence of natural laws, but in the knowledge of these laws, and in the possibility this gives of systematically making them work towards definite ends. . . . Freedom of the will therefore means nothing but the capacity to make decisions with real knowledge of the subject. . . . Freedom therefore consists in the control over ourselves and over external nature. . . ." [50]

Despite the residual vocabulary left from idealism (grating to the ears of British and American empiricists), this is a marvelously lucid statement of fundamental empirical tenets. The suspect term "necessity," freed from all its deterministic associations here, refers to the causal relations between phenomena. Without knowledge ("appreciation") of these, control is impossible. Without control, freedom disappears. Freedom, there-

---

[47] Marx, *The German Ideology*, p. 7.

[48] *SW*, II, 75.

[49] Auden refers to it in "Morality in an Age of Change," *Nation* (Dec. 24, 1938), p. 687, and again in notes to *New Year Letter* (London: Faber and Faber, 1941), p. 81.

[50] Friedrich Engels, *Herr Eugene Dühring's Revolution in Science,* trans. by Emile Burns; ed. C. P. Dutt (New York: International Publishers, 1939), p. 125. Generally known as *Anti-Dühring.*

fore, is control over nature, the appreciation of necessity. This is exactly the philosophical thinking that drifts in and out of Auden's poetry from about 1933 to 1938.

Of course empirical epistemology is not itself the subject of many Auden poems. It is the intellectual climate in which they have their being. The philosophy itself drifts in and out of them just as psychology did earlier—except that now the poetry is much less obscure than before and very much more skillfully controlled. Consequently philosophical thought itself is sometimes directly and purposefully present, though more often its presence shows indirectly in its effect on a variety of experiences. But there is a question to be raised before going farther: should Auden's empirical philosophy be called Marxism? Luckily the answer is not a crucial one. Auden's thought is what it is, whatever label one puts on it, and my concern is with its nature more than its source. But there is no particular point in avoiding the issue entirely, and several further questions will help clarify it. Is Marxism nothing but an empirical epistemology? No. Are all empirical epistemologies Marxist? Certainly not. Is Auden's empiricism then necessarily a Marxist empiricism? Not necessarily. Marx and Engels obviously share with a great many others the empirical principles described above, and when Auden's poetry displays only general principles he could just as well be called a Humean, or a follower of James or Dewey, or better yet a follower of no one—just a poet who generally accepts an empirical view of man and his place in nature. The common assumption that a writer's thought springs always from the pages of someone else is, of course, nonsense, however attractive that assumption may be to literary historians. Like most men, Auden had a mind of his own, lived in a world much like his predecessors', and might reasonably be expected to notice its character without their help. The empirical beliefs he developed are, in fact, much more general and widespread than the doctrine of repression and dialectical history displayed in his psychological period, and could go comfortably ungraced by any label, Marxist or otherwise. In fact, a reader unlearned in Marxism, or empirical thought generally, would find most Auden poems in this period readily intelligible. The early psychological poetry or the Kierkegaardian works of the 1940's would baffle this innocent reader much more. But all these disclaimers aside, it must be admitted that although Auden's beliefs need not have come from Marx and Engels, there is good evidence that some of them did. While the intellectual climate of Auden's 1930's *might*

have been Humean rather than Marxist, it was in fact the reverse. If the
poetry can be understood without reference to Marx or other writers,
Marx can help provide a useful description of its ideas. With these
cautious provisos kept in mind, then, the period from about 1933 to 1938
can be labeled Auden's "Marxist" period, just as the earlier can be labeled
"Freudian." If his beliefs arise, in part, from sources with nothing more
than a philosophical kinship to these famous generic names, so be it. The
names are useful, even generally accurate, labels for the intellectual
climates Auden passed through.

Marxist matter in Auden can be separated conveniently into two sorts,
philosophical and nonphilosophical, divisions that correspond roughly to
the two historical roles Marx and Engels played. While both wrote as
philosophers in the German tradition of post-Hegelian empiricism, both
were also what Marx called political economists, and at times spokesmen
for dissident social rebels and local causes, and on occasion activist
organizers and propagandists. If in *Anti-Dühring* Engels plays the role of
philosopher, in *The Communist Manifesto* both he and Marx write as
hot-headed polemical partisans. Some of Auden's friends (Day Lewis and
Spender, for instance) struggled to come to terms with this latter Marxism. For them the name Marx frequently raised an image of that political
organizer and activist agitator, the stern and ruthless enemy of an old
social order. From this fire-breathing figure there had evolved, by the
1930's, the rigid and perverted Marxist tradition today known as Stalin-
ism, and it had infected most European Communist parties. This brand of
Marxism (demanding suppression of the individual, brutality, and strict
obedience to authority), Auden's friends reluctantly tried to swallow and
often choked on. But Auden himself never showed much interest in any
of this. Aside from *On the Frontier* (perhaps mostly Isherwood's work),
his writing is not affected seriously by Marx the political economist, social
theorist, and revolutionary zealot. Auden, therefore, shows none of the
fence-straddling awkwardness his friends displayed, none of their agonizing indecision about Communism, none of their reluctance to forego
bourgeois traditions, none of their distaste for the crudeness of political
action. He simply pays little attention to these matters. Political Marxism
was not the sort of Marxism that interested him, in his writing at least.
(Some evidence indicates, beginning with *The Dance of Death,* that he
sometimes found Marx the champion of the underdog and political
sloganeer, and his later progeny, irrepressibly comic.) In *New Year*

Letter the speaker recalls that while Russian Communism attracted many in the 1930's, others "settled down to read / The theory that forecast the deed . . ." (*CP*, p. 285). Auden was probably thinking of himself when he made this second classification. His "Marxism" is much more a conception of human nature than a political theory, a diagnosis of social illness, or a partisan program for action.

Auden's revised conception of human nature shows up most elaborately developed in "In Time of War," a collection of twenty-seven sonnets and a verse "Commentary," published in 1939. In a sense, this explicitly philosophical poem is the culmination of the intellectual change that began about the time of "Here on the cropped grass of the narrow ridge I stand . . ." (1933). The first twelve sonnets look at the history of man from creation to the present (the creation myth here is completely secular, a handy, succinct metaphor). Expelled from Eden, man is overwhelmed by his new and bewildering freedom ("Freedom was so wild," *CP*, p. 319). Confronted by the meaningless buzzing and booming confusion around him, he must *make* his world by shaping observations into hypotheses. Even the observations themselves, sense perceptions, are simple hypotheses, called forth by man's need to control his environment: "The bird meant nothing: that was his projection / Who named it as he hunted it for food" (*CP*, p. 320). This illustrates what Engels meant when he wrote that all sciences "arose out of the needs of men." [51] ". . . nothing can have value without being an object of utility," Marx always claimed,[52] and all empiricists would agree. Auden's example shows the primal epistemological act itself. Sonnet III continues by illustrating beliefs first stated in "Here on the cropped grass of the narrow ridge I stand. . . ." If men do not choose at every point to gain knowledge and control their environment with it, the environment will control them instead. Faced with this weighty burden of action and choice, some Eden exiles, hoping the universe will automatically turn out right without their help, reject the responsibilities of being human. These become "abject, / And to [their] own creation became subject" (*CP*, p. 320). In the next sonnet something like this happens to a peasant. Unable to control his natural environment ("seasons" and "mountains"), he "changed little" and eventually "grew in likeness to his sheep and

---

[51] Engels, *Anti-Dühring*, p. 46.
[52] Karl Marx, *Capital* (New York: Modern Library Giant, 1906), p. 48.

cattle" (*CP*, pp. 320–21). If beasts originally became men by controlling their environment, the transformation is reversible. Failing to act, men lose the freedom control brings and become beasts once more, slaves to natural forces they can neither understand nor manipulate. Confronted by a post-Eden world in which they must act to know, know to control, and control to be free—and at every point must *choose* to do anything—men turn and twist to avoid their human lot. Two sonnets show how leaders emerge for awhile, then turn sick (*CP*, p. 321), and how philosophers begin properly by observing the natural world, but later turn hypotheses into philosophical abstractions and float up into the "imaginary lands" of idealism (*CP*, p. 322). (Foreshadowing much that is to come, though, this vice has some virtue. From his personal error Auden's philosopher learns about "human weakness," and with the humility born of his own imperfections, to accept it, *CP*, p. 322.) In another sonnet the poet, too, declines. Originally a pure voice of the tribe ("Their feeling gathered in him like a wind"), his very gift ultimately destroys him. Treated as a god, "worshipped" and "set . . . apart," he is denied the very wells from which his Muses drink. Once alienated from society, he turns private and introspective, "mistook for song / The little tremors of his mind and heart," and withers into a passionless technician: "Songs came no more: he had to make them" (*CP*, p. 322). (Marxists commonly accounted for the decadence of contemporary art with historical explanations something like this.) [53]

After Sonnet XII, "In Time of War" loses even the faint narrative structure of its early poems and much of its thematic coherence as well. But, after chronicling the rise and fall of religion, the emergence of modern science, and with it modern neurosis, the poem maintains what loose unity it has by showing various examples of unhappy man, refusing to accept or even recognize his human position. Hoping to escape the burdens of freedom, he refuses to take the responsibility for what he has become. And the more he tries to "turn away from freedom," the more feeble is his control over the world around him. "Machines" threaten to "push through into life." Connections between cause and effect fade into obscurity. No one can see, for instance, "how flying / Is the creation of ideas they hate" (*CP*, p. 327). In short, by failing to act, gain knowledge, and assert control, men have lost a freedom that must always be actively

[53] See, for instance, Christopher Caudwell, *Illusion and Reality* (London: Macmillan, 1937), pp. 117–18.

made and maintained. They become slaves of events, forces, and objects, thereby reversing the desirable relationship. *Things* come to life, and manipulate men: "A telephone is speaking to a man; / Flags on a map assert that troops were sent . . . ," "maps . . . really point" (*CP*, pp. 327–28); men "flinch from the horizon" (*CP*, p. 329); "Anxiety / Receives them"; "Freedom [becomes] hostile in each home and tree" (*CP*, p. 330). At the end of the sequence, the whole freedom-necessity-choice philosophy is summed up, explicitly, in philosophical language:

> Nothing is given: we must find our law.
>
> . . . .
>
> We have no destiny assigned us:
> Nothing is certain but the body. . . .
>   (*CP*, p. 332)
>
> We envy streams and houses that are sure:
> But we are articled to error; we
> Were never nude and calm like a great door,
>
> And never will be perfect like the fountains;
> We live in freedom by necessity,
> A mountain people dwelling among mountains.
>   (*CP*, p. 334)

A year or so earlier the very same ideas had shaped "Spain 1937," another fairly lengthy work. Though the poem certainly intends to align itself with the cause of Spanish liberals, the speaker actually talks less about Spanish politics than about matters of general human nature, specifically the subject of freedom-necessity-choice. He shows once again that in the midst of agonizing unpleasantness, when men fervently yearn for some change, they will turn everywhere but to themselves for a cure. Some god out of the machine, they hope, will turn up fortuitously to secure them: Christ, or a Freudian father figure, or an eighteenth-century deist God. "O descend as a dove or / A furious papa or a mild engineer," they cry, "but descend." Instead of coming, the life force replies with the old epistemological lesson petitioners wish to forget. "I am whatever you do. . . . / I am your choice," it whispers to unhappy ears (*CP*, p. 183). Men make their own fate, their own world, their own destiny, and none of their responsibility can be shoved off onto some nonhuman agent. Painful as it is, choices must be made, actions taken, control established, and freedom won. Choices and action in the Spain of 1937 were particularly unpleasant, but necessary: "Today the inevitable increase in the chances of death; / The conscious acceptance of guilt in the fact of murder . . ." (*CP,* p. 184). If such specific proposals sound, in the poem, rather crudely pompous, it is partly because the speaker feels much more at ease with the philosophy of human existence than with these special activist causes.

On the Frontier (1938), also built on a freedom-necessity-choice structure, contains even more of the activist Marx than did "Spain 1937." Various remarks indicate that in their collaborations Isherwood generally wrote the prose and Auden the verse.[54] If this is true, most of *On the Frontier* may be Isherwood's, since it is largely in prose. But whoever wrote it, the play does rest on the freedom-necessity-choice philosophy— underneath its topical propaganda. In *On the Frontier* dialectic becomes landscape again, perhaps for the first time since the early psychological poems. Now the landscape is political, a dramatization of that historical moment Marx had predicted, when capitalist society, its internal pressures perilously strong, finally explodes. Yet nearly everyone in the play, blinded by capitalist institutions and propaganda, misunderstands what is happening. When the states of Ostnia and Westland declare war on each other, ordinary folk in both countries believe the trouble started because of the evil nature of the other side. Valerian, the capitalist intellectual, knows this is nonsense. The war itself is a piece of trumped-up stagecraft, arranged by industrialists and leaders on both sides to keep the masses busily docile. But Valerian does not know everything, and in the end he and the common folk are equally mistaken. Though the war is genuinely trumped-up, forces larger than politicians and industrial magnates are at work in its turbulence. Such wars, the violent symptoms of capitalism's death rattle, herald a dialectical leap. Wise Valerian knows that a revolutionary proletariat exists, but the limitations of his own cultural experience prevent him from understanding their strength. They are, as far as he can see, merely "patient sheep, or silly crowing cockerels, or cowardly rabbits" (*OF,* p. 122). And so they are, but the dialectic of history, not to be thwarted, lends them its strength. The cowardly, ineffectual worker assigned to kill Valerian, though he bumbles tremblingly forward, does finally complete his job, and capitalism, in its final fascist stage, plunges into the backward abysm of history.

[54] See, for instance, remarks in B. C. Bloomfield, *W. H. Auden: A Bibliography* (Charlottesville, Va.: University Press of Virginia, 1964), especially p. 17.

While this dialectical plot clatters forward, Anna and Eric, the central characters, unfold a more philosophical one. Lovers—one from each country—they seek to elude the follies of their equally malignant homes by escaping to the frontier between, that theoretical line whose immateriality represents their mistaken decision. Eric knows that neither side is uniquely evil, but his explanation of the violent events, if philosophically more sophisticated than the version of his silly countrymen, is as wrong as theirs. Since both sides hate each other, hatred itself, he decides, must be the evil that blights human life. And since love is the enemy of hate, love must therefore be the only hope for salvation. His own dialectical view of existence, then, is fairly similar to the psychological one Auden had rejected some years before. Human history is a record of struggle between the hostile forces of love and hate, Eric believes. In attacking Eric's view, the authors reject the notion of love as a social cure-all, just as Auden had done before. And they show—again as Auden had shown before—that love can be a pernicious escape, a cause of cultural blindness. Love, the play demonstrates, is a spontaneous emotion that must be controlled by reason and empirically established values. But Eric assumes that since love is a universal panacea, it should also protect the healthy from social evils. The pure in heart, wrapped in their love, should be able to walk unharmed through a malignant world. "Locked in each other's arms, we form a tower / They cannot shake or enter," he says to Anna. "Our love is stronger than their hate" (*OF,* p. 151). Meanwhile, presumably, the world will take care of itself. In the play this doctrine is branded as irresponsible and false, a philosophy founded on nothing but wishful thinking.

Before the pressure of events, Eric's optimistic faith in love shatters, and he along with it. His foolish belief is simply part of an indulgent fantasy. He is one of those idealists party workers call "the clever who think that the world isn't real" (*OF,* p. 128).[55] But the world is real, and it rolls effortlessly over Eric and his beloved, crushing both, without even

---

[55] Marx and Engels were especially hostile to the notion that love, or any sort of private feeling or morality, could alter society without changing the environment. Engels attacked Feuerbach (whom he admired) for just such a Utopian illusion. Feuerbach had taken as his "starting-point . . . the liberation of mankind by means of 'love' in place of emancipation . . . through the economic transformation of production. . . ." "Ludwig Feuerbach and the End of Classical German Idealism," *SW,* II, 367.

noticing the love they had naïvely thrown up as defense against it. Just before he dies, though, Eric sees the truth and delivers the philosophical message the audience is to carry home. Marx had stated it many times. He wrote in "The Eighteenth Brumaire of Louis Bonaparte," "Men make their own history, but they do not make it just as they please; they do not make it under circumstances chosen by themselves, but under circumstances directly encountered, given and transmitted from the past." [56] Eric, failing to understand that men must make their destiny out of the environment at hand, had hoped to ignore the "circumstances directly encountered" and make a world from the utopia of his private wishes. "But I was wrong," he says at the end. "We cannot choose our world, / Our time, our class." The belief that love can cure social ills was but an unreal fantasy, he now recognizes. Instead, the world outside the individual must be transformed. Curative action must go on out there, not just in the minds and hearts of individuals. And the action demanded in the Ostnia-Westland instance is to destroy capitalist fascism. That act, enabling men to control their environment, will set them free. And at first it may very well call for hatred, not love. "Our hatred is the price of the world's freedom," Eric decides (OF, p. 189). Freedom demands the recognition of this necessity and, says Anna at the very end, "Thousands have worked and work / To master necessity" (OF, p. 190).

The works cited so far show how Auden's empirical philosophy can turn up in a variety of contexts. In On the Frontier political propaganda overshadows the empirical philosophy, but rests on it. "Spain 1937" reverses this emphasis. Philosophy is more important than incitement to political action, but both are still there. Partisan politics disappears completely in "In Time of War." The poem is entirely philosophical. The first two works clearly descend from Marx in his dual role of both political analyst and philosopher. Strictly speaking, "In Time of War" does not clearly descend from Marx in either role. Its philosophy could have come from any of several empirical thinkers or from Auden's own observations. But its philosophy, like that in "Here on the cropped grass of the narrow ridge I stand . . ." and the poems about love mentioned earlier, is identical to that found in Marx and Engels, and identical to the philosophy in Auden's politically Marxist works. Obviously the philosophy and the politics are closely related.

[56] SW, I, 247.

Three other poems deserve special mention because they show how this empirical philosophy contributed something permanent to Auden's poetry. One of these, "Fish in the unruffled lakes . . ." (1936), a personal love poem, describes the difference between men and beasts. Men, able to distinguish between self and environment, can choose between alternative actions. Animals cannot. Everything follows from this. While beasts swim, fly, and walk in innocent, unruffled perfection through the serene world of their instinctive lives, men suffer the inescapable consequences of free choice: agonizing indecision, the certainty of error, and guilty doubts about past decisions. Never able to escape the "shadowed days" of their anxious freedom, men naturally turn an "envious look" on "each beast and bird that moves." But if choice is a curse it is also a blessing. For choice can transform into love what in animals is merely a hunger. Men alone can bestow and receive "voluntary love" (*CP,* p. 202). (There is, in fact, no other kind.) Though men, granted free choice, will always use it imperfectly, they could not love if they were otherwise. The poem's philosophical thinking ends there, leaving implicit the next logical step —that since love makes life blessed, and since free choice alone makes love possible and men imperfect, free choice and imperfection are blessed as well. That imperfection is a blessing becomes the subject of "Lay your sleeping head, my love . . ." (1937), one of Auden's finest lyrics. Human love, necessarily faithless and flawed, nevertheless remains a joy untouched by relentless mutability and all the suffering, anxiety, and guilt caused by man's misguided choices. Though ever imperfect, life is blessed, and the speaker asks for his beloved the greatest gift men can receive— the mortal world itself. He hopes, in effect, that its imperfections will not obscure its blessedness. "As I walked out one evening . . ." (1938) states this message even more directly and urgently. Love, though imperfect, can and should be accepted. For all its imperfection, ultimately "Life remains a blessing" (*CP,* p. 198).

The view of human existence described in these three poems rests squarely on the freedom-necessity-choice philosophy at the heart of empiricism. Man's gift of free choice enables him to gain knowledge of the world, and, through it, freedom. But freedom never extends beyond the frontier of knowledge, always depressingly nearby, and it does not exceed man's power to control, always discouragingly small. And choices based on this small knowledge and incomplete control must always be imperfect. An empirical view of man, therefore, while it can (with Marx) optimistically celebrate the immense unrealized potentialities for human freedom, always shows just as clearly (as Kierkegaard does) why the freedom achieved will always be limited. "Fish in the unruffled lakes . . . ," "Lay your sleeping head, my love . . . ," and "As I walked out one evening . . . ," then, are closely related to *On the Frontier,* "Spain 1937," "Here on the cropped grass of the narrow ridge I stand . . . ," and poems about love cited earlier. All contain something of the same empiricism that, beginning about 1933, became a new current entering the main stream of Auden's intellectual development. In other ways these works may be very dissimilar. Private love is praised in some, watched suspiciously in others. *On the Frontier* is mostly a piece of topical political propaganda, while "Lay your sleeping head, my love . . ." is a love lyric, but an empirical philosophy supports them all. What Auden's career shows is that his philosophy soon left its political dress behind, but its naked self remained in all his later work.

If one were asked to describe *the* central Auden belief—a single idea that could be extracted from his entire body of work—that idea, beyond any doubt, would be "Life remains a blessing" (*CP,* p. 198), or *"Bless what there is for being"* (*N,* p. 70). Yet during the 1930's Auden's speakers very seldom said anything like this. More often, they spoke of contemporary life as though it were an illness rather than a blessing, something to be cured, and they frequently limited their remarks to clinical descriptions of the disease or prescriptions for the cure. That life remains a blessing was seldom openly stated. Yet, as I will explain in the next chapter, the message was often there nevertheless. Speakers sometimes said one thing and showed something else by their behavior. This difference might be described roughly by saying that part of Auden's "feelings" about life had not yet found a philosophical home. The psychological doctrine of repression and teleological death wish, with its stress on sickness, did not encourage the notion that current life could be accepted with pleasure. Marx the political revolutionary, eager to destroy social corruption, did little to support this feeling either. But Marx's empirical philosophy can be used to justify the feeling that life remains a blessing, and that is exactly how Auden uses it in the three poems cited above. The three lyrics, I suspect, show the first instances of a happy conjunction between a "feeling" and an "idea." Ordinarily Auden used philosophy to help his speakers disapprove of life. But when even the most disapproving social critic *feels* love, he temporarily accepts life as a blessing. If he should ever write about that blessedness we might expect to find it in a love poem. "Fish in the unruffled lakes . . ." is the first of this in Auden. Following this unification of feeling and thought we might also expect the poetry to show a sudden change, but Auden's does not. The general social unhappiness of the 1930's made such a change unlikely, and so did Auden's uncertainty about what poetry should be, as I will show later. But the change was not long in coming. "Fish in the unruffled lakes . . ." appeared in 1936. By 1939 "In Time of War" had gone a long way toward supporting a philosophy that accepted life with all its imperfections. "But we are articled to error," the last sonnet said, "And never will be perfect like the fountains" (*CP*, p. 334). The implication obviously is that since men are incurably imperfect they must understand and accept this. Nothing in the poem shows any of the reforming enthusiasm displayed in *On the Frontier,* "Spain 1937," or even "Here on the cropped grass of the narrow ridge I stand. . . ." Before long Auden's interest in changing the world faded and then disappeared entirely, while his emphasis on accepting life appeared in nearly every poem. This transition, already faintly noticeable in a few poems published between 1936 and 1939, was almost certainly speeded up by his discovery of Kierkegaard. In Kierkegaard he not only found philosophical reasons for accepting life, but a theology insisting that it must be accepted. Then he made his leap. Suddenly the supposed literary enemy of bourgeois complacency began to show some signs of believing that whatever is is right. Randall Jarrell and leftist followers gaped incredulously, and some became apoplectic. But in reality the leap had been only a small hop, and, in retrospect at least, anything but surprising.

V

Whatever the temperamental or psychological reasons for Auden's change, its nature can be described in philosophical terms. Having earlier drifted down the stream of post-Hegelian thought from the Freudian encampment to the neighborhood shared by Marx and Kierkegaard, he now shifted allegiance from the former to the latter. Or to put it less metaphorically, in Auden's early poems an inherently good and beneficially designed world had been made sick by men who repressed goodness and thwarted design. Although Auden never clarified this world view, it lay half realized in the thinking that drifted in and out of the poems. He belonged to this school of thought, whether he knew it or not. By 1933 he clearly knew it, and began to reject the school itself. Now the world began to look morally neutral, a thing men made either good or evil by their actions. Soon the various parts of the whole empirical epistemology began to appear. Men learned by acting, controlled by learning, and grew freer with each of these acts. If the culture were sick men had made it that way, and what had been made could be unmade. The choice rested with men, and in Auden's thought choice became the pivotal concept, that uniquely human thing—at once a burden and a joy, making error, anxiety, and suffering certain, love possible, and life blessed.

On all these philosophical matters Marx and Kierkegaard agree entirely. Auden could absorb both without conflict because both share the empirical philosophy I have described with the words freedom-necessity-choice. Of course Marx and Kierkegaard violently disagree about other matters, and these disagreements meant everything to some of Auden's leftist followers. From their vantage point Kierkegaard and Marx were enemies, the Christian transcendentalist worried about the wholly other, and the atheistic social revolutionary interested only in the right here. Caught up in this feud (not insignificant by any means), no one in the early 1940's backed off far enough to notice that Marx and Kierkegaard, members of the same intellectual family, fought inside the walls of one philosophical camp. Outside were the tents of their common enemies, and even most of them were brothers and cousins. Though all these advocates had their philosophical counterparts in Britain and elsewhere, in Germany the entire landscape of embattled partisans had a common ancestor in Hegel and had thrown up their separate fortifications in the latter half of the nineteenth century, when family feuds followed the *ur*-father's overthrow. Symbolically enough, both Kierkegaard and Engels had been present to watch the first rebellious act, as Professor Schelling attacked Hegel from a University of Berlin lecture platform in 1841.[57] From there Kierkegaard and Engels went separate ways to establish important subgroups in the large family of post-Hegelian German thought. The family later on came to be called the existentialists, and no one knows this better than Auden, who has spent his entire philosophical life moving within its capacious limits. Certainly he had never planned this from the start, but

[57] Reported in Paul Tillich, "Existential Philosophy: Its Historical Meaning," *Theology of Culture* (New York: Oxford University Press, 1959), pp. 76–111. I am indebted in a number of ways to this excellent article on nineteenth-century German thought.

by 1944 at least, he completely understood the nature of his own philosophical inheritance. At that time he wrote of Kierkegaard:

As a secular dialectician he is one of the great exponents of an approach, equally hostile to Cartesian mechanism and Hegelian idealism, to which the Germans have given the name Existential—though it is confined neither to Germans like Nietzsche, Jaspers, Scheler, Heidegger, but may be found, for instance, in Bergson and William James, nor to professional philosophers, for the same approach is typical of what is most valuable in Marx and Freud.[58]

In addition to sharing certain philosophical methods and habits these writers also have many peripheral things in common, so that anyone attracted to one may easily be attracted to the others. The psychologist Rollo May points out, for instance, that "Kierkegaard, Nietzsche, and Freud all dealt with the same problems of anxiety, despair, fragmentalized personality," [59] things that always interested Auden, even apart from their philosophical connections. "Freud saw this fragmentation of personality in the light of science," May says; "Kierkegaard and Nietzsche . . . were much more concerned with understanding *man as the being repressed* [who] suffers the neurotic consequences." [60] These matters, the very subjects of Auden's earliest poetry, are only a few of the many family traits Freud and Kierkegaard share. All the similarities can be summed up in May's remark that "it does not detract . . . from the genius of Freud to point out that almost all of the specific ideas which later appear in psychoanalysis could be found . . . in Kierkegaard in greater breadth." [61] So Auden could move easily from Freud to Kierkegaard. The move from Marx to Kierkegaard was even easier, the distance shorter. They shared not only a multitude of incidental interests, but an identical empirical philosophy. With Kierkegaard, Auden could live among familiar philosophical notions while he thought over the unfamiliar theological system accompanying them.

Kierkegaard divides existence into two very unlike parts—the human and the divine. Without its divine half, Kierkegaard's existence is much

---

[58] W. H. Auden, "Preface to Kierkegaard," *New Republic* (May 15, 1944), p. 683.

[59] Rollo May, *Existence* (New York: Basic Books, 1958), p. 33.

[60] *Ibid.,* pp. 24–25.

[61] *Ibid.,* p. 32.

like the one Marx and Engels described. Marx and Kierkegaard agree that
men make their own world from sense perceptions, that sense perceptions
are themselves hypotheses, and that human knowledge never extends to
any certainty beyond the hypothetical. When Kierkegaard says "the certainty of sense perception, to say nothing of historical certainty . . . is
only an approximation," he means that truth, a hypothesis, something
that men make, exists only in their consciousness.[62] Knowledge grows out
of the interaction between men and environment (subject and object).
"Knowledge" or "truth" independent of either has no meaning. By acting
men *make* truth. "When the question of the truth is raised subjectively,
reflection is directed subjectively to the nature of the individual's relationship; if only the mode of this relationship is in the truth, the individual is
in the truth even if he should happen to be thus related to what is not
true." [63] The idea struggling to free itself from this rhetorical quagmire is
the one Marx had set down succinctly two years earlier, in 1844: "The
question whether objective truth is an attribute of human thought is not a
theoretical but a *practical* question. Man must prove the truth . . . of his
thinking in practice." [64] Man is an empirical animal then, his earthly
freedom dependent upon control of his world, control a function of his
knowledge, both emerging from action on the environment, and every
step a new choice situation. Marx, Engels, and Kierkegaard all agree
about this.

But Kierkegaard's belief in God makes his description of human
existence entirely unlike Marx's, even while, in one sense, it remains the
same. Kierkegaard's philosophy is the Marx-Engels epistemology plus
God. Put simply, it is an empirical philosophy insisting, contrary to
empirical evidence, that God exists. That such a belief is logically contradictory and absurd is precisely Kierkegaard's point. Life *is* absurd, precisely
because though God exists men, confined to their empirical knowledge, cannot know him, or even demonstrate his existence. An unbridga-
ble abyss separates man from God. By nature limited to temporal experience, three-dimensional perceptions, empirical knowledge, men can never
leap across to the timeless, multidimensioned existence on the other side.

[62] Søren Kierkegaard, *Concluding Unscientific Postscript* . . . , trans. David F.
Swenson; ed. Walter Lowrie (Princeton: Princeton University Press, 1941), p.
38.

[63] Kierkegaard, *Unscientific Postscript*, p. 178.

[64] Marx, *The German Ideology*, p. 197.

And yet they are commanded to do so, and, in one sense, without moving an inch they can.

Since no intellectual gymnastics can resolve a paradox, any summary that turns Kierkegaard's avowedly paradoxical beliefs into a neat logical series is certain to be wrong. But if all human logic is equally wrong, neat error is often more useful and satisfying than untidy truth. So for my purposes it makes pleasing and useful sense to say that Kierkegaard's philosophy of human existence is identical to Marx's, while his beliefs about the divine are different. Of course Kierkegaard would immediately point out that this clear statement has more pedagogical merit than any other, since clarity increases with the distance from truth. Truth and incomprehension are inseparable. Things are like this because the divine can never be known in any clear sense by humans. In one sense, then, Kierkegaard says that all existence (the only one men can know) is in reality human existence—and on this he and Marx would agree entirely. But divine existence, out there contrary to all logical consistency, also completely modifies human existence in one way, and in doing so makes it a thing totally foreign to Marx and Engels. For when Marx and Engels say that man makes his own world from his sense perception, they are not speaking metaphorically. The world thus made is the only one there is. For Kierkegaard, the world thus made is the only one for man. Another exists, made by God. It may be unknowable, but the fact of its existence changes the world man does know. Marx's men make connections between themselves, objects, and events. Knowledge of these necessities, so called, can lead to control and freedom. Kierkegaard's men make connections between these "necessities" too, and also gain control and human freedom. But this is not the only kind of necessity in Kierkegaard's scheme, or the only kind of control and freedom. Though his men make connections between objects and events for their own uses, God has established connections independent of men's actions. The entire universe, in fact, moves serenely to some predetermined inscrutable design. Thus God, in a sense, predetermined existential necessity. In submitting to the arrangement of the natural world, men are ultimately submitting to the commands and design of Authority. Human choice therefore is free in one sense and not free in another. Since God's design is largely unknowable, men may seem free to choose, but in reality their choices move in harmony with the grand design. Ultimately they have only two choices: to submit to an unknown design or to try to try to rebel against it. (No one can reject God's design, but one may try to reject it.) Freedom, therefore, becomes control of a special sort. Since the universe and man's choices in it have been preplanned, men are not free to change anything ultimately. Freedom means, then, the absence of rebelling. It means submitting to God's design, moving in accord with its harmony. But this submission must be voluntary. When Kierkegaard uses the terms freedom, necessity, and choice, then, he means in one sense just what Engels meant when he said that "freedom is the appreciation of necessity." But Kierkegaard also means something quite different. Since only by submitting to God's design can men be free, human freedom is synonymous with religious faith: faith in the blessedness of God's design. Men can choose to have faith in that design. But since faith in an indiscernible design made by an unknowable designer will always be an incomplete faith, all the choices, finally, will be imperfect or wrong—or in religious terms sinful. Freedom is the recognition of that necessity too.

Auden wrote that he first read Kierkegaard sometime in late 1937 or early 1938.[65] About the same time he "began going, in a tentative and experimental sort of way, to church." [66] He apparently moved rather tentatively toward Kierkegaard too, at first learning from him how to clarify and extend the empirical philosophy he already had, only later taking in the theology. Some of this may even have happened early enough to affect parts of "In Time of War." Much of the philosophy there could have come from Kierkegaard as well as from Marx, since neither politics nor theology intrudes to rule out the affinity to either.[67]

[65] The exact date is conjectural. Auden returned from Spain in the spring of 1937. "Shortly afterwards," he says, he "met an Anglican layman" (apparently Charles Williams) who impressed him, and "presently, I started to read some theological works, Kierkegaard in particular," untitled essay in James Pike (ed.), *Modern Canterbury Pilgrims* (New York: Morehouse-Gorham Co., 1956), p. 41.

[66] Pike (ed.), *Canterbury Pilgrims*, p. 41.

[67] All this is of considerable interest, and I looked diligently into this matter before putting "In Time of War" into an earlier philosophical period—even though the designation is not crucial, of course, since the basic philosophy in both Marx and Kierkegaard is the same. Isherwood told B. C. Bloomfield that Auden wrote most of the sonnets for "In Time of War" during their China trip (January–July, 1938). (See *Bibliography*, p. 31.) Auden may have read Kierkegaard just before this. Yet nothing in "In Time of War" resembles Kierkegaard in any direct way—except for one intriguing line. The second sonnet contains the statement "freedom was so wild" (*CP*, p. 319). The most felicitous phrase in

But the first clear signs of change appeared in some of Auden's prose of the late 1930's. In 1936 he was still declaring that "a theology which stresses an absolute gulf between God and man, and the *inevitable* corruptness of the world is not really consonant with [Christ's] teaching." [68] Even as late as 1938 he cited Engels' famous definition to illustrate his empirical philosophy, one that as yet showed no Christian tinge.[69] But in 1939 he wrote that while "a purely religious solution [for human hopes] may be unworkable . . . the search for it is, at least, the result of a true perception of social evil." [70] And by 1940 he talked about how art, to be truly great, probably needed "an adequate and conscious metaphysics in the background," and he began to use Kierkegaard's terminology in his criticism.[71]

Even as a secular thinker, Kierkegaard might have seemed, to Auden, more helpful than Marx. For all his discursive style and baffling syntax, Kierkegaard scattered his philosophy less than Marx, who was much more interested in other things. In Marx, furthermore, the individual man, his inner workings and psychological self, got little attention, while such matters as compilations of death rates, economic analyses, and all sorts of social machinery got quite a lot. Though Engels seemed to have been more interested in the human individual, neither he nor Marx really could provide much help beyond a very general philosophy for a man primarily interested in human nature. Kierkegaard, on the contrary, was obsessed with the inner man. But most important for the new catechumen, fresh from existentialism's secular habitat, Kierkegaard's teaching could make it seem as though in the transition from secularism to Christianity very little had to be left behind. Kierkegaard's philosophy, by separating human from divine existence, and asserting that while both are necessary neither can be used to fathom or eliminate the other, has, to put it flippantly perhaps, the best of both worlds. Half of Kierkegaard's philoso-

---

Kierkegaard's *Concept of Dread* (Princeton: Princeton University Press, 1957), p. 55, but one that makes almost forgivable the unbroken turgidity surrounding it, is "dread is the dizziness of freedom." Such a redeeming phrase would surely not have escaped Auden's eye, had he read the book.

[68] Auden, "The Good Life," p. 36.

[69] Auden, "Morality in an Age of Change," p. 689.

[70] W. H. Auden, "The Public v. the Late Mr. William Butler Yeats," *Partisan Review* (Spring, 1939), p. 51.

[71] W. H. Auden, "Mimesis and Allegory," *English Institute Annual,* 1940 (New York: Columbia University Press, 1941), p. 19.

phy agrees entirely with empiricists, materialists, instrumentalists, prag-
matists, modern science, atheists, and secularists of all sorts—with all who
limit themselves to human experience, to that pragmatical pig of a world,
empirical existence. The other half offers something for the transcenden-
talists, idealists, and various religious thinkers, traditional or otherwise—
to all who believe in a reality beyond human experience. While moving
toward Kierkegaard, Auden needed to reject almost nothing, for nearly
everything could be reframed in the new language. Most of his secular,
scientific, empirical self could be salvaged. To the hostile outsider such a
change can seem a treasonous betrayal of principle, but to the new
convert the experience generally resembles a sudden expansion of old
perspectives. Former beliefs do not seem betrayed. Instead they appear to
be parts of a larger vision. In Auden's poetry there are no repudiations, no
agonizing reappraisals. No conflicting choices hold out equally tempting
pleasures to harass the postulant. Stepping across the frontier apparently
seemed to Auden to widen existing horizons, the sort of thing he described later in prose. ". . . I have come to realize," he wrote in 1956,
"that what is true in what [Blake, Lawrence, Freud and Marx] say is
implicit in the Christian doctrine of the nature of man [in that] each of
them brought to some particular aspect of life that intensity of attention
which is characteristic of one-sided genius. . . ." [72]

Nothing in *Another Time* (1940) shows any significant intellectual
change (though some new things are faintly visible in "Herman Melville," *CP*, p. 146; "Pascal," *CP*, p. 86; and originally untitled poems that
now appear in *The Collected Poetry* on pages 51 and 118). His general
public first glimpsed the truth in *New Year Letter* (1941). Even there
just what was happening must have looked confusing. The poem is not
completely a religious or philosophical work, and it does not seem to have
any definite organizational plan. [73] But parts of it clearly show Auden in
transition, building a religious structure on the old secular epistemology.
Kierkegaard's notion of the double man probably went into the founda-
tion. (In America the volume was called *The Double Man,* a phrase

[72] Pike (ed.), *Canterbury Pilgrims,* p. 39.

[73] In "Auden's New Year Letter: A New Style of Architecture," *Renascence,*
XVI (1963), 13–19, Edward Callan argues that *New York Letter* is organized
around Kierkegaard's triad—Aesthetic, Ethical, and Religious. I would like to
think so too, since the other long works of the 1940's are organized this way, but
I really cannot see that this, or any other, organization prevails.

Auden found in Montaigne.) "The reflection of inwardness gives to the subjective thinker a double reflection," Kierkegaard wrote. "In thinking, he thinks the universal; but as existing in this thought and as assimilating it in his inwardness, he becomes more and more subjectively isolated." [74] The hypothetical nature of all human knowledge disturbs Kierkegaard even as he insists on it, and where Marx and Engels stress the possibilities of expanding human control with these hypotheses, Kierkegaard often stresses their inevitable uncertainty. His statement emphasizes the fact that since men exist in time, they change constantly. Their conception of the world, then, constantly changes too, and nothing can be certain but the reality of ceaselessly shifting perceptions. Yet men think and talk as though their subjective experiences accurately reflect the outside world—as though subjective and objective truth are the same. Auden runs through this problem in *New Year Letter* in a passage more nakedly philosophical than anything he had ever written. Men have "no direct experience / Of discontinuous events," he wrote, that is, of any timeless existence apart from human perceptions. The allegedly "objective" world outside human experience can never be known. Even time itself is a subjective perception: "And all our intuitions mock / The formal logic of the clock." Since men can never escape their subjectivity, the old philosophical distinction between subject and object is unreal. Everything is subjective. Objects are only repeated experience patterns, "certain patterns in our lives." "All real perception, it would seem, / Has shifting contours like a dream . . ." and we cannot be certain of anything outside ourselves: "I cannot but express my faith / That I is Not-Elizabeth." But in spite of this, as Kierkegaard pointed out, we act and talk as though our perceptions and knowledge were objective and timeless. The stones we kick are really out there, we believe, whatever our philosophy claims. "We cannot practice what we preach," Auden writes, and so we are double men (*CP*, p. 278).

The philosophy here is old but the emphasis new. In the 1930's Auden usually stressed the positive, active possibilities inherent in the empirical epistemology. If the world is a thing of man's own making, then he should get busy at making it properly. Even if love were always faithless, hearts crooked, time destructive, guilt inevitable, imperfection certain, men could act to make an acceptable, even pleasurable world. Auden

[74] Kierkegaard, *Unscientific Postscript,* p. 68.

never loses this optimism, but under the influence of Kierkegaard he begins to emphasize more than before the inescapable causes of human failure. The uncertainty of human knowledge leads Kierkegaard close to the fearful solipsism of idealists he scorned and hoped to escape from. When he thinks of subjective man, forever trapped in a world no larger than the inside of his own head, he begins to display genuine symptoms of claustrophobic fright, and then despair. If nothing is certain, how can men presume to act at all, much less hope for knowledge about anything? Behind all this, of course, lies Kierkegaard's belief that a genuine non-subjective reality does exist, in God. But the vast abyss between that certainty and man's inevitable uncertainty forever kindles his desperation. Auden never broods about these matters as much as Kierkegaard, but the philosophical passage in *New Year Letter* shows him, more than before, emphasizing human subjectivity and uncertainty, and the inevitable error in anything man does or thinks. But *New Year Letter* shows other changes in Auden much more obviously Kierkegaardian than these. Auden now uses religious terms for the first time. One statement in particular shows the old freedom-necessity-choice beliefs of Engels and secular empiricists being converted to a religious conception. "To sin is to act consciously / Against what seems necessity . . ." Auden writes (*CP*, p. 283). Before, freedom arose from the recognition or appreciation of necessity, from knowledge of how events were connected. Not to recognize, appreciate, and know about these connections was slavery—and perhaps morally culpable in a society where control seemed so desperately needed. But in *New Year Letter* not to know necessity—or to know but ignore it—is sinful, and usually "necessity" means the connection between events *made by God.* To defy necessity is to sin. The statement appears in a discussion about the nature of choice. The passage shows that in a world without God (entirely evil) there can be no choice and therefore no sin, but that in a world with a God who offers a choice between good and evil, sin is inevitable, since imperfect men will always make wrong choices.

An even more important religious section begins in Part III, with the description of an evening of food, music, and friendship at the apartment of Elizabeth Mayer. This grateful account of a secular good place leads immediately to general discussion of the generic type, those moments of "accidental happiness," temporarily free from time and change, that can turn any place into a Good Place. Such moments, Auden points out, will not last. Destined to live in a world of perpetual Becoming, man can never escape for long to "the field of Being." Any attempt to prolong such nonhuman delights will spring "the trap of Hell," because man is in Hell when he thinks "Becoming and Being are the same" (*CP*, pp. 291–92). Auden here follows Kierkegaard's formulation of this familiar Christian doctrine. In the background lies Kierkegaard's entire many-sided attack on idealists of all sorts who hoped to discover (or invent) real forms independent of time. Even the notion of timelessness is nothing but an absurdity, Kierkegaard claimed, since men can never get outside time to perceive, understand, or even invent such a thing. Since "an existing individual is constantly in process of becoming," he wrote, therefore "existence is precisely the opposite of finality." [75] This means that religious experience, always human too, must take place paradoxically within time and the world of Becoming men can never escape. Even religious experience must be subjective and temporal. "It is subjectivity that Christianity is concerned with," he emphasized, because "it is only in subjectivity that its truth [like all human truth] exists. . . ." [76] Any attempt to flee from a world of subjective Becoming to the world of objective timeless Being, then, will only land one in hell, "Its fire the pain to which we go / If we refuse to suffer . . ." says Auden (*CP*, p. 292). Suffering, then, occurs when men submit to their temporal, limited human existence, and since only by submitting to this can men hope, even momentarily, to transcend it, suffering becomes a precondition of religious experience. ". . . suffering is posited as something decisive for a religious existence," Kierkegaard said; "the more the suffering the more the religious existence. . . ." [77]

The way up is the way down: Auden's thought grows out of the Kierkegaardian formulation of this Christian paradox, and Kierkegaard's formulation of it keeps the freedom-necessity-choice framework of his philosophical heritage. At least in Part III of *New Year Letter* Auden's philosophical conversion is complete. Freedom can exist only in the world of Becoming, since a state of Being, perfect in every way, allows for no choice at all. So man, just as Marx and Engels claimed, must choose, act, and gain knowledge within a material world bounded by the limits of human experience. But now this entire uncertain empirical life is some-

[75] *Ibid.*, pp. 79, 107.
[76] *Ibid.*, p. 116.
[77] *Ibid.*, p. 256.

thing that God created and planned. Man's limitations have been purposely set, and his "free" choices flow together to form some predetermined pattern. Within this plan men are "free" only to "choose" to
follow it, yet all their imperfect choices will ultimately be wrong. But
without wrong there can be no right, so that if human existence makes sin
inevitable, it also makes salvation possible: "In Time we sin. / But Time
is sin and can forgive. . . ." With this Auden comes to a Kierkegaardian
statement about life central to all his long works of the 1940's. Life is a

> . . . purgatorial hill we climb,
> Where any skyline we attain
> Reveals a higher ridge again.

But man is commanded to climb this topless range nevertheless, since
"mountaineering" is "the only game / At which we show a natural skill"
(*CP*, p. 293). By nature, then, men are destined both to climb and fall:

> Admitting every step we make
> Will certainly be a mistake,
> But still believing we can climb
> A little higher every time. . . .
>   (*CP*, p. 294)

Freedom is the appreciation of this necessity. To ignore it is to sin (to try
to escape into a world of Being). To accept it will mean inevitable sin
too. There is no escape. Like Kierkegaard's knight of faith, Auden's man
is destined to "make the movements upward, and fall down again. . . ."[78]
To climb upward is a risk, since falling seems unavoidable, but not to risk
is certain sin, the hell of confusing Being and Becoming.

For the next few years, all of Auden's major works rest on this
theological image of man, and man as inept mountain climber shows that
Kierkegaard's theology had allegorical as well as philosophical affinities
with Freud and Marx. All the long works of the 1940's after *New Year
Letter* are dialectical landscapes dramatizing the journeys men make to
get across frontiers separating Aesthetic, Ethical, and Religious existence
—Kierkegaard's dialectical triad. These famous terms mean just about
what their names indicate. In the Aesthetic life, action is governed by

---

[78] Søren Kierkegaard, *Fear and Trembling and The Sickness Unto Death*,
trans. by Walter Lowrie (Garden City, N.Y.: Doubleday Anchor Books, 1954),
pp. 51–52. Hereafter *Fear / Sickness*.

pleasure, in the Ethical, by reason, in the Religious, by faith. Most of the
time Kierkegaard regards these as an ascending hierarchy as well, Aesthetic existence least valuable and Religious most. Religious existence is
most subjective, too, since the best human experience is always a complete
submission to Becoming and least an attempt to escape to the objective
state of Being. Only by a leap of faith can men cross from Aesthetic or
Ethical to the Religious, and even the faithful leap only to fall back.
Kierkegaard provided a ready-made landscape of borders to cross, goals to
reach, failures to chronicle, and even a classification of human questers.

The landscape appears first in "The Quest," (included in the 1941
New Year Letter volume), with recognizable questers in nearly every
poem. The twenty sonnets might be called "Freudian" without serious
distortion, since at first glance they seem to be mostly psychological case
histories, sometimes described in religious metaphor. But in fact they are
closer to the opposite, religious case histories described in psychological
metaphor. Either way, the family resemblance between Freud and Kierkegaard never seemed clearer, but the psychology of "The Quest" appears to
come much more from Kierkegaard than from Freud. In fact the poem is
so overwhelmingly Kierkegaardian that many sonnets might be put
unchanged into *The Sickness Unto Death* to illustrate Kierkegaard's
categories of despair. The first three are less psychological. These show
that all the quests are journeys of the individual spirit ("Unluckily they
were their situation," *CP*, p. 251) and Kierkegaardian in nature: "The
journey . . . should take no time at all," yet "The time allowed made it
impossible" (*CP*, p. 252). This means that no amount of practice and
preparation will show anyone the Way. An infinite stretch of time will
bring the inept no closer to what the knight of faith can reach in an
instant. Yet if one is not blessed (and no one knows that he is), he must
try to reach in time what can never be reached by mere temporal striving.
Auden's sequence begins then with Kierkegaard's fundamental paradox
about "how the [timeless] eternal truth is to be understood in determina-
tions of time by one who as existing is himself in time. . . ." [79] No one
has a solution to this, so each must practice for a leap no one understands
how to prepare for. At best all quests will be bumbling and mismanaged.
Who knows what to take along, how to start, or where to go? Once
begun, the search for the Way must necessarily be unpredictable and
irrational, since no amount of study and skill will ever make a timeless

[79] Kierkegaard, *Unscientific Postscript*, p. 172.

God, or the road to Him, any less absurd to time-ridden men. And, as Kierkegaard drolly observed, "The absurd is not one of the factors which can be discriminated within the proper compass of the understanding. . . ." [80] Furthermore, if no one knows how to set off for the goal, neither do those who reach it have any idea how they got there. Later sonnets show this. Could success really have depended on those preposterous accidents and minor irrelevancies, one lucky contestant asks himself? "Suppose he had dismissed the careless maid," and so had missed the "cryptogram" as it "fluttered from the book." " 'A nonsense jingle simply came into my head,' " he declares, deciding, " 'I won the Queen because my hair was red.' " Questioned about his methods, another successful traveler returns nothing but wild absurdities:

> "What did the Emperor tell you?" "Not to push?"
> "What is the greatest wonder of the world?"
> "The bare man Nothing in the Beggar's Bush."
>
> (*CP*, p. 259)

His sullen neighbors finally give him up. "The true knight of faith is a witness, never a teacher," Kierkegaard said. "Humanly speaking, he is crazy and cannot make himself intelligible to anyone." [81]

Most sonnets describe the failures. Not since *The Orators* had Auden found such a chance to indulge his fondness for classifying neurotics. Sonnet IV describes what Kierkegaard called "despair at not willing to be oneself": ". . . the majority of men do never really manage in their whole life to be more than they were in childhood and youth. . . ." [82] Auden's character missed the Way because he could not "forget a child's ambition to be old / And institutions where it learned to wash and lie" or learn to "tell the truth for which he thinks himself too young" (*CP*, p. 253). Sonnet V comes under Kierkegaard's "despair of necessity": "The determinist or fatalist is in despair . . . because for him everything is necessary." [83] Auden's questers, "Seeking Necessity," fall because each believes "The nature of Necessity like grief" to be a pattern "Exactly corresponding to his own" life (*CP*, p. 253). Sonnet VIII illustrates what Kierkegaard calls "despairing narrowness": "getting engaged in all sorts

---

[80] Kierkegaard, *Fear / Sickness*, p. 57.
[81] *Ibid.*, p. 86.
[82] *Ibid.*, pp. 182, 191.
[83] *Ibid.*, pp. 170, 173.

of worldly affairs, by becoming wise about how things go in this world, such a man forgets himself, forgets what his name is. . . ." [84] When this happens to Auden's character, his forgotten self returns to torment him:

> . . . in an autumn nightmare, saw,
>
> .   .   .   .
>
> A figure with his own distorted features
> That wept, and grew enormous, and cried Woe.
>
> (*CP*, p. 255)

Sonnet VII describes the suicidal pride of a religious fanatic. Confusing dialectical with earthly leaps, this man lunges toward God from an upstairs window (*CP*, p. 254). Sonnet XVIII tells of a more genuine leap. In their soul's desert, ascetics trudge "The Negative Way toward the Dry," and at some point on their saintly journey leap from the alone to the Alone, "praising the Absurd with their last breath" (*CP*, p. 261).

These few examples make religion in "The Quest" appear more explicit than it really is. Auden's fondness for landscape details and clinical symptoms often draws attention away from the nature of both quest and illness. And the secular features of both usually leave the religious allegory more implicit than explicit. But this oblique sort of presentation disappears entirely in *For the Time Being*, subtitled "A Christmas Oratorio" (written in 1941–42). [85] Here Auden makes an explicitly religious landscape out of Kierkegaard's dialectical theology. The New Testament plot becomes a parable dramatizing the difficult leap from Ethical (Caesar's world) to Religious (Christ's). The oratorio's very first passage shows that Caesar's Ethical world, now decayed, its people full of despair, has gone as far as it can go. The moment for leaping is at hand. Philosophically, then, *For the Time Being* is simply a Kierkegaardian *On the Frontier*. In both, the dialectic of history is about to move on. But theological dialectic contains built-in difficulties Marx never had to face. The practical problems of leaping from fascist-capitalism to a Communist state, whatever their magnitude, seem puny alongside the theoretical difficulties of leaping from human to divine existence. Even if such jumps were possible, they could succeed only for a moment. The most successful rose garden illumination must fade before the necessity for remaining

---

[84] *Ibid.*, p. 166.

[85] For this composition date see Spears, *The Poetry of W. H. Auden*, p. 205. Auden's work was first published in 1945.

human. But, far worse, whether such jumps are possible or not is anything but certain, and it is not at all certain what they could conceivably mean, in any case. Floundering in the slough of theological paradoxes, worldly wise truth seekers sink deeper the harder they struggle to comprehend. Commanded to make an utterly irrational, absurd leap, the bewildered leaper will hesitate to make any move at all, and the more intelligent he is the more he hesitates. Forced to choose between a desperate present and an absurd future, everyone will feel baffled and terrified, and many will remain that way. Most characters in *For the Time Being* either illustrate this fright and bewilderment or talk about it. Directing what they say and do is a theology that accounts for the entire human condition (both historical and personal): its cause, its nature, and its paradoxical cure.

In theological terms, the cause of man's predicament is the Fall. It came, Gabriel explains, when Adam, filled with pride, stuck to a too narrow empirical epistemology.

> . . . Adam, being free to choose,
> Chose to imagine he was free
> To choose his own necessity. . . .
> (*CP*, p. 420)

In *On the Frontier*, Eric fell for exactly the same reason. The philosophical difference between that work and *For the Time Being* is exactly the difference between the secular and religious meaning of freedom and necessity. Eric failed to recognize that all acting and thinking must begin with the world as it is—the causally related objects of the environment we are all born into. Any changes must change this world. Freedom demands that its necessities be understood first. Eric ignored these empirical facts, and fashioned from his limited experience a completely imaginary world. In other words, Eric

> . . . being free to choose,
> Chose to imagine he was free
> To choose his own necessity. . . .

Therefore he fell. Adam and Eric live in the same world of facts, with one difference. In Eric's world natural forces have arranged them: evolution, the properties of matter. In Adam's world, God put the facts where they are, and connected them according to some master plan of His own. When Adam ignores these, choosing to believe himself free to make a world of strictly human design, he not only makes the same secular mistake Eric made, but an additional religious one. Eric must understand empirical reality before he can be free. Adam must understand and submit to God's design. For both, "Freedom is the appreciation of necessity." Since neither "appreciates" it, both fall, Eric into secular error, Adam into religious error (sin). Every man will repeat Adam's act, not because the Fall is either historically or genetically determined, but because as an empirical being each man will always imagine himself completely free to construct his world out of his own observations. The paradox is, of course, that being the creature he is, this is the only thing man can do, but now it is always wrong. (What is secularly admirable is religiously sinful; the triumph of Aesthetic and Ethical rightness will be Religious wrongness.)

In religious parable, these facts of human nature mean that since the Fall men, no longer able to understand God's design, have been commanded to understand it nevertheless. The distance between what they are commanded to do and what they actually do is the measure of their sin. But since no man can narrow the distance completely, all are sinful. The only choice, then, as Auden said in *New Year Letter,* is, in the face of failure, to keep trying to close the gap between human and divine or pretend that the divine does not exist. Those who choose the latter alternative will, settling into the secular world, impose on it their own designs, either Aesthetic (pleasing) or Ethical (rational), and ignore or deny the existence of God's built-in Religious design. And such acts will make life a hell—the more vigorously repeated the more hellish. Citizens in Caesar's Ethical Kingdom, a world patterned in its every part by reason and reason alone, have created around them just this hell. That is the cause of their predicament. And clearly in Auden's allegory, Caesar's world extends implicitly beyond that old Mediterranean bureaucracy and its colonial outposts. Simply to be human is to live in Caesar's world part of the time. For some it is to live there always.

An Ethical world is a rational world. Caesar's hell results from subjecting all existence to the scrutiny of human reason and rejecting whatever reason cannot comprehend. Such action, however sinful it may be, produces results—secular results at least—and Auden lists some, though with heavy-handed irony, among the "Seven Kingdoms" Caesar conquered. Here we find modern science, mathematics, chemistry, and other triumphs of rational thought, all burlesqued to indicate the ultimate puerility of such achievements (*CP,* pp. 432–34). The main apologist for these spurious monuments, and the outstanding proponent of the Ethical life, is that typical Caesarian administrator, Herod. He points proudly to the rational triumphs of the Roman world, civil order (rather than religious disorder), scientific knowledge (rather than religious superstition), and so on. For him, all human history has been a dialectical struggle between passion and reason, with the latter finally ascendant in Latin civilization. Yet the irrational lives perversely on, cropping up now and again to harass administrators busily oiling the machinery of state. Even in his own time a torrent of prophecies and miracles pours across the countryside, nearly drowning the reason of responsible men. Such perversity must be fought at every turn, Herod argues, because its social anarchy and epistemological chaos threaten human achievements at all levels: "Instead of Rational Law, objective truths perceptible to any who will undergo the necessary intellectual discipline, and the same for all, Knowledge will degenerate into a riot of subjective visions . . ." (*CP*, p. 458). In Herod's fine speech Auden accurately describes how absurd and irrational the Religious Way looks to an Ethical man. The point is that Herod's description is entirely right. Religion *is* absurd and irrational. But his evaluation is entirely wrong. Absurdity, anathema to the Ethical man, is a necessity for the Religious. But Auden's new religious zeal led him astray at the end of Herod's monologue, as it did in Caesar's seven conquests. After a brilliant speech, calmly and masterfully delivered, Herod begins to break down at the end, lose his assurance, whine, rail, and dissolve into quivering and infantile self-pity. Secular readers have sometimes felt, with dismay, that Auden breaks decorum to suit his theology, but in fact the theology breaks down too. The theology insists that no dialectical stage can be bypassed. No one can become Religious without being Aesthetic or Ethical first, and in fact *fully* Aesthetic or Ethical first. Brought to the absolute dead end of the Ethical Way, Herod in fact should be a first-rate candidate for the Religious leap. The conquest of Caesar's kingdom must come before Christ's, though certainly Ethical existence is genuinely lower than Religious. For a moment Auden's gleeful description of its lowness obscures his belief that it is also a prerequisite for anything higher, and thus shares in the general holiness of all existence.

But luckily this confusion lasts only briefly. *For the Time Being* could not survive much of it, since it undermines the work's main message: that the cure for man's condition lies in accepting secular life as a prelude (and postlude too) to anything else. The way up is the way down. No one can leap up to Religion without first having submerged himself fully in the Aesthetic or the Ethical (whether both are essential is not clear). Faith, the only equipment necessary for the leap, comes only at the end of a dialectical process. Only after discovering all the Aesthetic or Ethical byroads to be dead ends can the traveler find himself on the Religious highroad. In still different metaphorical dress, this doctrine appears early in *For the Time Being:* "For the garden is the only place there is, but you will not find it / Until you have looked for it everywhere and found nowhere that is not a desert . . ." (*CP*, p. 412). Simeon's rendition, ascetically disdaining metaphor, lays bare the dialectical structure: "Before the Positive could manifest Itself . . . it was necessary that nothing should be left that negation could remove" (*CP*, p. 449). Needless to say, such a cure may be even more bewildering than the disease, and almost as frightening. First of all, the doctrine directs sufferers to suffer more, until exhausted and limp with despair each desolate postulant may leap at the absurd, if he can finally accept the very irrationality Ethical man abhors. Put in this predicament, Auden's characters, like all men, squirm and hesitate, unable to take the cure once they see what it is. If only it were not so irrational, rational men complain. Everyone wants some sign, something to make reasonable the unreasonable and certain the uncertain. "We who must die demand a miracle," the chorus chants (*CP*, p. 411), and Joseph, his wife made pregnant by somebody else, is caught in the same human, only more comic, dilemma.

> All I ask is one
> Important and elegant proof
> That what my Love had done
> Was really at your will. . . .
> (*CP*, p. 424)

But no one gets any assurance. What Joseph and chorus ask for, and everybody wants, is for God to become more comprehensible, for Adam's Fall to be revoked, for the nonempirical to become empirical. But sin, human limitations, will not be lifted. The wholly other will never become just one of us, and the Religious Way must remain unintelligible and risky. The Word can be "fulfilled" only when it is "clearly understood as absurd," Simeon declares (*CP*, p. 451). And his dour pedagogy does nothing to decrease the forbidding ludicrosity of the cure: man "must decide which is Real and which only Appearance, yet at the same time cannot escape the knowlege that his choice is arbitrary and subjective" (*CP,* p. 450).

The title, *For the Time Being,* comes from the Narrator's speech at the end of the oratorio. The speech's content, its concluding position in the work, and the elevation of one of its phrases to the title all emphasize something important. Though Auden's basic theology is not original, he is by no means a nearly anonymous religious writer simply passing on another rendition of orthodox doctrines. The style, of course, is obviously his own, but his individuality shows in the thought too. Christians who believe that the way up is the way down still have an important free choice to make. They can choose to emphasize either the way up or the way down. From past decisions about this have descended whole schools, schismatic doctrines, traditions, and feuds. In the twentieth century, no one has stressed the importance of this basic choice more vigorously than Auden's friend and religious guide Reinhold Niebuhr. In his early books Niebuhr contemptuously denounced extremist advocates of either alternative. Some theologians, he said, by ignoring the vast gulf between human and divine, preach a gospel of fatuous optimism, as though perfection lay merely around some corner in the secular world, waiting to be stumbled on by a bright economist, psychologist, or politician. At the other extreme are equally misguided theologians obsessed with the gulf and with God as the Unknowable. For them, human suffering, the "injustices of society," are airy nothings, mere peccadillos of the fleshly world, by nature trivial. For theologians of this sort, Niebuhr charged, "Religion thus degenerates into an asocial quest for the absolute." [86] Though "degenerates" may cloud his distinction with emotion, this last category describes Kierkegaard fairly well.[87] Though Kierkegaard taught that secular life must be

[86] Reinhold Niebuhr, *Moral Man and Immoral Society* (New York: Charles Scribner's Sons, 1932), p. 70.

[87] This is true, I think, though in a later book Niebuhr puts Kierkegaard in a different classification. *The Nature and Destiny of Man* (New York: Charles Scribner's Sons, 1941) makes a great deal of the distinction between two theological camps labeled Classical and Biblical—latter-day modifications of Niebuhr's early description of theological opposites. The former, strongly Manichean, reflects a Hellenistic contempt for the flesh and works. The latter stems from the statement in Genesis that God found *all* his creation good. By ignoring Kierkegaard's strong "Classical" inclinations, Niebuhr manages to put him in the second category, where he becomes a major source for Niebuhr's own theology.

accepted as it is, acceptance for him was mostly a means to an end, necessary because it preceded transcendence. While both the way up and the way down are painful and unpleasant in his teachings, his enthusiasm for the way up surely far exceeds his enthusiasm for the secular world. Auden's emphasis is nearly the reverse. The temperament that had made him always suspicious of transcendental escapism (both religious and psychological) in the 1930's is still there in the 1940's. And so is his considerable contentment with life that sets him apart from Kierkegaard's despair and distaste for the world. No one can embrace both sides of a paradox with equal affection, of course. If men *must* accept the secular world in order to transcend it, everyone will still prefer either the transcendence or the acceptance, as every Christian has from Saint Paul on. Kierkegaard prefers one, Auden, the other. So at the end of *For the Time Being* the Narrator returns to emphasize that whatever he does no man can, for long, live outside the "Aristotelian city" of secular, Ethical existence. In the end leapers and nonleapers alike will live out most of their days in the world of Caesar and Herod, and though it promises a future "night of agony" no one can avoid, this world also offers a good deal of pleasurable contentment: "bills to be paid, machines to keep in repair, / Irregular verbs to learn"—in short, all of "the Time Being to redeem / From insignificance" (*CP,* pp. 465–66). By itself this secular life is no longer entirely "enough" as it was in "Lay your sleeping head, my love . . ." and the secular 1930's, but it is far from nothing. From now on Auden will always emphasize its worth—openly, explicitly, and with increasing fervor. The works of the 1940's all show that the human world is blessed in a religious sense. God made it. But its earthly satisfactions, while considerable, never quite deserve "blessed" as a secular epithet. After 1950 they do, and Auden will then not only affirm the need to accept secular life but will celebrate the joy of doing so.

In *For the Time Being* characters flounder in a collapsing Ethical world. These in *The Sea and the Mirror* (1945) sail from the collapse of an Aesthetic world. Inevitably, therefore, nearly everything in *The Sea and the Mirror* carries a message about art as well as about life. In fact, by writing about both at once Auden resolves temperamental conflicts for years unresolved. Thus the work is a very important one. It contains the best poetry Auden had yet written and marks a turning point in his entire development. His doubts about the value of all art, and bigger doubts about the kind he should make himself, his conflicting feelings about the attractions of life—in short, many of the opposing affinities that had split his temperament for years come into the open here to be examined and unified. But most of these matters must be put aside until the next chapter, while this one shows how in *The Sea and the Mirror* the pattern of Auden's philosophical development unfolds. *The Sea and the Mirror* contains another dialectical landscape where men journey from one frontier to the next, sometimes without crossing any. Launched out over seventy thousand fathoms, a whole shipload of characters from Shakespeare's *The Tempest* make their slow collective leap from Prospero's past and their own. On the far side of their watery abyss, one or two believe, Religion shimmers dimly in the distance. For others the distant shore is Ethical. Still others (and all but Antonio, in one sense) carry with them a private Aesthetic isle, from which they will never depart.

According to *New Year Letter,*

> Hell is the being of the lie
> That we become if we
> . . . claim
> Becoming and Being are the same. . . .
> (*CP*, p. 292)

The Sea and the Mirror is one illustration of that bare philosophical definition. The Aesthetic life always moves, even if surreptitiously, toward a world of Being where men, all mutability gone, might sing like golden nightingales in a life that moves but never changes. Since real men can never avoid being human, few ever sail very near such a place, but the fictional Prospero had sailed all the way, and on his enchanted isle had fashioned an Aesthetic paradise more perfect than any Yeats dared dream of. As a critic, Auden likes to show how the plots of almost any sort of literature can be turned into existentialist parables. *The Tempest's* final scenes yield easily. There Auden found all but two of Shakespeare's characters traveling a dialectical path from Aesthetic to Ethical or Religious existence. The two exceptions, Ariel and Caliban, the patron sprite of Aesthetics itself and his brutish counterpart, disorganized reality, fill out the fable. Shakespeare's cast on their final journey perfectly suited Auden's interests. In *The Sea and the Mirror* the old artificer Prospero speaks first, renouncing his Aesthetic life, bidding Ariel farewell. He, better than anyone, understands the sinfulness of confusing Being and Becoming. Attracted to magic since childhood, he defines it as "the power to enchant / That comes from disillusion" (*CP,* pp. 353–54). Aesthetics, in other words, by trying to create a garden of Being in a desert of despair, attracts those too weak to face the depressing realities of human existence. Seeking to escape these, talented unfortunates build around themselves an imaginary world of their own, perfect, organized, lacking the wildness of freedom, choice, and the erosion of time. In the center of these Aesthetic constructions, Godlike, sits the Aesthetic creator himself. So Prospero has built his enchanted isle, and in the fullness of his pride, completed his imitation of God by creating man, who would tender him "absolute devotion" (*CP,* p. 356). Unfortunately, like other men's, Caliban's devotion has been somewhat less than absolute. In fact Caliban's unruly reality is the only flaw in an otherwise perfect Aesthetic design. Thus even Prospero cannot entirely escape his human legacy. No man can, as Caliban points out later. The only perfect Aesthetician is God.

Considerably wiser now, Prospero, his magic books thrown in the sea, has renounced Being to embrace Becoming: "At last I can really believe I shall die" (*CP,* p. 352). His future life, he hopes, will follow what Kierkegaard called the path of "incessant becoming [which] generates the uncertainty of the earthly life, where everything is uncertain." [88] "I awake, and this journey really exists," Prospero exclaims with the new delight of the twice-born:

> And I have actually to take it, inch by inch,
> Alone and on foot . . .
> Through a universe where time is not foreshortened. . . .
>
> (*CP,* p. 358)

Prospero's destination, he hopes, will be not Ethical but Religious existence. Like Kierkegaard's knight of faith, he travels perilously suspended above one of the philosopher's favorite metaphors, the seventy thousand-fathom abyss Religious aspirants must leap. And in mid-leap, because "the entire essential content of subjective thought is essentially secret . . . and [therefore] cannot be directly communicated," [89] Prospero can explain himself only fitfully:

---

[88] Kierkegaard, *Unscientific Postscript,* p. 79.
[89] *Ibid.,* p. 73.

Sailing alone, out over seventy thousand fathoms—?
    Yet if I speak, I shall sink without a sound
Into unmeaning abysses.
                    (*CP,* p. 358)

He knows too, as Kierkegaard says, that "suffering is posited as something decisive for a religious existence," [90] and therefore that he must overcome his Aesthetic habit of making pleasing designs out of painful facts. He at least has hopes that he can

. . . learn to suffer
    Without saying something ironic or funny
On suffering.
    (*CP,* p. 358)

At first Prospero seems to be the wholly good man. But, pressed forward by his philosophical doctrines, Auden knocks him down in the next poem. The image of benign Prospero, built up through so many skillful lines, shrivels beneath Antonio's laconic scorn. With a contempt so diffident he scarcely bothers to utter it, Antonio mocks the very wisdom, humility, and good nature so attractively revealed but a moment before. In their place Antonio sets self-delusion and pride. Prospero moves in circles, he declares. The abandoned island, fading in the distance, fools only the nearsighted. Escape from Aesthetic enchantment has been an illusion. Prospero's magic wand, so ceremoniously broken, will rejoin, his sea-drenched books "soon reappear, / Not even damaged" (*CP,* p. 361). Even now the old Aesthetic conjuring begins; in fact it has never stopped. The forsaken island, the voyage, the characters paired off, raised or lowered, their futures bestowed—everything, the whole pattern of events, has been arranged by Prospero. And even now, dotted about the deck, kissing against the sails, the characters act out their parts in accord with Prospero's Aesthetic designs. "Yes, Brother Prospero, your grouping could / Not be more effective," Antonio mockingly observes (*CP,* p. 360). One Aesthetic existence left behind, Prospero now fashions another, and will never cease, Antonio insists. ". . . whatever you wear / Is a magic robe," he tells Prospero. You can "Never become," he says (*CP,* p. 361). The attraction of Being is too strong.

Antonio is spokesman for whatever makes human imperfection certain.

---

[90] *Ibid.,* p. 256.

In theological terms he announces necessity, God's design. Men must remain human. None escape. Without Antonio, Prospero's beneficently arranged world would seem peaceful and happy, the wrongs righted, the wounds healed, enemies reconciled, the young in one another's arms. Human perfection might seem just a few leagues off, rising in the distance across the seventy thousand fathoms. But such longed-for shores remain nothing more than a persistent human dream, Auden's philosophy insists. Imperfection and sin remain always, part of the human pattern. ". . . every step we make / Will certainly be a mistake," the speaker in *New Year Letter* declared (*CP,* p. 294). Even Prospero's cautious optimism goes too far, and Antonio's eagle eye notices the crack in every image, no matter how dazzling its surface appears. The dropped clue, the overlooked symptom, the telltale shred of pride instantly reveal to him the flaw in every human act and motive, even the best. Antonio's message is, nothing is right, or, rather, nothing has changed. If for God, everything that is is right; for man everything is wrong. Antonio plays the role of devil or genuine knight of faith. The two are mirror images, one almost perfectly good, the other almost perfectly evil. Neither is as perfect as God or as imperfect as ordinary mortals. *"Your all is partial, Prospero; / My will is all my own . . ."* Antonio declares (*CP,* p. 361), and he compares himself, in much the same way, to each of the other characters in turn. More than other men, devil and knight of faith sail alone outside the ordinary human condition, yet far from the divine too. *"Your need to love shall never know / Me,"* Antonio announces to Prospero; *"I am I, Antonio, / By choice myself alone"* (*CP,* p. 361). And the substance of this declaration, too, is repeated to each of the other characters. In the grand cosmic design, devil and knight of faith have a common purpose. The devil will "push us into grace," *New Year Letter* states (*CP,* p. 277), and the knight of faith can do the same thing. Our tiniest fault, exposed by the devil's cynical scrutiny, urges us forward to greater improvement. So does the impossibly high example set by the knight of faith. Impossible perfection is our goal, cries the knight of faith; perfection is impossible, whispers the devil. Responding to either, we redouble our effort (or fall at once, as all do in the end, devil and knight of faith included). Antonio, the voice of the nearly inhuman, reminds all men of their humanity, and therefore of their pride, delusions, and imperfections. So Prospero's image, shriveled as it is beneath Antonio's fastidious scorn, shrivels only to life size from its formerly too-large dimensions. Everything Antonio says is true, but his accusations do not set Prospero among the worst—merely among his fellow human beings. His imperfections are human limits, the necessity no one since the Fall can entirely escape. Prospero emerges after Antonio's deflation still the best of men, but always a man.

The other characters either remain fully enmeshed in their Aesthetic lives or believe themselves now to be moving on toward the Ethical or Religious. So far, Miranda and Ferdinand languish in a world of nearly perfect Being, a love that excludes external reality, though Prospero has already remarked on its impermanence (*CP*, p. 356). Trinculo and Stephano both find the real world too much and withdraw as best they can into Aesthetic realms of their own creation. Stephano's belly becomes his pleasure dome—bride, daughter, mother, and nanny combined. Trinculo, a more pitiful case, escapes into a landscape of satisfying childhood fantasy, just as Rosetta will do in *The Age of Anxiety,* a place of "Quick dreams" where "I / Was Little Trinculo" (*CP*, pp. 371–72). But long since his garden of Being has turned hellish, as *New Year Letter* informs us all gardens must. Trinculo's hold on existence is slipping, and in fact apart from Prospero and Antonio only Sebastian, Alonso, and Gonzalo confront human existence squarely enough to allow Auden to develop extended philosophical issues in their speeches. Both Sebastian and Gonzalo have just recently emerged from "The lie of Nothing" to the "Just Now" (*CP*, pp. 370, 371), and Gonzalo talks about this escape from the Aesthetic at some length. In the past, instead of trusting "the Absurd" and singing "exactly what I heard," this man of little faith had made songs more pleasing to his Aesthetic ear.

> Jealous of my native ear,
> Mine the art which made the song
> Sound ridiculous and wrong. . . .
> (*CP*, p. 364)

This is nothing more than Gonzalo's own repetition of Adam's fall, with Gonzalo, like Adam, believing himself free "to choose his own necessity." Gonzalo's pride ("self-reflection") ultimately makes his "Consolation an offence" (*CP*, p. 364), following a pattern Kierkegaard describes. "For what is an offense?" Kierkegaard asks, and answers, "it is an envy. . . .

The narrow-mindedness of the natural man cannot welcome for itself the extraordinary which God has intended for him; so he is offended." [91] But now "restored to health," his "subjective passion" once more vigorous, Gonzalo hopes he can move toward a Religious existence, a man whom "The Already There can lay / Hands on" (*CP*, p. 365). Pride, the cause of Gonzalo's (and all men's) fall, is just what Alonso warns against in an open letter to his son. Singling out for special emphasis the archetypal rudiments of pride, he tells how they grow out of that perennial wish: to escape the human condition. In believing escape from Becoming to Being possible, each man repeats Adam's mistake, imagining necessity to be entirely his own creation. Both mind and body can seduce, and Alonso warns against both. In one ear the Aesthetic "siren sings" of "water . . . / Where all flesh had peace," he tells his son, and in the other of

> . . . a brilliant void
> Where [the] mind could be perfectly clear
> And all . . . limitations destroyed. . . .
> (*CP*, p. 367)

But whether the Aesthetic bower of bliss originates in intellectual or physical pleasure, it will soon crumble and grow hellish.

The Sea and the Mirror is other things besides a philosophical or religious allegory. In fact, its characters, isolated in their monologues, do not really act at all, and perhaps a work without action should not be called an allegory. But action is implicit. The characters merely step out of *The Tempest* plot long enough to speak in *The Sea and the Mirror*, and their speeches turn that borrowed and off-stage action into an allegorical journey. Yet the work makes good sense without being read as a Kierkegaardian allegory, and the separate remarks about life and human nature in most speeches can be understood without a Kierkegaardian gloss. Taken as a non-Kierkegaardian commentary on art, rather than on the Aesthetic life, *The Sea and the Mirror* will yield a similar, though smaller, message. (For that matter, readers who have never heard of Shakespeare can understand much of it too.) Nevertheless *The Sea and the Mirror* is filled with the Christian view of man Auden fashioned with the help of Kierkegaard, and Caliban's dazzling speech presents this matter explicitly. Facing an audience of the Aesthetically and Ethically complacent, Caliban hopes to jolt them forward onto the Religious Way.

[91] Kierkegaard, *Fear / Sickness*, pp. 216–17.

After brilliantly lecturing for a time on the relationship of these triadic terms, he becomes more hortatory. Trying to escape from Becoming to Being, he tells his audience (most of whom have come to the theater to do just that), will lead to hell, and he takes evangelistic delight in illustrating this abstract theology with topographical details. "Cones of extinct volcanoes . . . plateau fissured by chasms . . . pitted with hot springs" await foolish sinners who hope to evade their human necessity (*CP,* p. 395). Simply understanding their predicament is not enough, he cautions. Since sin is not mere ignorance, Kierkegaard had stressed, wisdom is not salvation. Men *choose* to sin, and therefore must *act* to save themselves. So Caliban warns his audience of the "delusion that an awareness of the gap is in itself a bridge" (*CP,* p. 400). Knowledge of dialectic is no substitute for leaping. But after raising an "admonitory forefinger" for many pages, Caliban must begin to reverse himself as he approaches the heart of his message. The paradox there, avoided for so long, must now be faced, and his finger-wagging reproaches now must in one sense be withdrawn. After showing for most of his speech that neither of "the alternative routes, the facile glad-handed highway or the virtuous averted track," lead to anything but a "dreadful end" (*CP,* p. 399), he is now compelled to explain that these Aesthetic and Ethical roads must, in fact, be taken, and their hellish directions gladly followed right to the certain despair at their dead ends. Here too the way up is the way down, the way in is the way out, the way back is the way forward, so that if neither Aesthetic nor Ethical roads lead directly to the Religious, both lead there indirectly, and the indirect route is the only one there is. Only when all secular routes have been tried and found wanting can the Religious leap be taken. When "There is no way out . . . it is at this moment that for the first time in our lives we hear . . . the real Word which is our only *raison d'etre.*" Not that with a Religious leap men can escape human existence. Even the most successful leap only to fall back into a secular world in one sense completely unchanged. ". . . everything, the massacres, the whippings, the lies, the twaddle, and all their carbon copies are still present," Caliban reports, all "more obviously than ever." But in another paradoxical sense everything *is* changed by a Religious leap. Only after Religious illumination do we fully understand that "it is not in spite of [massacres, whippings, and lies] but with them that we are blessed by that Wholly Other. . . ." This is the Christian paradox at the heart of *The Sea and the Mirror* and all Auden's long works in the 1940's, and here as in all the others, Auden chooses to stress one side of it, the need to accept secular life. For all its sinfulness the Aesthetic-Ethical world of human existence must be lived in fully before Religious leaps can be made, and, if they are made after the inevitable fall backward. Men's greatest reward is not to transcend secular life but to experience its blessedness. That is the ultimate Religious illumination, Caliban says in conclusion, the recognition that "it is just here, among the ruins and the bones, that we may rejoice in the perfected Work which is not ours" (*CP*, p. 402).

The Age of Anxiety (1947), Auden's next big work, repeats this message, dramatizing the familiar ideas in a contemporary setting. Four New York residents suffer from much the same dread and despair their Roman forebears displayed in *For the Time Being*. Like their ancestors, these modern sufferers long to escape to something else. Only a Religious leap can relieve them, but none knows this. Instead they wish to be transported to some Aesthetic paradise, what Emble calls "The archaic calm without cultural sin" (*AA*, p. 10). Rosetta, hoping to reverse time and obliterate reality, drifts backward in memory to the Eden of childhood, a pure Aesthetic invention of her solicitous imagination. Emble pursues imaginary worldly success and prizes the ephemeral beauty of his sexual-athletic person, a feeble Aesthetic escape from the pressing realities of human necessity. Quant dodges despair by playing the fantastic, creating about him a comic, surrealistic existence, as though he lived in the center of a Dadaist poster. Malin, contemplative, intellectual, and Auden's main spokesman, is an Ethical man searching for something higher, but uncertain what or where it is.

Auden sums up his familiar view of the human situation in The Seven Ages. When each infant first believes he can control more than necessity permits, he repeats Adam's fall. "He jumps and is judged: he joins mankind" (*AA*, p. 29). As he grows, the individual learns to distinguish between self and nonself, between subject and object, and thus learns to recognize the human separateness that makes love possible and suffering inevitable. Eventually, punched and shoved about by the whole "real world of / Theology and horses," with its confusions and demands, he falls into despair, what Kierkegaard called the sickness unto death (*AA*, p. 39). He longs for some release but knows change to be unlikely. When despair is so great "that death has become one's hope, despair is the disconsolateness of not being able to die," Kierkegaard had said.[92] Emble describes it similarly:

> . . . a wish gestates
> For explosive pain, a punishing
> Demanded moment of mortal change,
> The Night of the Knock. . . .
> (AA, p. 40)

Yet, sick with dread the individual "muddles on, / Offending, fumbling, falling over" (*AA*, p. 41). Ironically, he may become a worldly success, though beneath the exterior facade his Aesthetically "Designed life" remains "A case of chaos," and he "pines for some / Nameless Eden" (*AA*, pp. 46–47). In brief, The Seven Ages describes the human condition in the Christian formulation Auden had first developed in *New Year Letter*. All four characters want to escape from this, and following the prescribed dialectical pattern, must try all the secular remedies before the Religious.

The "Nameless Eden" each longs for is an Aesthetic place, and in pursuing it each plunges in fantasy through the murky allegory in The Seven Stages.[93] Here, without knowing it, the characters begin that necessary chase down all the secular dead-end roads that must be tried before the desperate and exhausted traveler drops unexpectedly on the Religious. One by one Auden's characters try out and discard Ethical and Aesthetic possibilities, until in the Hermetic Garden a final paradise of Being turns hellish. Now, following the metaphor of *For the Time Being*, they have come to the desert's edge: "the garden is the only place there is, but you will not find it / Until you have looked for it everywhere and found nowhere that is not a desert" (*CP*, p. 412). But brought to the desert of despair, no characters in *The Age of Anxiety* can yet cross it, or even enter. None has yet reached the fullness of earthly dread. They are not yet ready for Religious leaping, and they do not fully recognize the need for it, though all hear rumors of "Oases where acrobats dwell / Who make unbelievable leaps. . . ." Malin, the most dialectically advanced, knows

---

[92] *Ibid.*, p. 151.

[93] For a Jungian interpretation of this see Edward Callan, "Allegory in Auden's *The Age of Anxiety*," *Twentieth Century Literature*, X (January, 1965), 155–65.

more than the others, but like Joseph in *For the Time Being* cannot shake off his Ethical habits. He still needs some sign, some empirical evidence to make a nonempirical, irrational faith easy to accept. About those acrobats, he reasons, "We should never have any proof they were not / Deceiving us" (*AA,* p. 94).

The Seven Stages, only a fantasy quest, is no substitute for a real journey, and after it the characters return from imagination to reality, definitely a step forward, though they do not realize it. Back in the world of dread and despair, the search for a nameless Eden continues, and everyone makes one last effort to believe this Aesthetic place can be found. They work hard to make something Aesthetically sacred out of the sexual attraction between Emble and Rosetta. Malin builds an altar of sandwiches, Quant pours liquor on the carpet, and in the midst of ritual, libation, and odes to the Queen of Love, everyone tries to conjure up the "millennial Earthly paradise" by mixing together what is really only "alcohol, lust, fatigue, and the longing to be good" (*AA,* pp. 116–17). Naturally all this fails. The Aesthetic vision Venus sends collapses when Emble, her earthly representative, passes out on the bed. But things have been moving dialectically forward all the time. This last failure brings Rosetta to the Aesthetic dead end that marks the beginning of the Religious Way. Having fulfilled the dialectical conditions, she now understands for the first time that escape from human existence is impossible, and for the first time accepts life as it is. Her role, she sees, is to

> . . . sit waiting
> On my light luggage to leave if called
> For some new exile. . . .
> (*AA,* p. 123)

She has made no Religious leaps yet but has now met the prerequisites, and in her last speech repeats the belief Auden had put at the conclusion of *For the Time Being* and *The Sea and the Mirror:* secular life must be accepted. "We must try to get on / Though mobs run amok and markets fall" (*AA,* p. 127).

In the epilogue, Malin elaborates on this. No one can avoid the suffering attendant upon human life, the confusion made inevitable by limited human knowledge and control, or the certainty of making wrong choices. In fact, no one can deny that on some unforseen "day / Of

convulsion and vast evil" humanity will disappear entirely (*AA*, p. 133).
Yet all this must be accepted, and without self-pity. The "noble despair of
the poets," tormented by doom and suffering, is nothing but a maunder-
ing self-pity, not noble at all—just fatuous. Malin says:

> . . . it is silly
> To refuse the tasks of time
> And, overlooking our lives,
> Cry—"Miserable wicked me. . . ."
> (*AA*, p. 134)

Far from being profound or dignified, such common laments are yet
another kind of escapism, practiced by incorrigible life-deceivers, who
"would rather die in . . . dread / Than climb the cross of the moment.
. . ." (*AA*, p. 134). For that is what must be done. Only by first
embracing all of secular Ethical and Aesthetic life can one hope to
catch a glimpse of something contained in neither:

> For the new locus is never
> Hidden inside the old one
> Where Reason could rout it out,
> Nor guarded by dragons in distant
> Mountains where Imagination
> Could explore it. . . .
> (*AA*, p. 135)

Only the "eyes of faith" can discover this "new locus," Religious existence
(*AA*, p. 137). When in his final speech Malin talks about the secular
world that must be accepted, he does not call it blessed as Caliban did, but
the fact of its blessedness is everywhere implicit. Auden nowhere else so
clearly states that all the mad confused suffering, so apparent to limited
human eyes, moves somehow to a divine grand design: "our least matter
dear to Him, / His Good ingressant on our gross occasions" (*AA*, p.
137).

Auden's poetry of the 1940's shows clearly that he belongs in the
tradition followed by Christians who emphasize accepting life more than
transcending it, but a further paradox splits the accepters into two additional groups. As Christian teaching has it, the secular existence to be
accepted is both sinful and blessed, made imperfect by man's Fall, yet in

the long run part of God's perfect design. Here again, unable to embrace both notions with the equal affection they theoretically deserve, every Christian will lean one way or another. If for a moment we ignore differences between the religious term "sin" and its secular equivalent "imperfection," we can see that during his career Auden first leans one way, then the other, and that the pattern made by his leanings over a period of about twenty-five years is one of the major patterns of his poetry. In one sense his entire career might be described as the result of his struggle to decide whether life was more sinful than blessed. After enjoying an uneasy ascendancy in work of the 1930's, sinfulness began to falter in the 1940's, and it collapsed in total defeat during the 1950's.

These rather abstract categories and subcategories can be illustrated handily (if not exactly) by comparing Auden's work to that of Eliot. By the early 1940's both men had essentially identical theologies. Yet this similarity seems almost irrelevant beside their enormous temperamental differences. Like Kierkegaard, Eliot's inherent distaste for the secular world nearly always made him look upon transcendence as a release from hell. (Admittedly Kierkegaard sometimes thought of divine existence as hell too, and of the divinity as devilish.) Where Auden shows more interest in accepting life, Eliot shows more in transcending it. But the paradox remains like the unmoving stone for both, and from "Ash Wednesday" on, Eliot's speakers are forced to admit that secular life must be accepted as well as transcended. Yet this acceptance in Eliot's work is almost unbearably painful, and his speakers seem to yield to it largely because theological paradox insists, because unpleasant acceptance is the means to pleasant transcendence. While his speakers describe transcendence with enthusiasm, with joy, and images of beauty, they take on the burden of secular life with resignation and prayer. Eliot accepts transcendence because he desires it, secular life because he must. Auden is not the direct opposite, but nearly. In the 1930's his speakers scoffed at transcendence, and while they often talked as though their sinfully sick world was unacceptable, their actions frequently belied their words (as the next chapter will show), and on occasion they explicitly accepted it as good, even blessed. In the 1940's Auden's speakers openly stressed the need to accept unregenerate life, even though descriptions of its sinfulness took up more space. But by 1950 blessedness not only got more emphasis but also more space than sinfulness, and Auden and Eliot, sharing the same Christian theology, became near opposites.

VI

By 1951 temperamental preferences evident in Auden's earlier work had become important enough to be called an intellectual change. When with *Nones* (1951) Auden began to stress blessedness overwhelmingly and almost exclusively, this did not move him into the camp of any new seminal thinker or cause him to reject religion or any other doctrine from his recent past, but it had a profound effect on the kind of poems he made. For nearly twenty-five years Auden's speakers had spent much of their time talking about the message of his poetry. After 1951 they begin to talk about other things. In many poems the speaker's subject and the poem's message no longer coincide. The poetry now begins less to proclaim a belief than to celebrate one. The poetry is less a statement that life is blessed than a celebration of its blessedness. As a result, poems can no longer be so readily described as a collection of ideas, and therefore the critical approach employed so far ceases to be very useful. Most of the discussion about poems published after 1951, then, must be put off until later chapters.

What ideas there are can be seen most clearly and completely in "Horae Canonicae," Auden's only significant religious work after 1947. "Horae Canonicae" makes explicit beliefs that are mostly implicit elsewhere. "Prime" tells again how men are forced to grope erroneously among the choices provided by divine necessity. But Auden now focuses on the ultimate sinfulness of everyone not in order to dwell on life's pain, ugliness, and defeat, but to insist on the inherent equality of all men. This corrects the doctrinal mistake made with Herod in *For the Time Being*. Whatever his earthly idiosyncracies, "Horae Canonicae" makes clear, no man stands above another in God's sight, as far as anyone can tell, and certainly none escapes his share in the common guilt. "Terce," "Sext," and "Vespers" work this out, separating Religious sinfulness from the secular peculiarities of Aesthetic and Ethical behavior. Sinful men may be Ethically good (the hangman solicitous for dog and wife) or Ethically evil. They may be either Aesthetically vulgar Utopians or fastidious Arcadians. But tastes in lamp shades and human engineering, like those in justice and truth, are ultimately all irrelevant. Before God all stand guilty; no man is sinless. But with this admitted, most sections in "Horae Canonicae" stress that life is blessed and delightful. Without those deplorable Utopians, without hangmen, judges, Caesars, and the world's Ethical power establishment, men would still be sunk in squalid Stone Age barbarism, "tethered for life to some hut village" (*SA,* p. 69). Next to that, civilization, though built with a sinful "cement of blood" (*SA,* p. 80), looks very good. Thus all civilized makers and doers come in for praise—cooks, surgeons, prosecuting attorneys, everyone who creates the texture of our guilty but delightful life. Each worker may be sinful, but he helps fashion a human culture more pleasant than unpleasant, and Auden singles out for special praise the mythological father of it all, some "first flaker of flints," or his anthropological analogue, whose devotion to craft freed us from our feral primacy, and started civilization on its guilty but glorious way (*SA,* p. 68). Even the repellent Utopian, dismantling beam engines, overshot water wheels, and other numinous antiques, is more good than bad in a poem that condemns nobody except the "poor s-o-b's who never / Do anything properly" (*SA,* p. 82). On the whole, "Horae Canonicae," a religious poem about man's inevitable sinfulness symbolized by the crucifixion, becomes mainly a hymn of praise to the blessings of secular civilization, filled as it is with

> basilicas, divas,
> dictionaries, pastoral verse,
>
> the courtesies of the city. . . .
>   (*SA,* p. 69)

Without sinful men, "there would be no authority / to command this death" (*SA,* p. 70), but there would be none of these glad things either, and the poem spends more time cataloguing them, praising them, and listing the speaker's self-delighting likes (and equally self-delighting dislikes) than in lamenting life's inescapable sinfulness. Toward the end, acceptance of life becomes even more joyous. A self-mocking comic prayer in "Compline" forgives everyone, speaker included, for whatever fumbling sins bewildering existence makes inevitable, and after enfolding all life in that benign embrace, the poem ends with a joyful hymn of celebration in "Lauds": "God bless the Realm, God bless the People; / God bless the green world temporal . . ." (*SA,* p. 84). Nothing in "Horae Canonicae," a remarkable performance, is more remarkable than this final cry of joy. How surprised Auden's early audience would have been could they have foreseen their grave and disapproving social critic in his middle age, blessing the whole unregenerate secular world with such unabashed ardor.

Auden's complete view of existence shows in "Horae Canonicae," but seldom, if ever again, in any poem after 1951 does he present the full philosophical panorama. Now that his religious conception of man is no longer something new to swallow and digest, but part of his blood, cells, and bone, Auden stops writing about religion. Kierkegaardian categories fade from the poetry, dialectical plots disappear, speakers no longer talk thinly disguised theology. Most of these things are gone even in "Horae Canonicae." No one there lectures on theology or winds his way along a dialectical journey. Though a religious poem, "Horae Canonicae" is about the holiness of sinful secular life. It says nothing at all about transcendence. So Auden's religious philosophy (urged on by temperamental inclinations), having caused him to write more and more about secular life, now causes him to write less and less about religious philosophy—until finally the subject itself nearly disappears. Though clearly descended from and rooted in religious beliefs, Auden's poetry after 1950 can be called almost completely secular again. Among the hundred-odd poems published in *Nones* (1951), *The Shield of Achilles* (1955), *Homage to Clio* (1960), and *About the House* (1965), only two aside from "Horae Canonicae" have explicit religious or theological subjects. And more important, among the hundred-odd only four or five poems stress the unpleasant sinfulness of secular life. All the rest, without ever denying men's ultimate sinfulness, celebrate life as a blessing. Auden's thinking in these might be summed up by saying that since to be human is to sin, nothing could be more common and less worthy of special attention than sin itself. The thing to remember, Auden reminds his reader everywhere, is that though there may be

> . . . reasons fast enough
> To face the sky and roar
> In anger and despair
> At what is going on,
>
> . . . .
> The sky would only wait
> Till all my breath was gone
> And then reiterate
> As if I wasn't there
> That singular command
> I do not understand,
> *Bless what there is for being.* . . .
> (N, p. 70)

In philosophical moods, then, when they survey life from a distance, Auden's speakers see all men as equally sinful, their every step equally wrong, yet their lives and the events and objects in them equally blessed. But while this serene vision hovers over nearly everything, affecting the poetry in dozens of ways, speakers seldom talk much about these large matters. Generally Auden puts speakers up close to the secular world, where caught up vigorously in its local sinful hurly-burly, they shun large philosophical contemplation, talk eagerly about parochial matters, and display all sorts of clay-footed prejudices. In the long view all men may be equal, but at short range Auden's speakers like some better than others. "In Praise of Limestone" is a good introduction to these preferences. Within its elaborate metaphorical landscape the poem considers four ways of responding to life. Limestone men live solely for pleasure. Their tribe spreads all the way from unsophisticated *ur*-man, living unspoiled in the natural state Rousseau dreamed of, to aesthetes in high civilizations graced by "Conspicuous fountains" and "formal vineyard[s]" (*N,* p. 11). Unable to imagine anything beyond their control, these attractive limestone types can experience neither Religious despair and joy nor Ethical good and evil. They are Aesthetic men, incapable of becoming either saints or Caesars. Saints live elsewhere, on "granite wastes," while "Intendant Caesars" prefer "clays and gravels" (*N,* p. 12). Saints are obsessed by time, death, chance, and all the uncertainties beyond human control. So they soon flee limestone lubricity for a gritty land where every austere outcrop reminds them of human puniness and limits. Caesars, like their limestone cousins, cherish earthly existence, but not for its pleasures. They thrive on power, and act to transform the earth, to control it, make it yield. So they seek out malleable builder's soil, gravel and clay. A "really reckless" fourth group prefers the ocean, in whose vast liquidity human aspirations sink without a trace (*N,* p. 12). The sea offers freedom by annihilation and guarantees that no human triumph shall mar its indifference to men's efforts. Those who prefer this freedom, the freedom of life-denial, are so completely uncongenial to Auden that he never mentions them again, even to disapprove. (The Eastern genius for confronting life by developing refined methods for ignoring it is, of course, completely alien to Auden's life-embracing temperament. The two worst fates he can imagine for his beloved citizens of the Mezzogiorno are "Taking the Pledge or turning to Yoga," *HC,* p. 82.) In "In Praise of

Limestone" Auden's speaker knows that under the eye of eternity all four of these responses are wrong and their devotees equally sinful, but with this briefly acknowledged, the poem goes on to evaluate them from the point of view of an ordinary mortal. From this position, Auden's speaker admits to a special affection for limestone men and indicates no personal affinity at all for Caesars and saints. Whatever their considerable short-comings, limestone men are at least ethically harmless, unlike their cousins the Caesars. In his fond moments, in fact, the speaker imagines the limestone world to be a model of paradise, wistfully longed for by men like himself, happily certain their wish to be innocent can never be granted.

In one form or another similar secular preferences become the subject of many poems. The mock longing for innocence, for instance, grows almost inevitably from Auden's contentment with a life in every way inescapably noninnocent. It showed up first as early as 1936 in "Fish in the unruffled lakes . . . ," where the speaker pretends to envy fish and swans from the safe distance of his human imperfection. This is a congenial theme for a man so pleased with life he can playfully pretend to wish, occasionally, that it were different. But against those Caesars who really would change life he stands the implacable opponent. This part of the "In Praise of Limestone" theme descends from preferences first defined in the Herod-Simeon contrast in *For the Time Being*. As Caesar's representative, Herod fathers a long line of Ethical offspring in Auden's poetry, all those latter-day clay and gravel citizens, the managers, administrators, deans, judges, Utopians, and Apollonians who earnestly itch to organize, administer, and generally modify things in the name of some Ethical principle —whether ecclesiastical, judicial, military, or rational. Auden the scrupulously fair philosopher admits the value of these people and shares their sinfulness, but Auden the imperfect mortal prefers life as it is, unchanged, and, if he must choose, likes limestone Arcadians much better than Caesars. Occasionally his speakers put forth a few moral arguments defending these preferences, but generally their judgments are not ethical but aesthetic. Speakers admit that Caesars are ethically valuable, since civilization is held together by judges, administrators and deans, but do not like them or their tastes. In "In Praise of Limestone" and "Under Which Lyre," the modern Herod appears as a scientist or a dean, and Auden attacks both from the position of a limestone man, something he knows (in sober moments) he can no more become than he can a fish or a swan. Auden approves when naughty gamins run their irresponsible ways in "In Praise of Limestone," jeering at scientists down their septic corridors. In "Under Which Lyre," the speaker himself adopts this raffish guise, scoffing at pretentious planners, attacking them with the limestone man's ten-point plan for planlessness: "Thou shalt not live within thy means / . . . Between the chances, choose the odd. . . ." Auden's academic Caesars, in their puritanic earnestness, look laughably puerile beside these Rabelaisian recommendations: "Nor, above all, make love to those / Who wash too much. . . ." (N, p. 62).

Clay and gravel men become the target in "The Managers" too, where after admitting their merits and their heavy burden of responsibility, the speaker reminds us of their privileges: they will have "places on the last / Plane out of disaster" (N, p. 33). In "Makers of History," history itself is reputed indifferent to the world's Caesars ("these mere commanders," HC, p. 23), and "T the Great" provides illustrative confirmation. T, the onetime terror of all he surveyed, survives finally only as an obscure name in a crossword lexicon, "II Down—a nubile tram" (HC, p. 25). An even more obscure fate, doubtless, awaits those lesser men of power pilloried in "Vespers," the ones whose eagerness to change and rule the world promotes their dreams of a New Jerusalem, where Auden's beloved krum-horns and gossip will be swept away by "cucumber-cool machine minders" turning out "special daily [newspapers] in simplified spelling" (SA, p. 78). Against these people who would change the world stand the speakers in dozens of poems who like it just the way it is, and who devote their entire speech in many cases to its blessings. Thus the period of Auden's odes begins, the poems of praise. After 1950, most poems are of this sort, and their praise of life easily outweighs whatever disapproval floats along their surface like fluff in a flood. They celebrate the large blessings—history (Clio), the earth (Gaea), and evolution (Dame Kind)—and the smaller natural forces and land forms (winds, woods, mountains, lakes, islands, plains, streams). Smaller yet, special places get their praise (Ischia, Austria, the Mezzogiorno), special people (Mozart, Verdi, Bellini), the blessed five (noses, ears, hands, eyes, tongues), and a host of miscellaneous items from battleships to lecture audiences ("God bless the lot of them," AH, p. 53), including every blessed room in Auden's Austrian house, a poem for each. The earth is the right place for love, all these poems assert, and they show over and over again that any sort of involvement in human existence is better than being removed from it.

When objects, experiences, and people are no longer things to be analyzed, manipulated, assessed, and modified, but things to delight in and celebrate, the nature of the poetry changes. "The impulse to create a work of art," Auden wrote in the midst of this change, "is felt when, in certain persons, the passive awe provoked by sacred beings or events is transformed into a desire to express that awe in a rite of worship or homage. . . . nothing is expected in return" (*DH*, p. 57). None of Auden's poetic speakers would dare the romantic ardor of this prose declaration, but it can be taken as an accurate account of what they feel on those rare unguarded moments when effusions overflow. Auden's intellectual journey through the terrain of Freud, Marx, and Kierkegaard had led him, by a somewhat cloudy route, ever closer to the acceptance of life that from the very beginning showed fitfully in his temperament, if seldom at first in his speaker's pronouncements. Now, with life openly declared to be delightful, the celebrating poetry begins, and almost every-thing from Sheldon's body types to limericks and clerihews testify to his enjoyment of the goodness in every mote. Like bathrooms and ears, these too must be numbered in the song.

There is no reason to trace the pattern of Auden's ideas further. The ideas go no further in any case, and the poetry after 1951 is less *about* ideas than at any time in his career. The intellectual search ended in the 1940's; the 1950's and 1960's celebrate what has been found: that life is blessed. As Auden accepts it all now—limestone men, Caesars, saints, Utopians—everyone, however awful their tastes and deplorable their ambitions, his dislikes become benign, his jibes playful. No disapproval however happily indulged threatens his large approval. Life is encom-passed, taken in, and celebrated. Men, all imperfect and sinful, are good. Imperfection and sinfulness themselves become good in a sense. They make life what it is, men what they are; and both are blessed. Fundamen-tal changes in all this are impossible, and any zealous tinkering with human affairs will probably make things worse. Auden wants no New Jerusalems built in his pleasant if not very green land. In a small way, of course, many things might be improved, but not man's imperfect nature, the certainty of his bewilderment, and his incorrigible error—and in any case these limitations make life more a delight than a painful burden. Human existence, therefore, not only cannot be significantly changed, but

Auden would not change it if he could. For him life is not just a religious necessity but a secular pleasure. The world, if not the best imaginable, is the best possible, and can be accepted with joy.

Most of this message no longer comes directly from what the speakers talk *about,* but from *how* they talk. The style carries the message, and that style, of course, is comic. After 1950 Auden becomes almost exclusively a comic poet, and this poetry with its comic message is his greatest achievement. But very little can be shown about it by tracing the pattern of ideas. Neither can this critical approach describe important things in the earlier work. It is time to look at Auden's poems as something other than a repository of ideas.

TWO

The Pattern of Personae

IN "NOCTURNE I," an otherwise unassuming poem in *The Shield of Achilles,* the speaker makes a most unusual public statement. He admits that he is pulled in different directions by highly contradictory impulses, and, dividing his personality in half, he gives separate beliefs and voices to each. While they squabble over apparent trivialities these voices carry on a familiar debate that for nearly thirty years had smoldered beneath the surface of Auden's poetry. These are the voices of two opposing parts of Auden's temperament, and their opposition, more than anything else, has made his poetry the kind of thing it is. In "Nocturne I" the moon, that old poetic stage prop, makes them flare up once more. " 'Adore Her, Mother, Virgin, Muse,' " begins one voice in full fustian, singing robes firmly in place, declaiming from some high podium. " 'You will not tell me,' " responds the other, feet and style solidly on the ground, " 'That bunch of barren craters care / Who sleeps with or who tortures whom' " (*SA,* p. 50). Labeled "heart" and "mind" in the poem, these two "natures" (Auden's term) in reality are the voices of much larger and more complicated parts of Auden's poetic self. I propose to call them Poet and Antipoet.

Since by nature language is a lively thing, the mere repeated appearance of the terms Poet and Antipoet will soon tend to turn these abstractions into metaphor, metaphor into allegory; and before long Poet and Antipoet will seem to be living entities romping around in some physical organism called "Auden," moving his hand across this line, choosing that image for his pencil, directing his every breath like Groddeck's It. This can threaten to turn a critical tool into an imaginative drama with a will of its own. I will begin then with some definitions and disclaimers designed to make tools remain tools. By "Auden" I mean not the flesh and blood mortal, but the Grand Persona, the Maker as he is fashioned by his own writing. While it is tempting to think this Grand Persona resembles the man (and some evidence suggests it does), to yield to this can invalidate every descriptive statement. Even the most confessional Romantic poet "makes" his poetry but not his life. And if Poet and Antipoet appear to be second and third parties living in a world called "Auden," this is critical allegory. The man in the Austrian house does not suffer from fugal personalities, as far as I know. My complete and only purpose, ultimately, is to *describe the poetry,* not the man behind it, and my critical terms are an apparatus to make this task easier. I want also to avoid building my description on some central "thesis" that, if shaky, may topple the whole descriptive structure. What I am setting up then is a model that is neither the "truth" nor complete. But it is useful; it works. And if incomplete, it is not false. If successful it will not be destroyed by, but incorporated into, later models that provide even more useful descriptive structures.

The things I want to attach to the words Poet and Antipoet vary a good deal—ideas, most obviously, beliefs and doctrines—but not just these. Ideas, beliefs, thoughts, philosophies, moods, feelings, experiences are all carried in a voice, and a voice is created by such things as syntactical habits, rhetorical patterns, levels of usage, favorite words, repeated figures, and dozens of such matters. Verbal behavior, rather than beliefs or ideas, often separates Poet from Antipoet. In short, they are more personalities than mere animated ideas, and like all personalities can be distinguished by a wide range of habits—regardless of what they believe or think they believe. For instance, though Auden's Antipoet is inclined to believe that Art is a small thing, to delight in mocking speech, low-brow diction, slangy abuse, jokes, and buffoonery, no one of these is essential to his existence. On special occasions he can praise Art or use the most elegant sort of diction and syntax. Some personality features remain to set him off from the Poet. What these are will emerge from the examples that follow.

II

Poet and Antipoet owe their existence in part to the difference between Art and Life, the cause of a moral dilemma Auden struggled with for much of his career. Reduced to its fundamental paradigm, the dilemma is that "Art is not life," and vice versa (*CP*, p. 267). If both seem valuable, how can their dissimilar virtues be connected? How can one cross from the aesthetic world where "heroes roar and die" to the mortal world where ethical choices must be made, where "Shall-I" must become "I-Will"—or I won't (*CP*, p. 351)? Wavering back and forth between the poles of this dilemma, never completely able to reconcile their opposing claims on him, Auden has at times favored Art, at times, Life. If the Poet preferred Art, the Antipoet felt "deep abhorrence" when he "caught anyone preferring Art / To Life and Love . . ." (*LLB*, p. 210). If the Poet believed his craft to be "The greatest of vocations" (*CP*, p. 268) and sang grandly at the top of his voice from Mount Parnassus ("O Love, the interest itself in thoughtless Heaven," *CP*, p. 89), the Antipoet generally countered with some wry observation: "none are lost so soon as those / Who overlook their crooked nose" (*CP*, 288). Pleasant though it may be, even "useful," the Antipoet remarks, Art is

> . . . not to be confused
>   With anything really important
> Like feeding strays or looking pleased when caught
>   By a bore or a hideola. . . .
> (N, p. 65)

Compared to Life, the Antipoet nearly always reminds, Art is a puny, feeble, insignificant pastime that makes "nothing happen" (*CP*, p. 50), a thing overlooked entirely by Gaea, Clio, and Dame Kind, those monumental makers and movers of Life. "I dare not ask you if you bless the poets," says the speaker ruefully to the muse of history in *Homage to Clio*, "For you do not look as if you ever read them / Nor can I see a reason why you should" (*HC*, p. 6). Poet and Antipoet owe their being and their temperaments, in part, to Auden's inability to conjure away his incompatible attractions to both Art and Life.

Whatever he believes about Art and Life, a poet's every poem will carry at least one inescapable message: poetry is worth while. A poem's very existence asserts this dogma. The poem's speaker, of course, may propose something quite different: I am unhappily in love, life is short, the world is evil, anything—even "Nothing is worthwhile." In such cases a work's total meaning, a composite of two messages, may be quite different from what the author intended. The type case is a poem whose speaker says, "Nothing is worthwhile." If all artifacts inevitably assert that "Art is worth while," no artist can convey the message "Nothing is worthwhile," or even a special case of this, "Art is not worth while." In serious jeopardy also, if not entirely ruled out, is "Art is less worth while than other things." What will happen if a poet puts such messages into his art? If he states in his poem that "Art has no value," or "I doubt whether Art has value," the message of his work will be: "The poet has mixed feelings," or "The speaker and the poet do not agree about Art's value." In either case personae begin to emerge from the split between what the poem *shows* and what it says. Obviously, the reader thinks, the speaker cannot be the creator—or at least not the *whole* creator—since what the speaker doubts or denies the creator asserts by making the poem. Poems of this sort suddenly become very complicated. Is the poet deliberately separating himself from the speaker, we wonder, and, if so, what further significance are we to draw from this separation? Or has he failed to recognize the distance between himself and his speaker? If the latter is true, we must watch the behavior of two personae within the poet, and just what his poems mean will not be easy to describe. The difficulty is in trying to resolve such contradictions into a single message. How does one weigh the meaning of what a speaker says against the meaning asserted by the artifact's existence? How does one reconcile *what* the speaker says with *how* he says it when the what and how conflict? If a speaker tells us nothing is worthwhile in an artful language overflowing with creative ebullience and delight, how do we describe what the poem means?

Only the most naïve artist, of course, will believe his speaker's message can remain unaffected by the material of its environment. Experienced artists have always known that a message antagonistic toward art must attack the medium itself. The total artifact, with its inescapable positive plea, must be destroyed. But since no one can totally destroy art by making artifacts, only more modest ambitions have any chance for success. If it cannot be annihilated, the medium can at least be maimed, cut up, spit on, or laughed at. Thus any artist with serious doubts about the value of his vocation will inevitably come to meddle, consciously or not, with the very bones, sinews, and tendons of the medium whose value he doubts. He must try to alter its built-in message. And, in trying, he will certainly produce an object that will appear odd, outlandish, or ugly to an audience nourished on artifacts made by men who never ceased to believe in the great worth of what they were doing. These elementary propositions will help the reader of Auden, in a variety of ways, to understand the kind of thing his poetry is.

Sometimes Auden translated his doubts about Art into philosophical and ideological doctrine—especially in his prose. Sometimes poetic speakers openly talked about these matters. But far more often his doubts caused him to bend, mutilate, twist, or in some way mock the very medium that insisted, by its implacable existence, that Art had great value. In the 1930's especially, the Antipoet in Auden believed Art might be an escape from Life, not a mirror held up to nature. He suspected that Art was magic, unreal. The Poet, on the other hand, preferred Art to anything else, and, if not held rigorously in check, moved further and further from Life. Peering down from on high with the eye of a detached authority and clinical observer, he remained aloof and superior, and spoke in a tongue far removed from lifelike speech. But the higher his song the more likely his fall. Lofty poetic flights threatened to attract the Antipoet, who enjoyed tumbling his opponent from the heights by pelting him with coarse chunks of Life, mocking, laughing, deriding, deflating his pretensions. On such occasions poems become a battleground. While all this is going on the speaker's utterance may seem peculiar and confusing, even trivial, to readers brought up on Milton, Wordsworth, Tennyson, Eliot— indeed, most English poetry. But what emerges is poetry nevertheless. All this battling, contradicting, canceling out, and self-mockery does not eliminate the poem line by line until it disappears. It adds line after line, and in doing so creates its own peculiar message.

The message of all these battles and twistings is, in part, "I, the maker of these poems, am troubled about the value of poetry, but not so troubled that I don't delight in writing it, and I am uncertain about the style my poetic speakers should use." In a very real sense this is the important message of many Auden poems from 1930 well into the 1940's. What the speakers in those poems talk *about* (Freud, Marx, love, cultural sickness—the things discussed in the first chapter) is often less important than what they reveal by *how* they speak. In extreme cases what these poems mean and what their speakers say is completely unlike. While the Poet may speak solemnly about cultural decadence, and the Antipoet taunt him for mouthing pompous pretensions, the poem itself may steadily show Auden's concern about the distance between Art and Life and his uncertainty about what to do about it.

But the split between Art and Life, simply by being examined, threatens to become too serious, too important. Described as a man set upon by doubts, Auden begins to sound like some anguished Romantic guiltily destroying his special gifts. Discussion so far may suggest that he rejects a heroic and exalted dedication to Art for heroic and exalted opposition to it. The full truth is much more complex. Though his doubts about Art are real, Auden is no more the agonized antiprophet than he is an orphic seer. As Antipoet he would mock the one as loudly as the other. Both are alike in imagining the poet to be some heroic figure, struggling magnificently against heavy odds to utter something Important. Just such pretentiousness is the Antipoet's main enemy. Auden's Antipoet is not so much against the artist, the Romantic, or the serious as against the pretentious. Auden is temperamentally the sort of man who can instantly notice the ridiculous side of everything. For people of this sort, blessed (or plagued) with a comic eye, every earnest human act may appear hilarious, the more earnest the more hilarious. They always detect the silliness in every solemn speech, dignified act, or venerable object or institution. They can never for long pretend that life is anything but fundamentally and helplessly preposterous. Among the slogans that help explain Auden's poetry, "I hate pompositas and all authority" (*LLB,* p. 203) is even more important than "Art is not life" (*CP,* p. 267). So if pompous claims about Art's sacred purpose are silly, so are smug pronouncements of the opposite sort. Gifted with comic sight, Auden seldom fails to notice how ludicrous is the sober Poet talking about anything in exalted terms. He must be brought down to recognize the innate foolishness of all human behavior, especially the absurdity of those who take themselves too seriously. To the Antipoet goes this educational task, and his deflating procedures are various. Sometimes he openly mocks or abuses the Poet; more often he parodies or burlesques. Sometimes the mere threat of his appearance seems to frighten the Poet into suicidal antics. This happens when the Poet, in the midst of solemn statements, ingenious analyses, sober diagnoses, authoritative classifications, pontifical judgments, suddenly seems to remember the Antipoet invisible in the wings, watching his performance with a fishy eye. Nervously listening for backstage snickers, the Poet, embarrassed by his own posturing, may suddenly begin to burlesque himself. "I am not really this pompous fool, this earnest bore, this smug poseur my performance suggests," he implies. "It was all a joke. I was fooling. It was an elaborate hoax, a comic parody you mistakenly took seriously. Look!" And he flies a bit higher, elevates diction and syntax a notch, and, sure enough, the heroic turns mock. We see it is all a farce. The Poet, destroying himself, turns into Antipoet, while the poem cracks in half, its message reverses itself, and the speech collapses around him in a comic heap—to the bewilderment and confusion of many readers. Even more disastrous than this are those times when the Poet unintentionally turns comic. He falls by rising, of course, since for him the way up is always the way down. If he steadily ascends increasing heights of solemnity, at some point he will soar into silliness. Sometimes he does accidentally fly too high, and wax, feathers, and all plunge into unintentional comedy.

Though poems may be nearly destroyed by these curious antics, Auden's destructive acts never reflect a temperament masochistically and soddenly bent on self-destruction, driven by some grim death wish. Quite the opposite. Auden was never a poet of defeat, continually emphasizing the gaping abyss, evil, the skull beneath the skin, getting perverse joy from self-torment and pleasure from despair. In an age when many have said no to life Auden has usually said yes. Even the Auden we see in the early poetry fits Louis MacNeice's description: "Who have felt the death-wish too, / But your lust for life prevails. . . ." [1] Auden's distrust of human pretensions in himself as well as in others is not a negative but a positive thing. Pomposity and authority, the enemies, dwell only amid the illusion that life is more certain than it is, that more is known about it than can be known. Thus the Poet, attracted to certainty, is forever tempted to turn away from confused Life to those twin certainties pessimism and optimism. In opposing this, the Antipoet's destructive violence (even though a poem may be ruined by it) is nearly always an act of healthy common sense, vigorous reality attacking the smug illusions of those who believe life to be either better or worse than it really is. The inflated optimist who sings "I'll love you, dear, I'll love you / Till China and Africa meet . . ." must be brought down (CP, p. 197). But so must those who believe the world to be a bleak sink of disgust and despair. Attacks on doom and neurotic despair, in fact, are more common in Auden's poetry than attacks on effusive optimism. Optimists often appear rather lovable innocents, deserving a gentle mockery. After all, soon destined to encounter those inescapable "Furies . . . / With claw and dreadful brow," simple naïfs may be treated kindly (N, p. 17). But the

---

[1] W. H. Auden and Louis MacNeice, *Letters From Iceland* (London: Faber and Faber, 1937), p. 261.

smugness of despair receives harsher treatment. Auden's Antipoet vigorously attacks narcissists who, crying they are not worthy, turn their faces to the wall.

Auden's compulsion to note the ludicrous in every solemn action, then, appears healthy rather than sick. Even the most casual reader, though he may not understand the change, will discover suddenly a great wave of liveliness sweeping across a poem when the Antipoet takes command. Suddenly, in the midst of often funereal surroundings, of dismal prophecies and prognoses of defeat, life asserts itself. High spirits, even joy, break forth. Auden comes alive when his Antipoet appears. His spirits rise, his speakers become delighted with their own vitality, energy, cleverness, intelligence. Their ostensible malice often turns kindly and sometimes becomes a disguise for love. His sober Poet holds life in check, suppresses high spirits, stifles health and joy. His favorite speeches are about cultural sickness. When the Antipoet bursts forth filled with lively abuse and ebullient skepticism, his very presence shows that life is good. If the Antipoet distrusts Art, his mockery of it is still a healthy mockery that in attacking anything too soberly Important is affirmative rather than the opposite. And since the Antipoet speaks poetry, he makes Art by championing Life. The resulting poetic object, therefore, does not carry a message of grim despair from its battlefield, but asserts the value of both Art and Life, and especially of the struggle between them.

III

One way of describing the whole body of Auden's poetry is to call it the result of his attempts to control and accommodate the opposing temperamental forces I have called Poet and Antipoet. In the early work he fluctuates between them, sometimes believing that his poems should be stern, solemn confrontations of important issues, yet at the same time suspicious of such grave pretensions and persistently delighted with high-spirited horseplay, mockery, and comic abuse of all sorts. In Auden we find twin paradoxes. He has been a prolific poet who distrusted poetry and a stylist with a great natural talent both for speech in the grand manner and for clowning, parody, and comic high jinks of all kinds. What sort of decent modern poetry could be made from such hostile impulses and incompatible gifts? No answer came easily. One solution was to suppress one or another of the incompatibilities. Often he tried banishing the Antipoet, and occasionally the Poet. But neither would stay exiled. Frequently he mixed them together in a variety of ways, intentionally or unintentionally. From these mixtures came successful poems and some memorable failures. But since he could not seem completely to reject either Poet or Antipoet, permanent success depended on finding some way to join the ill-fitting parts of his temperament. In effect, he had to learn how to make poems that mocked poetry, and how to believe in something that laughed at the pretensions of belief. When he learned how to do both, he made some extraordinarily beautiful poems. They were profound, moving, astoundingly skillful—and comic.

Before *Look, Stranger!* (1936) Auden swooped dangerously back and forth between his temperamental extremes. In *Poems* (1930 and 1933), the Poet prevails, though he must struggle hard for command against an Antipoet threatening almost everywhere to subvert him. While nearly half of the thirty selections are dominated by the Poet's voice, he is often close to self-parody, and sometimes collapses, punctured by burlesque. In *The Orators* (1932), *The Dance of Death* (1933), and *The Dog Beneath the Skin* (1935), as though exploding from his thralldom in *Poems,* the Antipoet runs riot everywhere, turning nearly everything into farce, and reversing the Poet's somber messages. We first see the Poet in the very first selection in *Poems.* Successfully fending off the Antipoet here, his performance carries to the end without disastrous incident. The persona is that of the clinical Dr. Auden, turning his microscope on the infections of his class and time:

> Will you turn a deaf ear
> To what they said on the shore,
> Interrogate their poises
> In their rich houses. . . .
>   (*CP,* p. 177),

The tone of voice, serious, solemn, but unemotional, rings with faint superiority, the diagnostician addressing his weakly receptive patients. The reader sees right away that the poem is a rather self-conscious performance. Diction, drawn almost too enthusiastically from several usage levels, is nevertheless severely formal ("Interrogate" for "question," "affectionate instant" for "companion," "porcelain filter" for "gas mask"). And everything is spoken in the rough, slightly queer, jerky syntax Auden borrowed from Anglo-Saxon. Though the Poet maintains decorum throughout, danger lurks everywhere. His performance, just a degree too high, shows Auden's strain. The collection of formal diction, slang, smart psychological coinages ("compulsory touchers") and straight-faced private allusions ("His favorite colour as blue / Colour of distant bells / And boys' overalls")—all hover near pretentiousness (*CP*, pp. 177–78). Though he keeps tongue out of cheek here, for a man unusually receptive to comedy this sort of production skates on thin ice. Burlesque lurks nearby. Nevertheless the early Auden sustains unblemished the Poet's role here and elsewhere, in "Sir, no man's enemy, forgiving all . . ." (*CP*, p. 110), and in other poems such as "Who stands, the crux left of the watershed . . ." (*CP*, p. 175). He even manages it in

> Love by ambition
> Of definition
> Suffers partition . . .
>   (*CP*, p. 78),

where the two-stress rhymed line, though it lends to his pronouncements an aphoristic terseness, shoves a jingling jerky meter into the stately syntax so essential to the Poet's gravity.

The Antipoet has a few poems all to himself, too. In one of the most notorious ("Beethameer, Beethameer, bully of Britain / With you face as fat as a farmer's bum . . ."), he throws coarse comic abuse at pompous pretenders: "Suckling the silly from a septic teat. / Leading the lost with lies to defeat . . ." (*O*, p. 62). His crude health still very much evident, but his manners slightly better, the Antipoet dominates again in "Get there if you can and see the land you once were proud to own . . ." (*P*, p. 73). This vigorous advocate of Life will tolerate no nonsense about the literature of sensibility, the delicate music of the refined aesthete, or about Art as a miraculous construction fulfilling its own ends. Using Tennyson's least refined meter, the Kipling-like speaker gives us a bouncing message about how to live properly in that no-nonsense world where robust men generally respond to intellectuals with distaste (to Newman, Plato, Baudelaire, and nine others). The Antipoet speaker says he likes intellectuals if they preach the superiority of Life (Lawrence, Blake, Homer Lane), but his tone betrays an affection for violent action rather than for the effete complexities of feeling and thought: "Shut up talking, charming in the best suits to be had in town, / Lecturing on navigation while the ship is going down" *P*, p. 76). The speaker here technically aligns himself with the sick by using, at the end, the rhetorical courtesy of "we." But the games-master tone in which he advises the "we," with its no-nonsense bluntness about straightening up properly, shows that in reality this Antipoet speaker thinks of himself as one of the healthy, a man who has little patience with the overeducated Oxbridge weaklings wavering on the precipice of decadence. The healthy gusto with which Auden creates this Antipoetic persona contrasts sharply with the restrained, unemotive intellectuality of his Poet's high-brow poems, composed with singing robes on. The excess energy released here shows, I think, with what delight Auden attacks intellectuals, the educated, and the overrefined, and with what enthusiasm he drops the highly formal diction and artificial syntax of his solemn poems—all suspected by the Antipoet of being pretentious.

As Antipoet Auden can maintain decorum and present a consistent message in several ways. One way is to make the Antipoet speaker a sick man. In this guise Auden can properly let flow all the clowning, joking, and jeering he likes so much. If the speaker's antics appear foolish, so much the better. He *is* foolish. He is sick. The poem beginning "It's no use raising a shout. / No, Honey, you can cut that right out . . ." is one of these (*P,* p. 52). Poems of this sort clearly separate Auden from the speaker. Though he lends the speaker his Antipoetic voice, he does so only to demonstrate the sick speaker's somewhat contemptible silliness, while the maker stands apart as one of the healthy, and mocks. Some readers, who find humor at the expense of the maimed tasteless, dislike these early poems with sick speakers. If Auden sometimes fails here it is partly because his allegory becomes too lifelike. These unfortunates eliciting his raucous scorn are usually meant to be mere types, ideas, cultural habits, or behavior patterns, turned into semihumans for the purpose of acting in his allegorical landscapes. But if they become too human, the reader may be repelled by the inhumanity of Auden's attack and the crude analysis of their faults. If they are really human, the diagnosis of their illness is sometimes so simple-minded as to be little more than an excuse for abusing them. The danger of the Poet lies mainly in his pomposity, that of the Antipoet in his crudeness.

Antipoetic speakers need not be sick to maintain decorum and consistency, of course. In the ode to John Warner the Antipoet speaker is neither comically neurotic nor abusively healthy, but something else, something very important in the history of Auden's development. Dropping entirely his mask of Poet and grave social critic, Auden appears here in the guise of a high-spirited, good-natured, playful speaker, full of open affection and good feeling, writing to a close friend on the birth of his first child. Nearly the whole poem is raucously mock-heroic, Antipoet parodying Poet. Yet the speaker is less interested in laughing at the high-style Poet or John Warner than at himself. The mockery itself is patently absurd. The travesty of celebrating infant Warner as a terror of the sick and hero of the healthy indicates neither the absurdity of little John (who in traditional mock-heroic would be the satirical target) nor the contemptible weakness of his enemies (the secondary target). The speaker is the foolish one, the man who constructed the whole thing, the mocker himself. By laughing at himself he achieves humility through self-abasement. Along with the friendly chaffing of little John and the good-natured exaggeration of his capacities, this humility denotes nothing but affection for the entire Warner family. This is the mockery of love, the first seedling of a technique that will blossom years later into some of Auden's finest poetry. Despite its friendly intent, though, this Antipoetic poem is destructive as well. There is no Poet present to be deflated, but his ideas are here. Throughout, the Antipoetic speaker plays prankishly with the notion that society is inhabited by the ill. This is one of the Poet's persistent messages, developed in many poems from 1928 on. Here it is treated as a good-natured joke between Auden and Warner. Castigation of the sick in high-style and pompous manner is a spoof, nothing more than the raffish poet playing Poet. Both the Poet's role of social critic and his pretentious manner are laughed at by a speaker apparently content with things as they are. As a result the world's alleged ills and dangers seem mere harmless bogeys. Little John Warner can solve everything in a minute with a wrench: "See him take off his coat and get down with a spanner / To each unhappy Joseph and repressed Diana . . ." (O, p. 100). That this speaker feels the world to be a good place, satisfying and comfortable, becomes explicit at the end, where everyday life at Helensburgh is talked about with an emotion and directness rare in the early Auden:

> We make ourselves cozy when the weather is wet
> With a shocker, a spaniel and a crystal set.
> The taps are turned off and the boys are in bed:
>   Drowsing I droop like a dying flower,
> But I'm going to sleep, not going to be dead. . . .
>   (O, p. 102)

Though this poem's message is internally consistent, Auden's attitude about his early themes is not. The Antipoet feels one way about them, the Poet another. The ode to John Warner simply contradicts, explicitly and implicitly, the "Auden" of the early Poetic poems. It is tempting, of course, to feel that this Antipoetic Auden is the "real" Auden, stepping for once from behind all the masks. He does seem more likable, personal, and human than the formidable Poet, pronouncing, diagnosing, condemning in so many early poems. And this temptation becomes almost irresistible when we know that benign speakers like this one will dominate Auden's poetry twenty years later, everywhere proclaiming life's blessedness. But this early genial Antipoet is not the whole Auden either. To present him, Poet and Antipoet must join. Apart they just contradict each other's message and style.

Auden's early poetry can be very confusing for even the most skillful readers. Even internally consistent poems can be puzzling enough, with their variety of speakers, allegorical landscapes, and private allusions. When inconsistent, they almost defy description. But since much of the complexity, and nearly all the inconsistency, is caused by the hostility of what I have called Poet and Antipoet, these terms now make it possible to describe more fully than the first chapter could the enormously complicated situation in these early poems. Schematic description will best simplify the complexities. If individual poems, though internally coherent, can contradict each other, let us consider the numerous possibilities for confusion in Auden's early work. His temperament is split into two forces or personae, Poet and Antipoet, each with its own style, beliefs, inclinations, predispositions, and habits. Within the allegorical landscape of these early poems are three classes of people who speak: the sick, the well, and the neutral observers. How may these five elements be combined?

First, a sick speaker may appropriately use:

   1. the Poet's voice
      —straightforwardly to confess and analyze his own sickness.
      —pompously to indicate indirectly his sick foolishness.
   2. the Antipoet's voice
      —to reveal his own clownish sickness or banality.
   3. awkward and contradictory combinations of the Poet's and Antipoet's voices

—to reveal his own confused sickness.

Second, a healthy speaker may appropriately use

    1. the Poet's voice

        —to analyze or denounce sickness and suggest a cure (but he must avoid the dangers of pomp and pretentiousness).

    2. the Antipoet's voice

        —to denounce and abuse the sick and show by his manner the healthy vigor of life (but he must avoid appearing foolish or banal himself, and he must avoid making what he attacks appear trivial by his comedy—or seem a complete spoof).

    3. awkward or contradictory combinations of the Poet's and Antipoet's voice

        —never (except to mock the Poet by mimicry. In this case the Poet must be clearly identified as one of the sick. If the Poet speaks as one of the healthy, accurately analyzing sickness, and is then mocked or parodied, the poem collapses).

Third, a neutral speaker may appropriately use

    1. the Poet's voice

        —to analyze, describe conditions, and suggest cures (but he must avoid the danger of pretentiousness and unintentional self-parody).

    2. the Antipoet's voice

        —only at its mildest (though he may be permitted enough wit and verbal dexterity to indicate his intelligence and rhetorical skill).

    3. awkward combinations of the voices

        —never (except when mimicking the frivolous or banal sick, and even this is dangerous).

Charts and lists may be unattractive substitutes for exposition, but I believe this one provides an outline of the major complexities of personae in Auden's poetry from about 1928 to about 1935, though it comes nowhere near exhausting all of them. Given his own temperamental fluctuations and this involuted web of subtleties in his personae, it is hardly surprising that time after time Auden sails along the edge of disaster and often falls over. I do not imply, of course, that he purposely, or even consciously, fashioned the tangle of dramatic alternatives outlined above. Many things (some perhaps inadvertent) contributed to its growth: his almost compulsive habit of allegorizing nearly everything he touched, from nouns to entire volumes; his continual use of speakers separate from himself; his uncertainty about the role of poetry itself. All these and other temperamental inclinations and gifts produced this almost fantastically complex poetic situation, filled with the possibility of suddenly dropping into an abyss of self-contradiction.

Poems examined so far, though they may contradict one another, have been internally consistent. Many others are not. I will not attempt to examine a failure for each type on my list, but the whole subject deserves some detailed attention. Poems that explode and collapse under pressure from the incompatible parts of Auden's temperament are among the most striking features of his early work and the seed ground for later growth.

Inconsistent and contradictory poems are appropriate if their speaker is sick, and therefore purposely made to look awkward and incoherent. In all other cases such poems are simply flawed. The *author* is disorganized and contradictory. Distinguishing between the two is not always easy. The most notoriously unclear case is the ode that begins "Though aware of our rank and alert to obey orders. . . ." Joseph Warren Beach, a perceptive reader, spent eight pages of his book mulling over the puzzle of this poem before he tentatively advanced a conclusion.[2] He decided reluctantly (but rightly I think) that the speaker is not Auden, but one of the sick. Auden is outside the monologue, more knowing than the speaker, healthier, showing some contempt for him. Yet Beach's problem—and everyone's—is that Auden's partisanship is too faint (indicated almost entirely by private myth details described in Chapter One). Since the speaker alternates awkwardly between the Poet's solemnity and the Antipoet's foolishness, no one who assumed Auden to be the speaker could decide for certain whether the speech or the mockery of it is the message. But if we assume the speaker to be sick, then the poem's contradictions are appropriate. This will explain why the speaker's pompous solemnity contrasts ludicrously with his clownish slips:

> Your childish moments of awareness were all of our world,
>
> . . . .
> At night your mother taught you to pray for our Daddy. . . .

(CP, p. 137)

[2] Joseph Warren Beach, *The Making of the Auden Canon* (Minneapolis: University of Minnesota Press, 1957), pp. 84–92.

To stand with the wine-dark conquerors in the roped-off pews,
    Shout ourselves hoarse:
"They ran like hares; we have broken them up like firewood. . . ."
                                    (*CP*, p. 138)

Interpreted this way the poem shows Auden standing outside the poem
laughing at the speaker's performance. But this is certainly not clear.
Even a careful reader could think Auden agrees with the speaker and
thereby reverse the poem's message. Apparently we are expected to
discover, without external comment, that the speaker is unreliable, that
the truth (or most of it) is the opposite of what he says. Yet his
unreliability is so faint as to be scarcely discernible. Maybe Auden simply
miscalculated (which is easy enough to do in such a case). Or he may
have written the poem for his friends, for whom faint clues were enough.
Or he himself may have wavered, unable to decide how foolish the
speaker was.

    If we decide that "Though aware of our rank and alert to obey orders
. . ." is a consistent poem whose consistency fails to be clear, what are we
to think of poems where the speaker's reliability is never established, even
by ultrasubtle clues? "Not, father, further do prolong / Our necessary
defeat . . ." is as interesting case of this. The poem seems to contain a
sick speaker solemnly requesting the quick destruction of his illness. But
how is the poet related to this speaker? If the poet stands apart (neutral
or one of the healthy) all flaws in the poetry—bad lines, pompous
diction, exaggerated hysteria, farcical behavior—reflect appropriately on
the sick speaker. But if the poet approves of the speaker, or if speaker and
poet are identical, all such lapses are either breaches of decorum or failure
of craft. I think this particular poem begins with Auden speaking as Poet,
soberly petitioning for health. But in trying to maneuver his grave formal
speech through some extremely involuted Anglo-Saxon syntax he stum-
bles into unintentional comedy:

These nissen huts if hiding could
    Your eye inseeing from
Firm fenders were. . . .
        (*O*, p. 110)

With some minute changes indicating that this comedy was intentional,
Auden could, without changing a word of the quoted lines, make this
utterance appropriate. The speaker could be made into one of the comic

sick, or into a healthy Antipoet parodying the pompous Poet. But without such indications the speaker's flaws are the author's flaws. Auden makes a mistake. The poem flounders. His Poet steps across the border between high dignity and comic pomposity, and decorum is broken.

"Consider this and in our time . . ." is a slightly clearer case. The speaker here is the Poet, neither sick nor healthy, but a neutral observer. Exalted and omniscient, he looks down on a sick culture. His language, extremely formal and rigorously abstract, borders on the pedantic. Describing a hotel dining room, he uses an idiom even Cowper might have blushed at. Through the window he sees

> . . . insufficient units
> .   .   .   .
> . . . constellated at reserved tables
> Supplied with feelings by an efficient band
> (CP, p. 27):

that is, while people eat, musicians play. Elsewhere the diction, though still stiffly formidable, may be accepted as proper for this very learned and correct Poet, who never calls a mountain a mountain if its proper classification is "massif," who says that clouds "rift," and speaks in phrases such as "life's limiting defect" and "derelict works." All these the tolerant reader might swallow, forgiving the Poet for being a bit of a stuffed shirt, but noting in his favor that he is unbending enough for a few happily low-brow clichés: "admire the view," "leisurely conversation," "within a stone's throw" (*CP,* pp. 27–28). But what are tolerant readers to think later on, when the idiom suddenly becomes undeniably pompous on the one hand and hilariously undignified on the other?

> And mobilize the powerful forces latent
> In soils that make the farmer brutal
> In the infected sinus, and the eyes of stoats
> (CP, p. 28),

the speaker says at one point. Do what with the soils? we exclaim. *Mobilize* their *forces?* To infect what? Sinuses and stoats' eyes? Can we accept this as serious speech? Can Auden, who later made high comedy out of just such incongruous juxtapositions, have stumbled accidentally into this preposterous style? If we believe so our credulity will soon get a further buffeting. Juxtapositions that follow are even more fatal to solemnity. After plunging from lofty dignity to sinuses and stoats' eyes, the

speaker next frightens the sick with the bogey of a destructive "rumour
. . . horrifying in its capacity to disgust," a rumor likely to become for
them "A polar peril, a prodigious alarm." In an earlier version this
mock-heroic utterance was then followed by a stanza that continually
demolished the stuffy speaker's decorum. And as his Poetic mask fell
away, to our great surprise we discovered underneath something of a
gleeful, naughty urchin issuing slangy low-brow threats ("The game is
up for you"; "It is later than you think"). He also showed a leering
fascination for queer neurotic symptoms, especially sexual, and was not
above making everything comic by purposely linking together the most
unlikely incongruities. For instance, among his list of doomed neurotics
were those "Who are born nurses, who live in shorts / Sleeping with
people and playing fives" (P, p. 88). The speaker, who began as a Poet,
turned into an Antipoet. Can Auden possibly have fallen unintentionally
into such comic circumstances? I think the answer is yes—that is, at *first*
the comedy was unintentional. Once it began, Auden purposely continued
it. The first lapses seem clearly unplanned. And even at the end the poem
struggles bravely to maintain some vestige of its formal idiom and Poetic
persona, as though retention of both were part of the original plan. The
disaster occurs, I think, because though Auden as Poet is forced to be
solemn, elevated, and seriously concerned with large weighty matters such
as the evolution of cultural collapse, he wears this mask somewhat
awkwardly. While he is fully behind it when the poem opens, it is
somewhat askew. The manner is not native to him and he gets it just
slightly wrong. The formality is misplaced in an epithet or two, the tone
is faintly too high, gravity rises into pomposity, pedantry replaces correctness, colloquial idiom slips in to mar the finish. The contrast between the
too-high and the mundane inadvertently threatens to create the very
incongruities at the heart of the mock-heroic. But when the Poetic speaker
steps accidentally across the line separating the formal from the comically
pompous, Auden begins to revel in the new possibilities. His exuberant
Antipoetic tendencies, longing to burlesque pretentiousness, take over.
Whenever his own speech releases a great deal of verbal energy, Auden's
Poet is in danger. High spirits begin to creep in, and Auden may begin to
play with the medium. "Watch this," he says, in effect, as he makes the
Poetic speaker perform an even more daring locution. Another step and
all will be burlesque. In the early poetry Auden often takes that step, by
mistake or by yielding to temptation. Then the Poet, with his dull gray

decorum, disappears. The Antipoet takes command. The stage is filled with clowning, parody, self-mockery, and verbal play of all sorts, while the Poet's message gets reversed.

The clearest case of Auden stepping across the line from Poet to Antipoet occurs in "The Argument" section of *The Orators*. The speaker, a sick gang member, begins solemnly enough, in prose not very different from much of Auden's rough-rhythm poetry. His monologue, with its free association, broken rhythms, and high serious tone of desolation, owes something to Eliot. Obvious echoes and borrowings from him appear throughout: "Speak the name only with meaning only for us" (*O*, p. 18). But very soon this tone becomes compromised and the persona confused. No sooner do lists of neurotic behavior appear than Auden's own healthy exuberance begins to show through the mournful gravity of his sick speaker ("one writes with his penis in a patch of snow 'Resurgam' "), while delight in cataloguing queer sexual behavior makes it particularly difficult for him to keep a straight face ("a douche for the unpopular member," *O*, p. 21). Behind the sober speaker the author's laughter becomes increasingly obvious. And once Auden the irrepressible comic breaks the solemn decorum, no matter how inconsistently, every utterance becomes suspect. The more sober it is the more hilarious it seems: "Theories inter-relating the system of feudal tenure with metabolic gradients" (*O*, p. 20). Did Auden intend this to be comic? It seems almost impossible that he did not. But whatever he intended when he began this section of *The Orators*, by the time his speaker gets halfway through his monologue Antipoet has replaced Poet. We are confronted by a purposely comic prayer, containing an unbroken string of ludicrous invocations: "O Goat with the Compasses, hear us," "O Marquis of Granby, hear us," "George, we beseech thee to hear us," (*O*, pp. 23, 25). This is something more than a sick narrator, in character, being foolish. Auden's Antipoet, after turning the Poet into a parody of himself, has simply run away with the performance.

A substantial portion of Auden's early work hovers on this line between solemnity and self-parody, an uneasy balance between Poet and Antipoet, so that in a single poem each may get the upper hand more than once before the end. In such cases the message, as well as everything else, seesaws from black to white and back again. In a sense the message has been destroyed. That is, the poem's opening message has been reversed by the end. But in another sense positive and negative messages blend to produce some third thing. For instance, when personae switch back and forth from Poet to Antipoet in "Under boughs between our tentative endearments how should we hear . . ." the final message is not just the opposite of the original one. It is something less than a complete reversal, some partial modification of what the speaker tries to make us believe. The poem begins with a highly serious clinical Poet, a speaker still present at the end, where in regal tones he informs us of his compassion for doomed neurotics: "Let each one share our pity, hard to withhold and hard to bear" (*CP*, p. 149). But these lofty Poetic sentiments are offset by an earlier description that displays something more like comic glee at the neurotics' plight: "their mind's constant sniffling, / Their blood's dulled shuffling." Along with an effective colloquial pun ("Fathers in sons may track / Their voices trick") these witty deprecations sound very much like the Antipoet, delighting in clever images, wordplay, and abuse. This identity is confirmed when the new voice tells us how the sick "May creep to sumps, pile up against the door, crouching in cases" (*CP*, p. 148). Certainly this is not the same speaker who finds his "pity" for these neurotics "hard to withhold and hard to bear." The Antipoet, drawn by the smell of joking, wordplay, and neurotics, is loose again. He does not sympathize with the Poet's pretentious royal forgiveness, and his brief appearances in the poem modify whatever the Poet tells us.

The best-known of Auden's confusing pieces, the "Address for a Prize-Day," is simply another case of shifting persona, probably unparalleled for creating an almost incredible tangle of irreconcilables. If the reader insists on making the "Address" coherent and consistent, he must decide whether Auden agrees with the schoolmaster speaker, whether he mocks him, or whether he can somehow manage both to mock and agree at the same time. Professor Beach, after considerable head scratching, decided that Auden agrees with the speaker, but mocks him to take the curse off his serious message. If this was Auden's intention he certainly fails disastrously. A fool's message is a foolish message, unless he is of the divine Fool sort, and Auden's schoolmaster is anything but that. Neither is he one of Auden's later speakers whose self-mockery establishes the honesty and humility of his own position. The "Address for a Prize-Day" is much more complicated than either of these possibilities. It is in fact such an unbelievable mixture of irreconcilable personae and messages, all given life with such attractive impetuosity, just as though the whole thing made perfect sense, that in a perverse way it succeeds in spite of itself. What could be more delightful, in a way, than Auden's boisterous audacity in presenting this amazing collection of comic self-contradiction for our solemn perusal. The poet who reminded the public that "he must beg / Permission now and then to pull their leg" (*LLB,* p. 24) pulls hard here—though the final joke, I suppose, was in publishing it in *The Orators* as the opening piece, where its position suggests a seriousness and direction it certainly lacks. As written originally (surely for Isherwood and the Gresham's School friends), it must have been a more intelligible joke, simultaneously parodying a Gresham's schoolmaster, schoolboy life, and Auden himself as a solemn Poet.[3] The schoolmaster is an awkward combination of Poet and Antipoet, a foolish mixture appropriate only for foolishly sick speakers. But the speaker cannot be a simple example of the foolish sick since he also presents Auden's familiar sober message about cultural decadence. When the speaker sometimes burlesques his own message, Auden's solemn themes appear silly too. Yet since Auden purposely laughs at his own Poetic messages elsewhere, even this behavior might still leave the speech internally consistent if no further reversals appeared. But they do appear. This speaker does not seem to *know* that his message is foolish, and thus his speech becomes inadvertently an attack on himself—Auden's old enemy—a certain type of public school mentality. (At the end it is the masters who are "to die without issue," stuffed into the stoke hole under the stairs by healthy boys, *O,* p. 17.) If this direction were consistently maintained, the malicious joke would be that, patently foolish as he is, the speaker believes himself healthy. But this message also collapses when Auden's delight in verbal mannerisms, clever inventions, and bizarre behavior so animates the speaker that his foolishness occasionally disappears and we come to admire his skill and wit. In short, "Address for a Prize-Day" is anything but a coherent social message. Put simply, the irreconcilable elements are these: The speaker is certainly not the author, but neither is he consistently anything else. Sometimes he speaks as Poet, sometimes as Antipoet, and each of these voices contradicts and reverses the message of the other. Auden could not make up his mind. Put in ideational terms, he could not decide what he believed. One part of him (The Poetic part) may have believed that

[3] Christopher Isherwood, *Lions and Shadows* (London: The Hogarth Press, 1938), p. 184, quotes Auden mimicking a Gresham's schoolmaster. The opening of "Address for a Prize-Day" is nearly identical.

"Address for a Prize-Day" should be a coherent artifact, with the sick speaker uttering a message that called for the destruction of others but implied that he should be one of the first to go. But another part (the Antipoet), caring little about artistic coherence, simply loved to clown, burlesque, parody, and play with words whenever he could. Neither part is subdued, controlled, or subordinated to the other in "Address for a Prize-Day," and as a result we see Auden's own temperamental inconsistency pulling the speech to pieces. Most of *The Orators* displays this sort of behavior.

Auden's early plays, *The Dance of Death* (1933) and *The Dog Beneath the Skin* (1935), are also fatally compromised by Poet and Antipoet battling for control—though in both the Antipoet wins easily. If we must decide finally whether *The Dance of Death* is a statement of or a parody of Auden's familiar evolutionary, death wish theme, surely we must choose parody (with a parody of Marx added). More accurately, the play wavers between social message and self-parody. Again in *The Dog Beneath the Skin,* whatever the authors' Brechtian beliefs about the viability of music hall drama, the play's social satire is hopelessly undermined by its vaudeville treatment of cultural ills. In this burlesque atmosphere, most evils become mere peccadillos, deserving no concern more urgent than laughter at their absurdities. Some deserve no concern at all. They are simply the unimportant subject for vaudeville gags. Part of this may be the mistake of excess. Jokes designed to take the curse off a solemn message may simply get out of hand and bury or destroy the message instead. But surely this does not explain everything. From the play's beginning the authors never seem totally interested in issuing their grave messages about a decadent world. Despite their persistent portrayal of illness and queer behavior, the play's atmosphere is generally benign. The world is all right, the play says; all this sickness is here to show how healthy and inventive and full of high spirits the authors are, and also presumably you the audience, who laugh. The social message seems to be there to make the comedy go rather than the other way round. Leaving the theater, the audience might well feel that the authors found their world not only acceptable but good fun. From time to time, in *The Dog Beneath the Skin,* the Poet puts in an uneasy appearance, but the Antipoet carries the day.

Auden's failure to unify personae and maintain decorum does not mean that each inconsistent creation is completely bad, or that his consistent works are always good. Many readers will surely prefer inconsistent Antipoetic poems to consistent ones featuring an overly pompous Poet. Occasionally we may rejoice when the Poetic speeches, growing tiresomely solemn, are shattered by the Antipoet leaping on stage to clown around. Better a flaw in decorum than a stuffed shirt Poet. In any case flaws are not fatal to art. Even the worst of Auden's early work usually exhibits great verbal energy, and verbal energy is the *sine qua non* of poetry. He may sometimes lose control, but at least there is an energy that needs controlling, and its mere presence is the most promising omen in the work of a beginning poet. Nevertheless Auden's incompatible swoops from Poet to Antipoet raise important doubts about his early philosophical themes. Much can be made of Auden the penetrating social analyst, who shows a profound understanding of both the sick and the healthy, and who surveys all from an omniscient hawk's-view perspective. But most generalizations made about this "Auden" are not quite right. The early Auden scarcely fits the image of that disapproving, sober cultural analyst built up by journalists and public. One part of his temperament seemed profoundly content with life as he found it, and when he spoke as a grave cultural diagnostician and activist leader, he sometimes had to invent personae whose earnest disapprovals were so alien to some of his own inclinations that he could scarcely keep from burlesquing them. Auden the social critic is only part of the total Auden. There is also an Auden who mocks social criticism. The messages in the early poetry are not merely inconsistent, then, but sometimes the complete reverse of each other. And these contradictions, since they clearly do not all occur accidentally, show something else about the early Auden. He often cared more about the liveliness of the total verbal performance than about philosophy, ideas, social themes, or his role of cultural critic. (In the long run, of course, this must be true for any good poet. Auden ruined some early poems by wrecking his speakers in order to play with their speech. But the skills learned from this made him a much greater poet later on.) His contradictions also raise interesting questions about the status of all his early themes. Subtle parody never deviates far from a straightforward treatment of the thing parodied. Without changing a single word, in fact, a sober speech can be parodied merely by placing it in a spoofing atmosphere. Such an atmosphere can be created by the simple knowledge that a given writer is a parodist, a leg-puller, a wit. When we know this we always have to look twice at everything he says, to make sure the clever jokester is not laughing up his sleeve while we earnestly mistake his parody for its solemn opposite. Auden's open parody of his own themes creates this atmosphere of doubt, and the careful reader will proceed cautiously. How seriously did Auden and his friends take some of those completely solemn poems, the ones with decorum intact, where the Poet dominates throughout? Since some poems show that Auden and his friends occasionally thought of the Poet's high-serious persona as a joke, is it not possible that in some others where the tone was diligently sober, the diagnosis oracular, the Poet's authority awesome, that these made the spoof even more hilarious? How often was Auden privately laughing at his public solemnly pondering those enigmatic utterances that apparently embodied grave profundities. Sometimes, surely, he pulled the audience's innocent leg. But whatever the prevalence of this (and it is interesting to notice that self-parody appears especially in those works most openly directed to the attention of Isherwood, Upward, and Warner), the Antipoet's appearance, briefly or in full performance, throughout the early years, shows Auden's wavering inability to take seriously either his Poet's messages or style.

Auden's own response to his early poems, ten or fifteen years later, shows something worth looking at briefly. When he went back over his youthful work in order to put together *The Collected Poetry,* Auden apparently found some of the early solemnity even more comic than before, and this brought forward his latter-day Antipoet in full force. His playful, irreverent, flippant, comic hand often shows clearly in *The Collected Poetry,* causing some of the things that upset Beach. This is especially obvious in titles given to early poems originally identified only by Roman numerals. Twenty-six of the thirty selections from *Poems* (1933) turn up in *The Collected Poetry* with new titles. Of these twenty-six titles, eleven are unmistakably comic, and nine others are probably comic. Only six are too bland or enigmatic to raise a smile. Of the eleven definitely comic titles, at least eight are quite obviously comments made by the Antipoet on rereading the old utterances of the Poet: "The Questioner Who Sits So Sly" (*CP,* p. 177), "Something Is Bound to Happen" (*CP,* p. 34), "Venus Will Now Say a Few Words" (*CP,* p. 109), "We All Make Mistakes" (*CP,* p. 152), "Make Up Your Mind" (*CP,* p. 22), "Do Be Careful" (*CP,* p. 151), "Such Nice People" (*CP,* p. 92), and "Two's Company" (*CP,* p. 5). Though inconsistencies appear in some, all eight poems are written mostly in that solemn voice and high idiom of the early Poet, gravely surveying his world and time and dismayed at finding both bad. To the Auden of 1945, whose Antipoet found his world good, the early dismay a fashionable pose, and the solemn high style pretentious, these poems apparently seemed unintentionally comic, as his new titles indicate. The best example probably is "Doom is dark and deeper than any sea-dingle. . . ." Many readers, responding to its elegiac tone (rare in early Auden) and to its general suggestions of exile, alienation, and fall from brightness, regard this as Auden's best early poem. It contains no inconsistencies in persona or lapses in decorum. Nevertheless, to this rather poignant poem, pleading for a wanderer's safe return to a forsaken homeland, Auden affixed his flippant comment for title: "Something Is Bound to Happen." This remark suggests that the poem's pathos is maudlin, its situation probably melodramatically contrived, and its poignance sentimental. Found guilty of pretentious bathos, both Poet and protagonist are condemned by the Antipoet in Auden. Full of brisk healthiness, he looks with disdain on their self-indulgent suffering and flips at both the unsympathetic title, which says by its tone, "Cheer up, buddy, something is bound to happen." The solemn Poet receives an equally deflating puncture from the title of "Watch any day his nonchalant pauses, see. . . ." Completely grave, the speaker in this poem tells of an outwardly poised neurotic, whose inner terror makes his every action a precarious balance between "shocking falls on razor-edge" (*CP,* p. 152). This mighty sufferer and his somber biographer are cut down to minuscule size by an Auden who sees the posturing of each as comic. "We All Make Mistakes," he says in the title. To the sober, indecisive bumbler who speaks in another poem, Auden says, "Make Up Your Mind" (*CP,* p. 22). In still another title, he remarks ironically of neurotics the Poet once took seriously, "Such Nice People" (*CP,* p. 92). The most attractive of these titles (if I understand it correctly) is the one affixed to that puzzling ode from *The Orators* originally subtitled "To My Pupils" (*CP,* p. 136). Turning to this baffling piece of schoolboy mystification (probably after he had first gone through the earlier *Poems,* making wry comments), Auden in his late thirties may have said to himself, with amused exasperation, "For God's sake which side am I supposed to be on," and left the last eight words as its title. If this guess is wrong, the other alternative, reflecting a similar amusement, is that he addresses his readers in the title, saying to them, "Guess which side I am supposed to be on."

Titles from *The Collected Poetry* provide an amusing insight into Auden's habit of noticing the ridiculous in every pretentious speech, particularly his own. But I am not claiming that the Antipoet of 1945 provides evidence for the existence of an Antipoet in 1928–35. That earlier existence needs no support from such after-the-fact evidence. Auden apparently took his Poet more seriously in 1928–35 than he took him in 1945, but the Antipoet is very much alive in both periods and frequently cavorts through the early poetry. *The Orators* (though it has little artistic value) provides an endlessly fascinating insight into just what sort of unique person Auden was behind that Poet's mask he so often donned for his early performances. The more one ponders *The Orators,* the more striking becomes its real oddity and queerness, and attractiveness too. A great deal of it resembles the free association of an irrepressible clown, mimic, and wit. Ebullient energy runs around everywhere, and a fantastic inventive imagination. In every corner are pack-rat collections of gifted wordplay, half-finished constructions, and odds and ends of situations. The whole book resembles a mixture put together by some irresponsible, precocious, and very talented schoolboy. We almost seem to get a glimpse into the wordy storeroom of an artist's unconscious, where constructions lie about every which way and energy, disconnected from order, rushes from side to side assuming a variety of strange shapes. To understand the later Auden fully, readers must immerse themselves in the Auden that could make *The Orators.* (Erudite comparisons to the works of Rimbaud and Blake probably just obscure the book's nature. The most important model, I would guess, was Mortmere, that endless schoolboy saga.) That all this untidy, attractive rush should somehow lie behind or beneath the grave, responsible, authoritative Poet is most significant. The puzzling behavior of many later poems can be explained as the result of this irrepressible energy, baffled, gagged, and banished with great difficulty, bursting through.

IV

A note Auden attached to *Poems* (1933) tells that all its selections were written before 1931. Most of *The Orators* (1932) seems to come from this same early period, when Auden's public apparently consisted mainly of Isherwood, Warner, Spender, Day Lewis, Upward, and a few others. *The Dog Beneath the Skin,* though written later, owes much to the early schoolboy atmosphere as well, and so does *The Ascent of F.6* to a lesser degree. The old schoolmates' collaborations always trailed clouds from an earlier existence among the private worlds of Mortmere and public school. But *Look, Stranger!* (1936) marks a surprising change, even though its selections (1932–36) show no gap in Auden's production. Before, never completely comfortable either as Poet or Antipoet, Auden kept getting too pretentious as Poet and too farcical as Antipoet, and seldom joined the two in a single poem without the threat of mutual self-destruction. In *Look, Stranger!* whether by design or not, Auden subdues the Poet and nearly banishes the Antipoet. The Poet, that sometimes pompous clinician, always in danger of floating away on the farce of his own elevation, is controlled mainly by being lowered.

As speakers descend in English verse from, say, the Milton of *Paradise Lost* to the Wordsworth of "Tintern Abbey," their intentions remain highly serious, but their diction, syntax, and voice move toward the informality of speech. Yet, while their podium falls from awesome heights to the stage of their own meditative minds, their tone is still oratorical. Singing robes flash less conspicuously perhaps, but the poem remains a solemn performance. Since Auden's Poet never dares scale Miltonic heights without self-burlesque, he must settle in some middle elevation to escape onslaughts from the Antipoet. Poems in *Look, Stranger!* seem to be an attempt to discover how high the Poet should go. At what heights can serious intentions safely be combined with sober tone? Considerable loftiness is still possible, several poems show, but in general the Poet occupies lower levels than those attempted earlier, as Auden moves his Poet toward the more informal relaxed styles of meditative verse. No extended exploration of the Antipoet's limits appear. These had probably been discovered in *The Orators* or in *The Dance of Death.* The lessons learned there may very well show up in *Look, Stranger!* where Antipoet, usually kept off stage, is substantially meeker when he appears. Though all of these developments probably took place no more than half-consciously in Auden, they make a logical pattern, as though directed by a conscious purpose: Poet and Antipoet seek reconciliation by moving away from their extremes toward the middle. Many poems show a Poet near enough to the middle to escape censure from the Antipoet, who in these mild circumstances can be suppressed. Several others show something destined to be even more promising. Occasionally the two hostile forces fuse momentarily in a middle style, where their very antagonism itself becomes a kind of unity.

"Perhaps" displays the highest elevation in the volume, with its invocation ("O Love, the interest itself in thoughtless Heaven"), invocative exclamation ("Yet, O, at this very moment"), formal diction, inverted syntax, high declamation, and long epic simile at the end (*CP*, pp. 89–90). Yet by eliminating the oddities of Anglo-Saxon style and the forced Latinate diction of several former failures, by including real rather than mythical landscape (Glamorgan, Dumbarton, Rowley), and some mundane imagery ("netted chicken-farm"), the poem avoids the pretensions that marked earlier Poetic heights. The Antipoet's snickers, therefore, are kept at bay—though Auden teeters dangerously once or twice: once when he describes barrows as "mounds like a midget golf-course," and again when he nearly lets an inventive patch run away with the solemnity,

> Under whose fertilising flood the *Lancashire* moss
>
> Sprouted up chimneys, and *Glamorgan* hid a life
> Grim as a tidal rock-pool's in its glove-shaped valleys. . . .
> (CP, pp. 89–90)

The book has a number of other successful Poetic performances too. "Our hunting fathers told the story . . ." (*CP*, p. 95) is one of these and "Look, stranger, on this island now . . . ," with its rare perceptual images and no joking or cleverness, is another (*CP*, p. 214). In "Hearing of harvests rotting in the valleys . . ." (*CP*, p. 47), the Antipoet appears only briefly in the speech of the foolish sick. The poem is essentially all Poetic and successfully so. And a poem such as "Easily, my dear, you move, easily your head . . ." succeeds in being Poetic too, partly because, as a love speech directly addressed to someone, it is less formal than usual. The Antipoet's brief buffoonlike appearance does no harm, then, and it probably would go unnoticed by anyone not watching especially for a glimpse of him: "The boiling tears amid the hot-house plants, / The rigid promise fractured in the garden . . ." (*CP*, p. 37).

Auden also makes attempts to lower his Poet to an even more familiar, informal middle range, with varied success. Pitched some degrees lower, the same voice that speaks in "Perhaps" appears again in "Here on the cropped grass of the narrow ridge I stand. . . ." This Poetic speaker, still obviously formal and declaiming, nevertheless uses the first person pronoun, looks at real landscape, and speaks in the manner of nineteenth-century meditative verse ("When last I stood here I was not alone; happy

. . . / Each thought the other . . ." *LS,* p. 42). Though still declaiming, the Poet, in "To Christopher Isherwood," speaks directly to a friend. His grand manner is hardly colloquial ("Nine years ago, upon that southern island / Where the wild Tennyson became a fossil . . ."), but wit reduces his stuffiness, and reminiscences about place, events, and people create some illusion of informality (*LS,* p. 63). Yet even here burlesque hovers dangerously near in several places: "gaga Falsehood highly recommended," "Among the well-shaped cozily to flit" (*LS,* p. 65). How to lower the Poet without resorting to Antipoetic farce: that is the problem Auden works at in *Look, Stranger!* As a beginning poet he could make solemn high speakers and unsolemn low ones. The problem was how to write in the middle, how to make a poem with a rather low or informal manner yet serious intent and tone. The poem to Isherwood, a verse letter to a close friend, called for just such a middle style. But the poem Auden wrote, attractive as it is, does not yet solve his problem. Its manner is still too formal, if its matter is not. This very disjunction always threatens to produce mock-seriousness, and Auden narrowly escapes several times, particularly in his personification outburst toward the end: "Scandal praying with her sharp knees up, / And Virtue stood at Weeping Cross" (*LS,* p. 65).

The Antipoet, threatening to break out in the Isherwood poem, does burst through elsewhere occasionally to cause Auden's familiar destructive wavering. The clearest case (and the only poem in the volume published as early as 1932) is in "Brothers, who when the sirens roar . . . ," where the Poet, even with the original cry of "Comrades!" changed to "Brothers," collapses before half a dozen lines have passed, overpowered by an Antipoet who finds this pretended brotherhood preposterous and the supposedly "common" diction much too comical to pass up ("By cops directed to the fug," *LS,* p. 34). Much more significant, though, are the beginnings of a reconciliation between Poet and Antipoet, in poems where Auden moves toward a middle style that avoids the mutually destructive extremes of each. The earliest of these, "To settle in this village of the heart . . ." (1933), is a landmark in Auden's development. This modest little poem is the first one where the speaker explicitly expresses his healthy genuine love by exposing his foolishness (Auden had done this implicitly once before in the John Warner ode). In doing so he completely reconciles the hostile temperamental forces I have called Poet and Antipoet. The Poet, all solemn high intentions, considers himself Important. The Antipoet, farcical foe of Importance, shows that life is ridiculous. At their extremes each insists on ruling alone. If life is wildly farcical it can scarcely be highly solemn at the same time. One must give way to the other. The presence of both makes a self-contradictory poem. But as Poet and Antipoet grow calmer, and move away from their extremes, the solemnity of the one becomes less pretentious and the comedy of the other less farcical. On middle ground either/or fades. Life or Art, it appears, may easily be both slightly foolish and yet modestly important and serious. In fact, most honest speakers can scarcely deny that both are true. In "To settle in this village of the heart . . ." the forces of Poet and Antipoet have been embedded in a speaker who, wishing to express his love as honestly as possible, must acknowledge the presence of both personae in himself. Therefore, though he is serious about himself and his love and believes both to be important, from another angle he can see that he and his feelings are flawed, awkward, and foolish. But his vices become virtues. The speaker asks that his very imperfections and foolishness be accepted as lovable and that his exposure of them be proof that his love is sincere: "O can you see precisely in our gaucheness / The neighbors' strongest wish, to serve and love . . ." (*CP,* p. 145). From just this sort of behavior, nearly twenty years later, will come the message of most Auden poems. Imperfection here becomes a blessing, almost the *cause* of love. Auden's philosophical themes are partly forced on him then by his rhetorical needs and his split temperament. The mere joining together of Poet and Antipoet automatically creates most of his philosophical message.

But "To settle in this village of the heart . . . ," though a milestone, showing Auden one way to unify his warring inclinations, is not itself one of his great triumphs, good poem that it is. Unity here is achieved by nearly annihilating Poet and Antipoet, by eliminating their extremes, even their recognizable voices until nothing is left but their ideas. Later unity comes from a much more exciting procedure. The voices of Poet and Antipoet will be pushed further and further outward toward their extremes, the very movement that tears apart some of the earliest poems. Unity will come from the dialectic of their clash. But before he learned how to do this, Auden sought unity by moving Poet and Antipoet in the opposite direction, toward each other, into the middle. Put another way, before he could develop his high-style comedy he had to learn how to make a successful middle-style poetry. Or if "had to" sounds too deterministic, at least that is what he did. Both styles are made by unifying Poet and Antipoet, though one moves them together and the other apart. But neither grew immediately or even steadily from Auden's first early successes. Poet and Antipoet, unjoined, appeared separately again in some fine poems, and in many not so fine. Auden started down quite a few dead-end roads before he found the way up to the right one.

Three poems in *Look, Stranger!* show the beginnings of his middle style. "Out on the lawn I lie in bed . . ." contains the most formal speaker, and its stanzaic demands (six rhymed lines of three and four feet) force him into some fairly stilted locutions: "To gravity attentive, she / Can notice nothing" (*CP,* p. 97). But on the whole the poem moves skillfully through this difficult stanza with a meditative, ruminating personal directness new in Auden:

> Out on the lawn I lie in bed,
> Vega conspicuous overhead
>   In the windless nights of June. . . .
> (CP, p. 96)

The persona's speech is usually no more formal than the public utterance of an average educated intellectual, and it is filled with references to events in a definitely placed world (June, windless night, Vega, Oxford, Big Ben, churches). These help keep him from ascending the summits of the oratorical high Poet. At the same time Antipoetic tendencies are restrained, not allowed to become too self-consciously clever, to run away with the performance. Instead they seem fitting wit for an educated man not too far removed from contemporary life: "The sexy airs of summer," "The dumpy and the tall" (*CP,* pp. 96, 97). Even more successful (perhaps because its five-foot lines and off-rhymes throw up fewer obstacles to informal speech) is "The earth turns over; our side feels the cold . . ." and its companion piece "Now from my window-sill I watch the night. . . ." Both are unusually personal for Auden ("I . . . / Son of a nurse and doctor," *LS,* p. 26), and display a Poetic formality suitable for the seriousness and emotion of the subject and enough Antipoetic wit and humor to hold the Poet's solemnity in check ("My father as an Airdale and a gardner / My mother chasing letters with a knife . . ." *LS,* p. 25). In "Now from my window-sill I watch the night . . . ," where the Poet is higher the Antipoet is more unrestrained also, even permitted a mock-heroic passage, "O Lords of limit, training dark and light / And setting a tabu 'twixt left and right . . ." (*CP*, p. 84). But in both poems Poet and Antipoet are unified by being set in the persona of a single speaker. Serious intent and educated tradition are joined with a sharp wit, contemporary speech, slang, humor, and a refusal to take life too solemnly. Neither poem is a masterpiece of its kind. "Now from my window-sill I watch the night . . ." particularly, by allowing both Poet and Antipoet to stray farther from center, comes dangerously close to the lines that separate high from too high and low from farce, and probably slips into each at least once. But both are fine poems, and both begin the development of a genre extremely important in Auden's total work—his middle style. All three poems display great skill (one need only glance at the single earlier piece of this sort, "It was Easter as I walked in the public gardens . . ." in *Poems* to see Auden's enormous improvement). They also show Auden's great indebtedness to Yeats, whose discursive poems are obviously models for these three, and the earlier one as well. If Auden's later middle-style poetry owes something to Dryden, Horace, Marianne Moore, and the tradition of English and Latin Augustan poetry, it had its roots in Yeats.

On the whole the personae in *Look, Stranger!* are strikingly different from those in *Poems* and *The Orators*. Speakers in the early volumes, with their rough choppy rhythms, dissonant rhymes, telegraphic elisions, and generally abrasive music, seemed to the early public to speak in a new poetic style (Hopkins was not yet widely read). *Look, Stranger!*, though it everywhere contains patently Audenesque traits, is a different kind of poetry. Most of the Anglo-Saxon heritage is gone. Grammatically scrupulous formal syntax replaces the early gruff ejaculations, traditional syllable-stress meter the choppy stresses. Nearly every poem is shaped by patterned stanzas, sometimes of rather elaborate rhyme and metrical formulations. Four sonnets appear, along with a sestina using rhyme words from a Philip Sidney double sestina (*The Orators* contained an earlier sestina). A new meditative tone in "Here on the cropped grass on the narrow ridge I stand . . ." is reminiscent at first of "Tintern Abbey." A rhythm from Shelley sets the pattern for "Fish in the unruffled lakes. . . ." Hardy supplies a line for "O what is that sound which so thrills the ear. . . ." Several poems and a number of separate phrases show Auden's close attention to poetry of Yeats' middle years, the Yeats who could "talk" across long stanzas of metered lines. None of Auden's poems is tastelessly derivative; they are all very much his own. But unlike his earlier work, poems in *Look, Stranger!* are a familiar kind of English poetry. A reader brought up on seventeenth-, eighteenth-, and nine-teenth-century verse, who might find Hopkins, Eliot, or Pound bewilder-ing, and the earliest Auden crude and prosaic, could respond with famili-arity to the poetry in *Look, Stranger!* This volume introduces the Auden of the classic English style, an important and recurring part of his total work. The speakers are educated, literary, formal, and of serious de-meanor. Their syntax is Standard British, their diction elevated, their speech metrical. The poetry relies heavily on the reader's familiarity with the traditional media of English poetry. The art here is the art of mastering traditional practices. Auden now delights by his skill in polish-ing, manipulating, and extending the familiar (in *Look, Stranger!* polish-ing prevails; extending becomes more important later). Primarily this poetry is oratory, declamation, public speech, the poet speaking from the stage or rostrum. Its ground and fiber are logical discourse, rhetoric (the sort Rimbaud and Pound wished to break the back of). The speaker's voice, its pitch, tone color, and rhythm, determines the degree of solem-nity and high seriousness. His voice can elevate even the plainest words, the most unembellished line to the level of intense emotion. Most English poetry is this sort of thing, though symbolist practice and theory made it unfashionable in the early decades of the twentieth century. Yet Auden's work in *Look, Stranger!* is not hopelessly academic. There are many good poems in the volume. The point is that something significant happened to the personae after *Poems* and *The Orators. Look, Stranger!* is an abrupt change.

Tastes vary, and even today some readers, disappointed by Auden's turn in *Look, Stranger!* and what it heralded, take him to be a poet whose very early innovations and youthful gusto held a promise unfulfilled as he sank dismally into being the Good Gray Academic Poet, a man whose col-lected work, a museum of English prosody, displays all our worn-out poetic history. For others, *Look, Stranger!* makes a big forward step. The youthful Auden, fantastic and pretentious, wavering between pomposity and buffoonery, uttering strange grunts in gnomic riddles, writing private jokes for friends, now masters his material, becomes sure of his audience, and develops a responsible voice. Large evaluations aside, however, noth-ing in *Poems* hinted at the enormous mastery soon to be displayed in *Look, Stranger!* Many of the poems in this volume are simply fine poems of their kind, however one feels about the kind. Nobody can say that of the selections in *Poems* or *The Orators,* I think. The earliest Auden showed a powerful explosive force, a personality addicted to words and their play, all the encouraging symptoms, in fact, of something unusual, the very sort of verbal explosion from which a major poet might develop. But the poetry itself was as yet often inchoate. He had not yet found a style—or a *kind*—of poetry suited to the diversity of his temperamental interests, inclinations, and predispositions. In *Poems* and *The Orators* the impulses I have called Poet and Antipoet created voices and styles hostile to each other. In *Look, Stranger!,* with the few exceptions noted, Auden controls these by employing levels of the Poetic voice similar to those in past English poetry. Along with these speaker's voices, of course, came the whole media of traditional English verse—prosody, rhetoric, grammar, and so on. Though these traditional Poetic voices remain always with Auden, they satisfy only part of his total temperament. When they dominate, the Antipoet must be banished or suppressed. And had he completely killed his Antipoet, Auden might indeed have become simply academic, the voice of English poets in modern dress. But the Antipoet, very much alive, always lurks in the wings while the Poet speaks. *Look, Stranger!* is Auden's best collection of Standard English poems.

V

In the six years after *Look, Stranger!* Auden produced two long middle-style works. One, "Letter to Lord Byron" (1937), is dominated by his Antipoet. The other, *New Year Letter* (1941), is a balanced mixture of Poet and Antipoet. Between these large and important works, the Antipoet appeared by himself in only a small handful of insignificant poems, while the Poet performed alone in a great many. In this period, while he searched diligently for a satisfactory yet original style, a voice for his solo Poet, Auden wrote some of the worst poetry of his career.

As Poet and Antipoet move toward each other to create a middle style, their differences begin to blur. Nevertheless the temperament of one or the other nearly always dominates, providing a basic voice, style, tone, even intent. "Letter to Lord Byron" is clearly the Antipoet's work. There are occasional fleeting appearances of a very subdued Poet, but the poem is seldom a true mixture of the two. Yet I prefer to call it middle style because it is so clearly a further development of Auden's attempt to move away from the extremes of Poet and Antipoet toward some central informal style that could easily occupy the space between the two, moving without strain from one to the other. If the subdued low-level Poet scarcely shows up at all, at least his counterpart, the Antipoet, also a restrained, modest performer now, comports himself with some dignity, never venturing too far toward the antic clown of former days.

As befits an Antipoet, in "Letter to Lord Byron" Art is ostensibly reduced to its least pretentious, while the poem is everywhere flooded with Life. The allegorical or mythical character of Auden's "reality," disappearing rapidly in *Look, Stranger!,* is completely gone now. In its place is the genuine substance of England and the world of the 1930's. There are hundreds of references to places, people, events, customs, dress, language, and fads from mundane reality: Gary Cooper, Father Coughlin, Duke Ellington, insect repellent, Sunlight soap, Aertex underwear, plate-glass windows, chrome-plated furniture, Kodaks, tennis, golf, Ely Culbertson, The Croydon aerodrome, and on and on. None of these is gathered for our solemn edification. The Antipoet prefers to delight rather than teach, and though we are told at great length what the real world is like, no stern lessons are derived from it. Cultural sickness, its causes, symptoms, cures, the sober problems of human existence—subjects for the Poet—are nearly all banished. The Antipoet holds life to be a blessing, and has little inclination to dissect and condemn. No criticism appears stronger than the teasing mockery of love and some good-natured laughter at the amiably silly. "Letter to Lord Byron" must have disillusioned early admirers who had manufactured from his Poet's appearances the myth of Auden as a grave social critic, political activist, and rebellious leader dissatisfied with twentieth-century life. The Antipoet, everywhere the reverse of this, can scarcely be ignored or dismissed as a brief aberration in "Letter to Lord Byron." He appears at great length, in full view, in the most autobiographical poem Auden ever wrote, and his detachment from political and cultural partisanship is apparent everywhere. Here was a speaker in 1937 casually joking not only about the home-grown Fascism of Mosley ("That you would, hearing honest Oswald's call, / Be gleich-geschaltet in the Albert Hall") but even about Hitler himself. That "Teutonic / Führer-Prinzip," the speaker laughingly agrees, might actually have appealed to Byron:

> "Lord Byron at the head of his storm-troopers!"
>   Nothing, says science, is impossible:
> The Pope may quit to join the Oxford Groupers. . . .
>   (*LLB*, p. 57)

Here, just shortly before the Poetic Auden wrote "Spain 1937" (surely one of his most falsely pretentious pieces), the Antipoetic Auden appeared in print with only the faintest passing reference to the "United Front" and all the European crises. (Elsewhere in the volume Auden's enormous noninterest in the Spanish War shows in the following letter from "W.H.A. to E.M.A.": ". . . there was one first-class diver. I cannot conceive of anything else I would rather be able to do well. It's such a marvellous way of showing off. Have just heard for the first time of the civil war in Spain. Borrowed two volumes of caricatures, which are really my favourite kind of picture, and spent a very happy evening. . . .") [4] When the speaker in "Letter to Lord Byron" turns a bit solemn and worries briefly about contemporary world affairs, he shows no more knowledge of or interest in their causes and cures than the average middle-class man who reads the newspapers. In fact the poem shows considerable sympathy for just such middle-class men, particularly in a long discussion on pages 55–56. For all his shortcomings (his "Scratches for self-esteem," and sly "pecks . . . in the neighborhood of sex"), twentieth-century middle-class man is thought to be an improvement on "John Bull of the good old days," the "swaggering bully" with the "meaty neck." He is far more humble and passive, a victim rather than a victimizer, a "little Mickey [Mouse] with the hidden grudge," kicking tyrants "only in his dreams" (*LLB*, p. 55). The speaker rather likes him, indeed clearly thinks of himself as middle-class. He jokes about being "An intellectual of the middle classes" (*LLB*, p. 201) and remarks near the end that "In bed, asleep or dead, it's hard to tell / The highbrow from l'homme moyen sensuel" (*LLB*, p. 234). Auden's Antipoet, educated though he is, distrusts high-brows, and in this poem thinks of himself as just an ordinary sensual man, the very sort of person the clinical Poet usually classifies as sick. But the Antipoet does not think of himself as sick, and he does not worry about the class system, monopoly capitalism, or other evils of reactionary democracy. On the contrary, in "Letter to Lord Byron" he remarks, "We've grown, you see, a lot more democratic, / And fortune's ladder is for all to climb . . ." (*LLB*, p. 53). He is mocking here, but he accepts the statement as true. Decayed industrial landscape, old mills, slag heaps, pieces of machinery, the very

---

[4] Auden and MacNeice, *Letters From Iceland*, p. 123.

things that are symbols of cultural sickness in the early poems, are now listed as objects the speaker loves most (*LLB*, pp. 50–51). This Antipoetic Auden, whose explicit love for England ("With all thy faults, of course we love thee still," *LLB*, p. 233) is evident throughout, is a persona not interested in cultural sickness or European affairs or politics. He seems content to remain " 'A selfish pink old Liberal to the last' " (*LLB*, p. 203).

The Antipoet's other beliefs and temperamental inclinations appear everywhere too, particularly those concerned with Art. The speaker who hates "pompositas" (*LLB*, p. 203) and abhors those who prefer "Art / To Life" (*LLB*, p. 210) everywhere attacks exaggerated claims about the importance of Art. In his own poetry he aims simply "to please, find everything delightful" (*LLB*, p. 21) and favors *Don Juan* as a model because he wants a muse both "gay and witty." For after all Art ends "In an attempt to entertain our friends," he says (*LLB*, p. 103). In fact, in a brief literary history he claims that poetry went bad when it stopped being written for patrons. After that it turned "arty" and "private." Patrons had kept poets to their proper task: pleasing, entertaining, and speaking a familiar language (*LLB*, pp. 105–6). Accordingly the Antipoetic speaker praises "light verse," and as a poet himself says he prefers the lower slopes of Parnassus where he can pasture his "few silly sheep with Dyer / And picnic on the lower slopes with Prior" (*LLB*, p. 22). Poking good-natured fun at the high Poets " 'Daunty, Gouty, Shopkeeper, the three / Supreme Old Masters,' " he would most prefer, he says, to write like "Firbank, Potter, Carroll, Lear" (*LLB*, p. 202). For after all Art is not much compared to Life, and poetry is not even as important as the novel (*LLB*, p. 20). Self-deprecatory always, the Antipoet chooses a "cotton frock" for singing robe (*LLB*, p. 101).

And in cotton robe he speaks a language never too far from Life, though its syntax and grammar are impeccably proper. His stylistic ground is the very informal language of the educated man, everywhere avoiding pomposity (except for mockery), and easily including colloquialisms and slang:

> . . . in case the book's a flop,
> Then from the critics lest they should be hard on
> The author when he leads them up the garden. . . .
>   (*LLB*, p. 24)

Though the former wild clowning is mostly gone, comedy is everywhere. The speaker plays with his own poetic form by making comic rhymes, fashioning comic epigrams out of the couplets, and laughing in the loud *sotto voce* asides the *Don Juan* style encourages. He plays with his subject too, purposely jamming together incongruous topics to be funny: "And death is better, as the millions know, / Than dandruff, night starvation, or B.O." (*LLB,* p. 52). And convinced of the foolishness of everyone, especially himself, he makes comedy from the good-natured mockery of others and himself: "The mountain-snob is a Wordsworthian fruit; / He tears his clothes and doesn't shave his chin . . ." (*LLB,* p. 102); "In games which mark for beauty out of twenty, / I'm doing well if my friends give me eight . . ." (*LLB,* p. 201). Everywhere there is the genial self-disparagement of a man who always guards against taking himself too seriously. In short, "Letter to Lord Byron," both in manner and doctrine, is a huge display of Auden's Antipoetic temperament. None of the tinkering he did with *The Collected Poetry* begins to equal the distortion created by omitting from it his two longest Antipoetic works, *The Orators* and "Letter to Lord Byron." Readers who think only of his Poetic voice when they think of Auden create a false image of the poet, and critics who do this generally deplore his comedy as a trivial aberration.

But the Antipoet is no more the total Auden than is the Poet, and what the speaker says about Art, Life, and current affairs in "Letter to Lord Byron" cannot be simply quoted as "Auden's views." One year after its publication Auden saw human events less pleasing and delightful, when he toured the battlefronts of the Chinese-Japanese War, and again wrote a long sequence, this time exclusively as Poet. "In Time of War" (1939) is the low point in Auden's career. Its poetry is bad, and this creates special critical problems because bad poetry is nearly always harder to dissect than good. In a good poem almost any feature can be singled out and said to be helping to cause the goodness. But single elements taken from bad poems often prove on examination to be innocent of ill effect. Taken by itself each feature of a bad poem may appear healthy (in fact the very device may operate splendidly elsewhere) and yet the sum still be bad. Whatever the cause, verbal excitement is missing from "In Time of War." Did Auden's adopted persona destroy the verbal excitement or the verbal dullness, the persona? If the former, why did he adopt such a persona in the first place; if the latter, what made the dullness? Answers must be tentative—even speculative. Yet careful scrutiny would suggest some things pretty clearly. "In Time of War" is not weak because hostile personae or the author's hostile temperamental inclinations battle each other. The Poet is in command everywhere. Weakness appears to come from the way he speaks. In other words, something goes wrong with Auden's technique, with the Poet's style, and detailed examination of this must be postponed until the next chapter. But why does something go wrong with the Poet's voice? His intent is solemn, his subject serious and large (the nature of man), his clinical, analytical, explanatory mind is at work. His syntax is still formal and correct. Yet the elevating tone of voice that can give emotion or intellectual excitement to even the plainest line and flattest diction is missing. The poems are filled with lines like "And the age ended, and the last deliverer died / In bed, grown idle and unhappy; they were safe . . ." (CP, p. 325). Auden sounds like a man forcing himself to write when his powers are at low ebb. The serious voice is lifeless, tired, prosaic. The formerly lively verbal play is reduced to a multitude of forced allegorical images, dead personifications, and strained similes. Scattered everywhere are such things as "Only a smell had feelings to make known" (CP, p. 320); "He was the Rich, the Bountiful, the Fearless" (CP, p. 321); "They carry terror with them like a purse" (CP, p. 329); "Anxiety / Receives them like a grand hotel" (CP, p. 330). After inventing voices for more than ten years, it is as though Auden suddenly could find no voice at all. What remains is a huge heap of rhetorical devices living on after their speaker is dead. Most of the pleasure one gets from these poems comes entirely from their thought.

Auden's difficulty surely is part of his unsuccessful ten-year-old search for a suitable Poetic persona. Such explanations should not be pushed too hard, of course. Journey to a War was a commissioned travel book. Perhaps forced to meet a deadline while caught in a slump, Auden may simply have ground out the poems as best he could. (His own comments in Letters from Iceland, another commissioned book, show his comic dilemma at finding himself, money already advanced, with nothing to say. The idea for a Byron letter came, apparently, as a lucky accident. In China, perhaps, his luck ran out.) But whatever contributed to the difficulties of "In Time of War," the persona problem there is part of a familiar pattern in Auden's work. The Antipoet is gone, and along with him his lively, genial, mocking spirit. The Poet, left alone, must somehow put on an exciting verbal performance by himself, and Auden had not yet found a thoroughly suitable Poetic voice. The search for it, though, is one of the most obvious features of his poetry from about 1933 to 1940, despite statements in some of his prose from this period that might suggest just the opposite. Readers will be misled who swallow whole Auden's stepped-up campaign, about this time, for light verse and poetry-as-entertainment. Some of his critical essays are exactly the sort we would expect the Antipoetic speakers in his poems to write. Whatever they may reveal about Auden's willingness to settle down comfortably at Parnassus' foot as an entertainer, flattered by the company of Dyer, Prior, and the like, his practice from 1933 to 1940 belies this humble ambition. Though his Antipoetic inclinations were certainly real and strong, he also wished often enough to align himself with the English tradition of high serious poetry, and no amount of protestation to the contrary can offset the fact that in this period, more often than not, he tried to write as a Poet. Why then should Auden, in "In Time of War," have abandoned the Poetic personae he developed in *Look, Stranger!*, who speak with emotion and liveliness in a number of poems? I have said before that apparent dissatisfaction with his earlier Poetic speakers had led Auden, in *Look, Stranger!* to write closer to the manner of a familiar English tradition. I suggest that, consciously or not, he felt discontented with his *Look, Stranger!* Poet partly because he spoke something like Standard English poetic speech in a Standard English poem, that for all his Audenesque traits, he was too much like an amalgam of his ancestors and not enough like W. H. Auden. So Auden kept trying to move his Poet away from the safe but familiar to something more his own. Whether this speculation about motives has any factual validity or not, as a description of what the poetry looks like it is surely accurate. The poetry *does* move in a number of directions from the Poet of *Look, Stranger!* And "In Time of War" certainly does make the Poet sound less like Everybody Else's Poet and more like Auden. It does so by exaggerating those very stylistic traits that are most Auden's own (allegorical ornament and incongruous juxtapositions) and by subduing features that are everybody else's. The result is a flat, mannered verse, producing the illusion that it is made of almost nothing but a few rhetorical habits. But these, without any doubt whatsoever, belong to nobody but W. H. Auden.

Another Time (1940) shows no significant poetic development, but both Poet and Antipoet are clearly present. Auden divided the volume into three sections, the first and third (thirty-seven poems) containing mostly Poetic speakers, the second (thirteen poems), Antipoetic. Despite his obvious desire (shown by this distribution) to write as Poet, no new or particularly successful Poetic style turns up here. In at least eight selections the Poetic voice is essentially the one from "In Time of War," with its defining, declarative sentences, forced cleverness, and plethora of allegorizing. Most of these are sonnets. Although in the course of his career Auden completely dismantles the sonnet and reassembles its parts in just about every possible combination, this virtuosity is offset by the strikingly similar persona who appears in many of them. It is almost as though when he writes sonnets Auden frequently puts on his "sonnet persona." Whatever new sonnet arrangement he thinks up, much the same voice comes through it all, unaffected by the formal ingenuity. "The nights, the railway-arches, the bad sky, / His horrible companions did not know it . . ." (CP, p. 121): this Poet in "Rimbaud" is the same speaker who says in "In Time of War," "They are and suffer; that is all they do; / A bandage hides the place where each is living . . ." (CP, p. 328). Twenty years later this voice is still recognizable (though not identical) in an Homage to Clio sonnet, "Words": "A sentence uttered makes a world appear / Where all things happen as it says they do . . ." (HC, p. 20). In Another Time this Poet seldom flies very high, and on occasion, his few rhetorical devices gone, speaks entirely unornamented lines:

> Hell is neither here nor there
> Hell is not anywhere
> Hell is hard to bear.
> (CP, p. 51)

Surely one of Auden's least successful inventions, this Poetic voice is part of his attempt to develop a speaker who is solemn but not too solemn, who can speak something like the language of ordinary men without joking around with it, a Poet who moves in the direction of the Antipoet but can stay dignified and talk about sober matters soberly.

But Auden yearns for a higher Poet too, and in Another Time he tries again to elevate the Poet in some of his solo performances. Indicative of this new escalation, at least twelve poems contain the invocative cry: "O Pride so hostile to our Charity," "O in these quadrangles," "You alone,

O imaginary song" (*CP*, pp. 134, 80, 6). If some of these pass as decorous and unobtrusive (as do four of them in "As I walked out one evening . . ." *CP*, p. 197), others seem arbitrary and rather unsuccessful attempts to raise the level of emotion and solemnity by simply sticking in that familiar symbol for emotional intensity, "O": "O had his mother, near her time, been praying," "O when she saw the magistrate-in-charge" (*CP*, p. 86). Praiseworthy as Auden's search for a high Poet's voice may be, his talents and temperament simply prevent him from speaking well as the Romantic persona he imported here for a cry or two. Given Auden's habits, before long a completely solemn Poet was absolutely destined to say something like "O little restaurant where the lovers eat each other" (*CP*, p. 100). That great admirer of *Don Juan* and Firbank, Auden's comic Antipoet, asleep when that line emerged, could scarcely doze forever if the Poet began to fall regularly on the thorns of life with such unlikely cries. Very much awake, the Antipoet speaker parodies just such practices in "It's farewell to the drawing-room's civilized cry . . ." ("O were he to triumph, dear heart, you know," *CP*, p. 60). Even in the extremely sober "Spain 1937" such invocative exclamations are uttered only by the foolishly deluded, "O descend as a dove" (*CP*, p. 183). Their speech is being mocked. The two best Poetic performances in *Another Time* avoid both the Romantic cry and the deluge of rhetorical ornament used in "In Time of War." "Lay your sleeping head, my love . . . ," like its less-perfect predecessor in *Look, Stranger!*, "Fish in the unruffled lakes . . . ," is simply a fine philosophical love lyric, traditional and restrained (*CP*, p. 208). "Musée des Beaux Arts" succeeds by keeping the Poet well away from the invocative heights. Down near the slopes of middle style where he can be both completely serious, yet informal and colloquial, Auden's Poet produces an excellent poem (*CP*, p. 3).

The Antipoet speaks alone in a number of poems that while attractive, even extremely funny, show no advances that need examining here. In passing it is worth noting, though, that at the very time Auden tried to raise his Poet he lowered his Antipoet to levels of antic clowning not seen since *The Orators*. "O tell me the truth about love . . ." is one of these cases, a love-song parody where Auden appropriately lets loose all the zaniness so often bottled up: "Does it [love] look like a pair of pyjamas / Or the ham in a temperance hotel . . ." (*AT*, p. 89). Just a bit more subdued, the same persona shows up in "It's farewell to the drawing-room's civilized cry . . ." (borrowing its meter from "The Night Before Christmas," *CP*, p. 59), "Roman Wall Blues" (CP, p. 221), and elsewhere. In a few places the Antipoet still pops up inappropriately in a Poetic poem, when the wit, play, and invention get out of hand and threaten decorum. At least one poem, "The Unknown Citizen" (*CP*, p. 142), shattered by this difficulty, is left with a completely confused message. But except for one kind of interesting exception, Auden's Antipoet is generally controlled and kept in his place.

The exception is in some of the portrait poems. *Another Time* contains ten poems about real people (plus three portraits of invented characters, two of general types, and four of cities). Portrait poems have always figured in Auden's work, and since they show some interesting personae problems, and since there are so many of them in *Another Time,* this is a good place to consider them. Portrait poems create rather special personae situations for Auden, since they all descend from a common ancestor— poems about the sick. In the early portraits the person shown was always sick, usually psychologically sick. The neurotic in "Watch any day his nonchalant pauses, see . . ." (*CP*, p. 152) was one of these. So was the figure in "Control of the passes was, he saw, the key . . ." (*CP*, p. 29) and the airman in *The Orators,* and there are many more. I do not wish to re-examine these early portraits, but to call attention to two things: they portrayed sick people, and the techniques Auden developed in them were techniques designed to analyze the sick, condemn them, and laugh at, threaten, and abuse them. In doing this Poet and Antipoet played many roles. When the speaker himself was sick, Poet and Antipoet became high pompous proclaimers, low foolish clowns, and all sorts of absurd decadents in between. But when the speaker was not sick, Poet and Antipoet sometimes became partners in a sense. Instead of attacking each other, for once they joined to attack someone else, the sick neurotic being portrayed. The clinical Poet analyzed the nature of his sickness while the Antipoet abused or mocked him. Portrait poems in *Another Time* are usually more subtle and sophisticated than their early ancestors, and they usually express admiration rather than contempt for their subject. But they often show their heritage nevertheless. "Edward Lear" is a type case. The Poetic speaker admires Lear (Auden has often praised him): "And children swarmed to him like settlers. He became a land" (*CP,* p. 77). But strange things mar the Poet's praise. Lear "wept to himself in the night, / A dirty landscape-painter who hated his nose" (*CP*, p. 76), and

> . . . he was upset
> By Germans and boats . . .
> But guided by tears he successfully reached his Regret.
> (*CP*, p. 77)

With his queer phobias, his comic appearance, eccentric behavior, paranoid self-consciousness, and dirty habits, Lear is clearly as neurotically sick as anybody in the early portrait poems. And though Auden's Poet may admire him and find his sickness attractive, the Antipoet (nearly always dangerously excited by neurotics and odd behavior) gets carried away, as often before, with cataloguing his illness. As a result Lear surely becomes more of a sick comic fool than the Poet intended. Poet and Antipoet again make a poem inconsistent.

The reader who does not separate Antipoet from Poet, but takes the poem as "Auden's" utterance, will automatically respond to the inconsistencies I mention as though they are part of a coherent, unified message, something that can be called "Auden's attitude toward Lear." That message makes Auden rather unattractive. Lear, turned into a figure of fun, seems to be nothing more than a few superficial traits dished up by the amateur Freudian, Dr. Auden. These are then paraded for ridicule. If the reader laughs, he laughs uneasily, for in spite of the admiration at the end of the poem, the author's contempt seems to lie too close to the surface to be ignored. I think this reaction to "Edward Lear" is nearly inescapable, but I believe it to be the result of an unfortunate mistake. I do not think Auden intended to be either abusive or contemptuous. When he writes a portrait, he begins almost automatically to use his old portrait practices, left over from a day when all the figures were queer neurotics to be pilloried. The Poet's old habits of clinical analysis and classification tend to make all the portraits caricatures, with the subject reduced to a few superficial traits and features. The Antipoet's habit is to seize these for comic purposes, and in no time at all his comedy becomes abuse and the figure is held up for ridicule. When this happens the poem's speaker can seem smug, proud, even cruel. But the flaw is not in Auden's cruel heart, but in his failure once again to control Poet and Antipoet. This failure, though not always fatal or even important, is common in the portrait poems. The people in all Auden portraits, even in his elegies, are caricatures, and they are all, whether flagrantly or faintly, sick. Housman

Kept tears like dirty postcards in a drawer;
Food was his public love, his private lust
Something to do with violence and the poor.

                          (*AT*, p. 24)

For Rimbaud, "His senses systematically deranged," "Verse was a special illness of the ear" (*CP*, p. 122). Melville suffers from a wild terror (*CP*, p. 146); Pascal, whose "misery was real," builds "a life upon original disorder" (*CP*, p. 87). Arnold is destroyed by his father (*CP*, p. 54). Freud, like Prufrock, is "at times absurd" (*CP*, p. 166). All are sick, even if only slightly and beneficially so. Miss Gee, James Honeyman, and Victor, of course, are flagrantly sick—the latter two insane. Not that each of these is treated with comic contempt or wildly abused; the real people are all genuinely admired, and in some cases (Freud's particularly) sickness is a very minor and insignificant item. But all the portrait poems contain traces of the old "neurotic-portrait" poems, and I think all fail to be first-rate partly because of this taint, another casualty of the split between Poet and Antipoet.

If "Edward Lear" shows Auden's unfortunate habits most clearly, "In Memory of W. B. Yeats" shows them least, and therefore is a good test case. Though it is one of Auden's more famous portraits, admired by a great many readers, this poem too suffers from Auden's old methods. Like the others, the Yeats portrait emphasizes sickness, weakness, and flaws—though Yeats's deathbed behavior, not his neurosis, is stressed. Foolish actions, the raw material for many Auden poems, are reduced to the barest minimum here ("You were silly like us . . . / The parish of rich women"). But they are still here. In fact, small as it is, this remark about Yeats's silliness is the only statement in the entire poem that shows anything about his personality, character, or life—except for the observation that his poetry is the product of a wound: "mad Ireland hurt you into poetry" (*CP*, p. 50). Elsewhere, like Lear, Yeats becomes simply dehumanized in the Dickensian fashion characteristic of Auden's portraits—where bodies behave as objects. Here there is no comedy perhaps. But Yeats's dying body, turned into a geographical trope too clever and too long, moves in that direction. A few more lines, just a little more delighted play with the landscape figure, and the Antipoet would emerge, revealing too much interest in the clever performance. As it is, the too much interest is just barely (but clearly) perceptible. If the Yeats elegy avoids making its subject comic, if it avoids flagrant caricature, if the portrayed figure is not made completely inanimate and totally bizarre, the shadow of these familiar Auden habits falls on the poem. Yeats the man scarcely appears and is undignified when he does; faintly embarrassed we watch a clever allegory of his death rattle. The section on Yeats himself is exceedingly cold. Emotion appears only in the final quatrains, really a separate poem about time, poetry, and impending war. These subjects (unlike the subject of Yeats) move Auden's Poet to some of his most attractively impassioned verse, in the manner of Blake. Poet and Antipoet are at odds in this portrait of Yeats, even if only faintly so. Either the Antipoet has betrayed Auden's real wish to admire and praise, or Auden's genuine feelings of disaffection for Yeats show through the Poet's mask.[5]

The Antipoet in Auden is healthy, though sometimes this healthiness obscures Auden's usual awareness that he shares with others an existence of universal silliness. On such occasions Antipoetic speakers look out upon the sick, the weak, the failures, the hesitators and doubters, even on the slightly flawed with a comic scorn not very well hidden. Luckily this happens seldom. But it happened rather often in the early portraits and survives in the later—attractively (maybe) in "James Honeyman" and "Victor," less attractively in "In Memory of W. B. Yeats" and "Miss Gee," still less in "Matthew Arnold," and not at all attractively in "A. E. Housman" and "Edward Lear." Turned on himself, the Antipoet's mockery produces humility, tolerance, love for all those, like himself, who are flawed and absurd. Turned on others, his mockery can become arrogant and merciless. In these latter poems, perhaps by mistake, Auden's speakers can appear smug, proud, even cruel.

VI

At the time of its publication *New Year Letter* (1941) was Auden's greatest artistic achievement. Poet and Antipoet, at war for more than ten years, were here completely harmonized in a major work. Without elimi-

---

[5] Auden's reservations about Yeats, published in a variety of articles over a period of nearly thirty years, generally show a good-natured twitting of Yeats's theatrical Romantic side, a role Auden's Antipoetic self finds comically excessive. But the reservations were less good-natured about the time of Yeats's death. See the 1939 article "The Public v. the Late Mr. William Butler Yeats," *Partisan Review* (Spring, 1939), pp. 46–51.

nating either, without allowing either a major eminence, Auden curbed the destructive excesses of each. Each moved toward the other until at the center there lay a unified style and voice, a speaker who could contain them both as opposing poles of his own integrated temperament. *New Year Letter* is the great triumph of Auden's middle style. "Letter to Lord Byron," for all its success, by allowing the Antipoet, however mild, to dominate nearly everywhere, had eliminated too much of the Auden temperament to be completely satisfactory. The Auden well-read in dozens of intellectual fields, continually expanding his ideas about man's place in the cosmos, above all a poet constantly trying to produce an art more significant than that of Firbank, Carroll, and Lear—the whole Auden simply could not appear in a work dominated by only part of his personality, the Antipoetic part. *New Year Letter* provides him with a much wider persona to swim in. With an almost balanced mixture of Poet and Antipoet, *New Year Letter,* whatever its aesthetic and entertaining achievements (and they are great), clearly sets out also to offer a serious criticism of life.

In a middle-style Auden poem "unity" means that the speaker believably contains both Poet and Antipoet in his own person. When this happens the speaker becomes a man who can see Life and Art, everything, from two sides. He sees the solemn and the ridiculous, the importance and the supreme unimportance of everything. (It is no accident, obviously, as I suggest in a later chapter, that Auden's artistic success and his Kierkegaardian philosophy appear together.) As long as Poet and Antipoet stay modest and restrained, hovering around the center, such unity is fairly easy to maintain. But artistically and philosophically, there are good reasons for moving both away from the middle toward their extremes. As Poet and Antipoet move away from safe center, the speaker's personality seems to grow. He knows more about unlike things, his thoughts range over a greater variety of experiences, his feelings expand. He is a larger and more interesting personality. At the same time (in fact this is the same thing described differently), his voice begins to show greater variety. His speech style can leap from one rhetorical manner to another, his diction can come from an expanding usage pool. In short, the poem becomes a more aesthetically exciting verbal artifact. (Even Auden's continual return to the Poet in solo performance surely reflects his need to get out away from the tame restrictions of a safe middle style to the exciting outer reaches.) The *New Year Letter* speaker never lets either Poet or Antipoet stay at their extreme outer limits for long—out where unity is threatened and excitement is greatest. (Later high comic poems do that.) But they do range further than in any previous unified work. As a result *New Year Letter* is much larger (takes in more experience), more flexible and elastic than anything before it. Its unity is so solid that anything—the Poet's highest solemnities, the Antipoet's lowest clowning —can briefly be included without destroying the persona. That is the Muses' gift to the poet who for more than a decade had abandoned neither Poet nor Antipoet, even when they wrecked his poems, but had learned how to speak in both voices.

The Poet's ideas, thoughts, and feelings, (mostly excluded from "Letter to Lord Byron," or laughed at) turn up thoughout *New Year Letter*. Art is important, the poem says and shows. Poetry is called "the greatest of vocations" (*CP,* p. 268), and a pantheon of "Great masters," summoned up at the very beginning, remind Auden to write his very best. In the opening sequence of more than one hundred lines, calling upon the great poets to sustain and direct by their example, Auden's twentieth-century speaker commits himself, with this old epic device, to the whole tradition of poetry. Life is important too, for this Poet, and he ponders its enigmatic panorama right after the invocation: "The situation of our time / Surrounds us like a baffling crime" (*CP,* p. 271). When his contemplation of both Art and Life ends, he tells us in a separated twelve-line stanza just what we could have guessed. Both Art and Life are important. Art can even be a criticism of Life: may "the good offices of verse" be "the dispatch that I intend / . . . to all / Who wish to read it anywhere . . ." (*CP,* p. 274). This is a modest wish, as befits a modest middle-style Poet, but in its own way, nevertheless, it is the Poet hoping to be an unacknowledged legislator and critic of life. In what follows, the Poet wanders across an enormous range of life, seriously attracted to and examining landscapes, friendship, art, music, writers, intellectuals of all sorts, and the most erudite matters of epistemology and theology. There is no subject—no matter how high or low, weighty or not—that may not fittingly be examined, without devastating pretentiousness or pomposity, by this Poet.

Auden's Poet owes his success and his freedom to the restraining presence of the Antipoet, who just by being there threatens to destroy him with laughter if he starts getting pretentious. For the Antipoet's ideas, beliefs, and feelings are everywhere also, reminding that "Art is not life" (*CP,* p. 267), that ultimately language is "useless," that anything too solemn is probably wrong ("Yet truth . . . resents / Approaches that are too intense"), and that, since existence is essentially ludicrous, wisdom may come "through the Janus of a joke" (*CP,* pp. 273–74). So if poetry and its great masters demand obeisance, they are also comic, as dozens of references say and show. Most poetry developed from "Soiled, shabby, egotistic lives," the speaker says (*CP,* p. 268), and the people who made it were generally, in some way, absurd—Rimbaud, "The adolescent with red hands" (*CP,* p. 270); Rilke, "The Santa Claus of loneliness"; "horrible old Kipling" (*CP,* p. 271). Looked at from one angle, philosophy and theology are comic too, and in his frequent Antipoetic moods the speaker looks from just this angle. For instance, Bishop Berkeley's achievement is that his "modest Church-of-England God / Sustained the fellows and the quad" (*CP,* p. 279). Even the Devil himself is comic: "The Devil, as is not surprising— / His business is self-advertising . . ." (*CP,* p. 281). And Hell, though defined with considerable ingenuity by the Poet, has a lively comic energy about it:

> Emerging into view and groping
> For handholds on the low round coping,
> As Horror clambers from the well. . . .
> (*CP,* p. 292)

And the divinity himself does not escape being ludicrous. In the guise of "Truth," he cavorts like the absurdity he is: "The *Lex Abscondita* evades / The vigilantes in the glades. . . ." (*CP,* p. 287).

Nearly everywhere in Auden, of course, Poet and Antipoet are less beliefs than temperaments, more often revealed by how speakers talk than by what they say. And as many of the above quotations have already demonstrated, Poet and Antipoet show distinctive voices in *New Year Letter* as the speaker moves back and forth between them. The Poet can move successfully to the very high, in a lyric of intense emotion and artifice such as "O Unicorn among the cedars" (*CP,* p. 315), or at a modestly low Wordsworthian elevation (but with no less emotion) in addressing Elizabeth Mayer, "Dear friend Elizabeth, dear friend" (*CP,* p. 316). The Antipoet's range is equally wide. He can indulge himself with extreme intellectual slapstick:

> . . . Baudelaire went mad protesting
> That progress is not interesting
> And thought he was an albatross,
> The great Erotic on the cross
> Of Science. . . .
>   (*CP,* p. 303)

He can joke about Marx's triumph over Hegel: "The Dagon of the General Will / Fell in convulsions and lay still . . ." (*CP,* p. 286). Or he can simply speak with a mild wit: "Has learnt what every woman knows, / The wallflower can become the rose . . ." (*CP,* p. 279). But the distinction between Poet and Antipoet now separates not the incompatible forces of Auden's temperament but the two sides of a coherent and unified temperament. On his Poetic side he chooses (and this is very important to the meaning of the total artifact) to speak in metered and rhymed lines made up of grammatical sentences and Standard English syntax. He uses diction drawn from formal usage and from dozens of erudite and technical disciplines, plus several foreign languages. On his Antipoetic side, across these metered lines he runs prose rhythms that often ignore both rhyme and metrical stresses, and he scatters among the formal sentences colloquialisms, slang, puns, wit, jokes, and wordplay of all sorts. The result is a poetry that laughs at itself (its form is almost continuously mocked), but not so much that its seriousness is destroyed. The persona knows that if all men are absurd, the serious matters of their lives are no less real for this. If their speech is comic and needs to be laughed at, it nevertheless says something worth-while. And in fact what the persona shows by his speech is the very paradox that will soon become Auden's explicit philosophical message: If life is everywhere absurd, it never ceases to be blessed. In a sense Poet and Antipoet, by fighting with each other, have always been saying something like that. If they had not been present in his temperament from the beginning, no Kierkegaardian philosophy could have seemed so right to Auden. In *New Year Letter* Poet and Antipoet show by their behavior that life is blessedly absurd. Before long, through other speakers, they will be saying so openly, and throughout nearly all of Auden's poetry from here on—and certainly in his greatest poems—they will show by their performance alone, by *how* they speak, that what they say is true. It is no accident that Auden's greatest themes, as well as his greatest skills, emerge only when he unites Poet and Antipoet in a single speaker. In the long run, of course, skill and ideas are not separate entities. Such statements say in another way that Auden is best when all his temperamental parts are working fully and coherently together. This tautology accounts for the fact that at the time it was written *New Year Letter* was Auden's greatest work.

Auden is not a great sonneteer. "The Quest" confirms this. For one thing, the sonnet is too short for him. There is no time for a speaker to reveal a complex personality, no time to speak in a variety of voices, no time to look at experience from a number of angles. A single voice, a single subject, no more than two attitudes (one in the octet and another in sestet or final couplet)—these, if not absolutely demanded by the sonnet, seem to work best. And of course there are very few comic sonnets. That single voice and subject and the two attitudes are nearly always solemn. The sonnet is a Poet's form. In "The Quest" the sonneteer Poet is the familiar Auden clinician again, presenting a collection of psychological case histories, not unlike some of the portraits in *Another Time.* The Strange Case of Edward Lear or A. E. Housman becomes now The Singular Account of Patient X, Suffering from Dread—portraits of general types, like those in the early poems. The exaggerated rhetorical devices from "In Time of War" are prominent again. Inanimate things constantly spring to life, "The library annoyed him with its look" (*CP,* p. 254). Everything in sight acts out an allegory. But since these stylistic habits appear in *New Year Letter* too, the perplexing critical problem is that "The Quest" and *New Year Letter,* though so similar in most ways, are different in quality. Again I think description of the personae problem supplies most of the answer. The same words spoken by two different men are not the same. "To be or not to be" printed separately as an occasional poem will not produce the effect of Hamlet speaking from the heights. We know that the *New Year Letter* speaker lives in New York, among friends, in a world at war, reading certain books, listening to certain music. We can also see in him a wide temperamental range. He can be sober, moved by lofty sentiment, learned, verbally accurate, and so on. He can also be full of fun, play, exuberance, invention, irreverence. The speaker widens into a full-scale personality, with a variety of moods, feelings, and thoughts, none of them the essence of his person. This diversity prevents any one part of his temperament from becoming exclusively important. Our response to what he says and does in one place is very much conditioned by what he says and does in another. Does he speak here a pompous line? We know from elsewhere how he would laugh at himself were it pointed out. Does that pun seem unworthy, that allegory or wordplay rather tasteless? We know from elsewhere how he mocks his own weaknesses, and from still another place that he is neither coarse nor crude. The pompous line exists as only an insignificant part of a much larger unpompous personality. Extremes of pun, allegory, or indulgent wordplay are only a small part of the man who can also be noble and restrained. The slapdash and too-glib analysis are products of a speaker who laments both failings in himself. He can laugh at his excesses, recognize his faults, mock his weakness and indulgences. As a result his faults become almost endearing. His vices are virtues. Shown to be imperfect, like us, he is more attractive for having them. All men have faults; he acknowledges his. The flaws establish his humanity and their acknowledgement his goodness. But the sonnet is too short a form for all this. Excesses of Poet and Antipoet cannot be offset by redeeming practices elsewhere. There is not much time for the humility of self-mockery or for the wide range of emotions, thought, and speech that will show each flaw to be a mere peccadillo in the grand scheme of a complex personality. What would a seven-line botch count for in a poem of seventeen hundred lines, or even one of a hundred? But a sonnet will be forced to organize its entire self around anything as big as a seven-line mistake, and present it neatly crystallized for us to look at. Theoretically, maybe a sequence of sonnets could escape this limitation, but Auden's does not. Each fourteen lines is too much a self-contained unit. Each poem is a new beginning, a new formal problem, a new plot. As a result there is no feeling in "The Quest" (or in "In Time of War," for that matter) that a single persona speaks across hundreds of lines divided into fourteen-line units. The speaker ends and a new one begins with each poem. The voice is the same in each, but the personality is no larger than fourteen lines.

While speakers in "The Quest" might, with suitable manipulation of rhyme and meter, utter their speeches with complete decorum in *New Year Letter,* set apart in little fourteen-line worlds the same speeches produce special effects. As speakers grow Poetic, they become Auden's familiar clinical analyst looking into human failure, illusion, and sickness of all sorts. And sometimes they are likely to be rather smug, pontifical, and too slickly diagnostic. The Antipoet, with his mockery, wit, buffoonery, and healthy scorn for sickness and pretension, cannot, in the cramped space of the sonnet, turn mockery on himself, outsiders, and the Poet at the same time. He can usually concentrate on only one, and all too often he chooses to attack those very specimens already sprawled helpless under the Poet's microscope. As a result the Antipoet's imperfectly veiled contempt, when it gets out of hand, reinforces the Poet's clinical smugness. As for "style," with Poet and Antipoet joining hands against the outsiders, neither keeps the other in check. Free from the Antipoet's puncturing barbs, the Poet may become pretentious (not in speech so much here as in his diagnostic assurance and clinical classification). The Antipoet, unrestrained by the Poet's sober taste and his own self-mockery, runs free to indulge his excessive fondness for clever allegory and inventions. My description perhaps exaggerates all the faults by singling out the flaws (far fewer than in "In Time of War") and ignoring successes. "The Quest" is a good deal closer to the genial, learned, good-natured middle style of *New Year Letter* than was "In Time of War," and shares a good many of *New Year Letter*'s virtues. But Antipoet and Poet seldom work at their best in portrait poems or in sonnets, or when analyzing the sick. And "The Quest" is a collection of sonnets portraying the sick. When flawed characters speak for themselves, as they do in *For the Time Being* —and particularly in *The Sea and the Mirror*—most of Auden's shortcomings vanish.

By themselves the forces of Poet and Antipoet urge Auden to speak through a variety of personae whose speech and personalities range from the formally high to the informally low. This might indicate that the drama is his proper medium. But the realistic stage, with its warm, breathing, unique individuals moving through the furniture of a sensible world, is something foreign to Auden's dramatic talents. He can animate ideas, and people if they are thinking—and thinking people can be moving, emotional figures. But he has no real capacity for making these people react to one another as bodies rather than minds. He is far too much the conceptualizing, allegorizing poet. In the 1930's the charade and German expressionist theater supplied a tradition more suitable to his temperament. Unfortunately, born some five hundred years too late, he missed the genre perfectly fitted to his talents, the morality play. As a dramatist Auden needs a form where characters can be general types, where without pretending to be real visceral organisms, they can step to the front of the stage to deliver set speeches—or where, completely disembodied, they can become *only* speeches, just voices alone. He needs something like a pageant, an opera, or a radio play. *For the Time Being* (called by Auden an "oratorio") could be produced as any one of these.

In *For the Time Being* Auden brought together Poet and Antipoet by inventing a multitude of voices through which they could fittingly speak at a variety of levels, from the highest and most solemn to the very low. In the "Chorus," for example, the Poet sometimes rises safely to heights he could seldom manage before:

> Where is that Law for which we broke our own,
> Where now that Justice for which Flesh resigned
> Her hereditary right. . . .
> . . . Gone. Gone.
> (*CP*, p. 411)

Such elevated declamations, rather like those of some Shakespearean king, could probably be used in an individual poem only as parody. (An identical voice in "The Truest Poetry Is the Most Feigning" is mock-heroic: *"Those raining centuries it took to fill / That quarry whence Endymion's love was torn," SA,* p. 44.) At the other end of the scale, the Antipoet disguised as "Soldiers," frolics around appropriately if not very attractively amid the most vulgar slapstick:

> Prospecting for deodorants among the Eskimos;
> He was caught by a common cold and condemned to the
>   whiskey mines,
>   But schemozzled back to the Army.
> (*CP*, p. 461)

Between these extremes, characters speak on all sorts of levels. There is quite formal simplicity ("The Garden is unchanged, the silence is unbroken / For she is still walking in her sleep of childhood . . ." *CP*, p. 418), Mary's frightened confusion ("Light blazes out of the stone, / The taciturn water / Burst into music . . . / What sudden rush of Power / Commands me . . ." *CP*, p. 419), and Joseph's breezy colloquialism ("My shoes were shined, my pants were cleaned and pressed," *CP*, p. 421).

Although Poet and Antipoet appear harmoniously together in *For the Time Being,* they are united by being distributed among the characters, not by being joined within a single speaker as they were in *New Year Letter.* No doubt this is fitting. A drama cannot have the same kind of unity a verse essay, a narrative, or a lyric has. But with Antipoetic and Poetic Auden fragmented among his characters, more is lost than is gained. The individual characters seldom come to life as the speaker does in *New Year Letter,* as a man who contains in himself all the complexity distributed in *For the Time Being* among various speakers. None of Auden's long dramatic forms of the 1940's, successful as they are at uniting the hostile forces of his temperament by assigning them to different characters, completely solves the problem, as did *New Year Letter,* of uniting these forces within one person. Coherence in one person is what Auden needed. Yet the one person in *New Year Letter* did not completely satisfy all Auden's needs either. The middle-style speaker there had a limited range. Poet and Antipoet were permitted only brief excursions into the outer limits of their possibilities, excursions that held the promise of a more exciting poetry. The main line of Auden's development, after the middle style, is in the creation of single personae in whom Poet and Antipoet can move further and further away from the middle. In *The Sea and the Mirror* that persona is Caliban; in *For the Time Being,* the Narrator.

Like the speaker in *New Year Letter,* the Narrator is an amalgam of Poet and Antipoet. Learned and formal, issuing clinical analyses and serious messages, he can still be colloquial, slangy, witty, sometimes playful and clownish. But he does not usually speak the middle style of *New Year Letter,* except at the end. His idiom and verbal capacities are moving modestly in the direction of Caliban and the speakers in Auden's later comic poems—toward the extremes of Poet and Antipoet. His manner is often both higher and more comic than that of the *New Year Letter* speaker. He slips back and forth between straightforward elevated utterance and deliberate self-mockery, self-parody. As yet though, in his self-parodies he is only pretending to be one of the ridiculous. In *New Year Letter* the speaker *was* one of the ridiculous, but since his self-ridicule seldom strayed very far from the center it was mild and genial. The Narrator's ridicule moves further from the center, and he is not yet willing (as many later speakers are) to admit that *he* is one of those preposterous Average Men he so likes to mimic. Yet in his last speech, in a quieter moment, when he speaks in the middle style of *New Year Letter,* when the silliness of the Average Man seems far less extreme, we see that he is—that whatever the distance between them, the Narrator and Average Man, both human, share the same inevitable foolishness.

The Narrator speaks first as the collective voice of sick civilization. But though he never abandons this guise to appear openly as himself, we are always made aware that this is a mask with someone behind it, that there

is a distance between Narrator and Narrator-assuming-voice-of-the-sick.
The distance is indicated by irony and mockery. By faintly burlesquing his
mimicry of Average Man, the Narrator makes him appear foolish. The
Average Man's colloquial idiom is handled with faint distaste. His earnest
thought, delivered in solemn clichés, seems silly: "and between us we
seemed / To have what it took" (*CP*, pp. 409–10). The Narrator maliciously joins incongruous low illustrations to high solemn actions and
baffled cogitations:

> Perhaps that mysterious noise at the back of the brain
> We noticed on certain occasions—sitting alone
> In the waiting room of the country junction, looking
> Up at the toilet window—was not indigestion
> But this Horror starting already to scratch Its way in?
> (*CP*, p. 410)

By assuming the guise of the sick, the Narrator mocks them by mocking
himself. Though he never speaks in his own voice, his obvious mockery
tells us that he has one. In his second appearance he does speak, at the
beginning and end, in his own voice. He delivers an explanation and
command to Joseph: "you must now atone, / Joseph, in silence and alone
. . ." (*CP*, p. 424). Between beginning and end, he mocks Joseph and all
unredeemed men by again assuming momentarily their own foolish
voices. What this adds up to is that while the analysis and logic are his,
the idiom is theirs. Thus he can mock and analyze accurately at the same
time. The message comes to the reader directly from the Narrator's
analysis and indirectly (in reverse) from his mockery. Such lines as the
following make a true statement and maliciously mimic a foolish idiom at
the same time:

> For likening Love to war, for all
> The pay-off lines of limericks . . .
>
> . . . .
> Today the roles are altered. . . .
> (*CP*, p. 425)

This is all handled very skillfully here and will be used over and over
again in many comic poems later on—where the message of the style
becomes even more important than what the speaker talks *about*.

The Narrator's third speech is similar, except that this time, in the first seventeen lines, speaking as pompous Average Man, he pushes the self-mockery out even further toward burlesque:

> . . . the Committees on Fen-Drainage
> And Soil-Conservation will issue very shortly
> Their Joint Report. . . .
>   (*CP*, p. 435)

At the stanza break, the burlesque stops and the Narrator, speaking in a middle style, provides an accurate analysis of the Average Man's predicament: "In our bath, or the subway, or the middle of the night, / We know very well we are not unlucky but evil . . ." (*CP*, p. 435). This voice continues all the way through the Narrator's final appearance, the last speech in the drama:

>   Once again
> As in previous years we have seen the actual Vision and failed
> To do more than entertain it as an agreeable
> Possibility. . . .
>   (*CP*, p. 465)

Throughout, in every speech, the Narrator's mockery is more friendly than hostile. The Average Man, it implies, is blind, misguided, foolish, but understandably so—even on occasion attractively so. By virtue of his greater understanding, learning, and verbal skill, the Narrator stands apart. He is not misguided and not foolish, yet he clearly delights in his burlesque mockery. Instead of just condemning, he enjoys some of Average Man's foolish antics. Finally, in his last speech this comes more out in the open, and the Narrator and his target, Average Man, come even closer together. There is still some good-natured fun at Average Man's expense ("Not that we have much appetite, having drunk such a lot, / Stayed up so late, attempted—quite unsuccessfully— / To love all of our relatives . . ." *CP*, p. 465), but the mockery now is completely affectionate. The Narrator's analysis shows foolishness, bafflement, secular vulgarity to be inevitable—to be human. If most often he only pretends to be the Average Man whom he attacks by comic self-parody, at the end, with the attack very mild, and the foolishness recognized as inescapable for all men, the Narrator and Average Man are nearly identical. Anthologized, as it often is, out of context, this final speech can be read with no important distortion as though the speaker is talking about himself.

With the Narrator, the handling of persona and voice becomes extremely subtle, and my description will probably be only half comprehensible to anyone who does not look closely at the speeches. And they deserve a close look. The Narrator's four speeches are the most interesting and successful things in *For the Time Being,* and they show an important stage in the development of Auden's personae. They are, in effect, nothing more than modest extensions of the middle-style speech of *New Year Letter.* In both, a single speaker contains Poet and Antipoet within himself. By switching back and forth between them he is able to move either toward their extremes or toward the middle where they are scarcely distinguishable. Both the *New Year Letter* speaker and the Narrator maintain the extremes only briefly, since the very high and the very low are dangerous threats to a speaker's coherence and trustworthiness. Yet the Narrator dares more than the *New Year Letter* speaker. He goes both higher and lower—but only when he pretends to be mimicking someone else. This is safe. If that other person seems ridiculous, the Narrator does not. After all, he was only pretending. Only when he retreats to a safe middle style will he permit himself and that other person to become nearly identical. Then both are foolish but not very much so. This is an intermediate evolutionary stage in Auden. With the next step speakers will admit that they are foolish. Caliban drops the pretense. He never implies that only the others are comically absurd. He never retreats to the safe middle style. He performs always at the very outer reaches of both Poetic and Antipoetic idiom, where neither can be anything but burlesques. Caliban is wildly, gloriously, and grandly foolish all the time. His self-mockery, far more than anything the Narrator achieved, is monumental. In Caliban the extremes of Poet and Antipoet rush constantly back and forth—or rather exist simultaneously. And yet these dangerous forces do not destroy him. As soon as this happens, of course, the philosophical message of Auden's poetry completes its evolutionary leap.

When Poet and Antipoet are at odds in the early poetry, the message of an entire poem will switch back and forth. At times Life will seem to be unpleasant, sick, in need of reform, and Art to be a solemn instrument for analyzing the disease and urging on the cure. At other times Life, though ridiculous perhaps, will seem to be a pleasant healthy delight, something to be accepted without any reform or cure, and Art, equally ridiculous and frivolous but also pleasant. In later poems when Poet and Antipoet join in a single speaker, Life becomes both serious and comically absurd at the same time, both sick ("sinful" after 1941) and a joy, in need of reform and yet a thing to accept as is, unregenerate, and ultimately unchangeable. In short, the mere joining of Poet and Antipoet in a single speaker makes Life both sinful and blessed. As Poet and Antipoet move toward their extremes, the single persona containing them will become increasingly comic, and Life therefore will seem more absurd than before, a thing of joyous foolishness. And the speaker himself will be most foolish of all, since his extravagant style will be inevitably self-mocking. At this point satire stops. A comically foolish speaker cannot seriously condemn anything. He accepts everything. His style alone forces acceptance on him. Thus the temperamental forces I call Poet and Antipoet were pushing Auden toward his Kierkegaardian message long before he read Kierkegaard. But when he did read Kierkegaard, and found his own inclinations crystallized there in philosophical form, the poetry became unified for the first time. That is another way of saying it became better. All such descriptions really mean is that Auden's poetry shows the same kind of thing whether it is described as a repository of philosophical ideas or a dwelling place of personae. Personae create ideas and ideas, personae. When Poet and Antipoet riot at their outer limits, certain ideas come into being—or when certain ideas come into being, Poet and Antipoet riot. This begins to happen in the Narrator's speech, and it happens everywhere in Caliban's. Not only does he appear as a unified, coherent, believable persona, but in the midst of his ceaseless burlesque, he somehow communicates, both by what he says and by how he says it, Auden's most serious and profound message about Art and Life. The straight line of Auden's development runs from the *New Year Letter* speaker through the personae of the Narrator and Caliban. The line traces Auden's discovery of how to combine Poet and Antipoet in a single speaker—of how to unify his own temperament in his art. The development itself is rapid; from the *New Year Letter* speaker to Caliban is a leap. And the leap, of course, is toward Auden's greatest achievement—comedy. Soon after Caliban, nearly all Auden's poetry becomes comic.

VII

The Sea and the Mirror is Auden's first masterpiece, more daring and exciting than *New Year Letter,* and larger than later comic poems that equal it in brilliance (perhaps only "Bucolics" exceeds it). No part of Auden's temperament is excluded from *The Sea and the Mirror.* His highest Poet, his lowest Antipoet all have their perfect and appropriate

speech. More important, his mixtures of Poet and Antipoet, from Prospero's flawless middle style to the high comic speech of Caliban, surpass
anything of this sort he had done before. In Prospero, Poet and Antipoet
blend again to produce a speaker directly descended from *New Year
Letter* and the Narrator of *For the Time Being*. In many places the three
speakers are identical:

> When I am safely home, oceans away in Milan, and
> Realise once and for all I shall never see you again,
> Over there, maybe, it won't seem quite so dreadful. . . .
> *(The Sea and the Mirror, CP, p. 358)*

> . . . Who
> That ever has the rashness to
> Believe that he is one of those
> The greatest of vocations chose,
> Is not perpetually afraid
> That he's unworthy of his trade. . . .
> *(New Year Letter, CP, pp. 268–69)*

> We look around for something, no matter what, to inhibit
> Our self-reflection, and the obvious thing for that purpose
> Would be some great suffering.
> *(For the Time Being, CP, p. 466)*

The speaker in these passages is an intelligent educated man whose native
formal idiom in relaxed moments becomes an easy, supple, middle-style
soliloquy (still more declamation than conversation). Colloquial speech
mixes with modestly correct syntax and learned vocabulary. On occasion
he may rise to a high style or, when more playful, skillfully parody,
mimic, joke, and clown—all without losing the authority and dignity of
his self. As Prospero he can speak with high poetic artificiality (". . . and
with your first free act / Delight my leaving; share my resigning
thoughts / As you have served my revelling wishes. . ."). Or with colloquial ease: "In all, things have turned out better / Than I once expected" (*CP,* p. 352). Or with playful comedy: "You, I suppose will be
off now to look for likely victims; / Crowds chasing ankles, lone men
stalking glory . . ." (*CP,* p. 355). Or with affectionate mock-stiffness:
"Stephano is contracted to his belly, a minor / But a prosperous kingdom" (*CP,* 356). Poet and Antipoet are again united in a single personality, who seems larger, more lifelike and attractive for their being there.

The unification produces in Prospero's speech a poem surpassed by nothing Auden had made before. By 1944 Auden had become, like Dryden, complete "master of the middle style" (*CP*, p. 271).

The startling contrast between Prospero and Antonio is even more remarkable for the fact that Antonio speaks a style almost identical to Prospero's own, in the voice Auden had developed in *New Year Letter*. How can Auden create such unlike personae out of the same style? The answer lies in something observed before. Antonio, detached, looks at "others" with contempt. Prospero, detached, looks at them with love. Antonio's Poetic voice scornfully analyzes the ills, follies, and flaws of others; his Antipoetic voice mocks them with cruel jokes. Parodied and mimicked, their actions and idiom look fatuous:

> Two heads silhouetted against the sails
> —And kissing, of course—well built, but the lean
> Fool is quite a person, the fingernails
>
> Of the dear old butler for once quite clean. . . .
>
> (*CP*, p. 360)

The tone of voice is heavily sarcastic. Prospero's Poet, detached from the "others" only by being more intelligent and articulate, mostly analyzes his *own* follies and shortcomings. When he mocks others, he does so with the awareness that they and he share the same sort of foolishness—the inevitable absurdity of being human. His mockery is the mockery of love. Turned inward the Poet's analysis and the Antipoet's mockery create a persona tolerant and affectionate. Turned outward the very same Poetic analysis and Antipoetic mockery create a persona a bit smug, contemptuous, and too knowing. Magnificent in Antonio where decorum demands it, this persona is not very attractive in earlier poems where it seemed to be Auden. Prospero's humility and self-mockery are always attractive. The rhetorical style of both may be the same. Their personae are near opposites.

Stephano is another mixture of Poet and Antipoet. The Poet in him, though his intelligent analysis is not wrong, is just a shade too high, so that his formality becomes comic, especially set against his low subject: "Embrace me, belly, like a bride; / Dear daughter, for the weight you drew . . ." (*CP*, p. 362). His Antipoet is low ("Wise nanny, with a vulgar pooh," *CP*, p. 362) and makes him seem silly. Stephano descends from those sick speakers in the very early poems, made appropriately

foolish by an awkward combination of Poet and Antipoet. The difference
now is that Auden's compassion has increased. The intelligence of his
Poetic voice and the humbling self-mockery of his Antipoetic make
Stephano more attractive than not. He may be foolish, but he is not
deluded.

Several removes further from Prospero's middle style, the Antipoet
performs alone in the song given to Master and Boatswain. Its downright
meter and perfect rhyme, its balladlike pattern, straightforward idiom
("We drank our liquor straight"), and literary parody ("The nightingales are sobbing in / The orchards of our mothers . . ." CP, p. 369)
assert the claims of the Antipoet as average sensual low-brow against the
literary pretensions of elegant and highfalutin Poets, such as the one who
precedes him in Alonso's speech. The magnificent success of Alonso as
Poet is, in fact, more striking in some ways than the middle and low styles
of Prospero and his inferiors. Though Prospero's speech is probably
Auden's best middle-style performance, and the speeches of Stephano and
the others appropriate and nearly flawless, Auden had successfully done
these kinds of things before. But in Alonso's speech the high Poet's voice,
often reached for but usually missed, succeeds better than ever before.
Alonso's persona is that of a Prospero removed from the library (where
over after-dinner brandy and cigars, indulgent and relaxed, he speaks to a
beloved friend) and placed on stage before a formally dressed audience.
No matter if the "Dear Son" opening suggests a letter or fatherly talk,
Alonso, every bit the courtly rhetorician, puts on a deliberately high-style
public performance. By greatly elevating the Poet, by dropping the
Antipoet's mockery but retaining some of his wit and jokes, Auden
creates a persona whose elegant language and clever tropes are an appropriate display of rhetorical skill by a master orator:

> So, if you prosper, suspect those bright
> Mornings when you whistle with a light
> Heart. . . .
> . . . the park so green,
> So many well-fed pigeons upon
> Cupolas and triumphal arches. . . .
>   (CP, p. 367)

For once Auden has combined his own temperamental tendencies to
produce a speaker of truly remarkable elevation. Alonso is a high Poet,

who takes himself, but particularly his performance, seriously. But the formal locutions set against wit and cleverness, the very things that make other speakers seem foolish, in Alonso become the marvelous constructions of an orator so confident of his rhetorical skill that he dares to range outward to the borders of mock-heroic, knowing that fully in control he will never slip over. If his delight in his own skill shows through, we delight with him. Only a short distance separates serious Alonso from comic Caliban, but that is the distance between heroic and mock-heroic speech. Alonso provided Auden with just what the Poet in him had yearned for all along: a verbal performance in the grand manner where wit and cleverness would enhance rather than defeat the elevated idiom, where all Auden's delight in rhetorical skill for its own sake could be appropriately indulged in a high-style performance.

The Poetic performances of Gonzalo and Sebastian are lesser achievements, partly, I think, because unless they were to be indistinguishable from Alonso's, their rhetorical range had to be limited. As a result, though each speaks appropriately and well, their poems are not as exciting and dazzling as Alonso's. In both, Auden eliminates the daring near-comic cleverness that distinguished Alonso's speech. Except for one unlikely lapse in Gonzalo ("I whose interference broke / The gallop into jog-trot prose . . ." CP, p. 364) both are nearly pure sober Poets, and Sebastian is particularly high:

> O blessed be bleak Exposure on whose sword,
> Caught unawares, we prick ourselves alive!
> Shake Failure's bruising fist! Who else would crown
> Abominable error with a proof?
>   (CP, p. 371)

These are dangerous heights. This speech is not supposed to be mock-heroic, yet such questions cry out for Antipoetic answers that begin: "Dear Sebastian, your splendid query deserves a plain reply. A great many unscrupulous sorts, given the proper chance, would be only too happy to crown Abominable error with. . . ." But Auden's Antipoet is out of sight here. The allegorical images Sebastian plays with are not used to mock himself or anyone. His rhetorical embellishments are closer to metaphysical practice than is usual in Auden's writing:

> The lie of Nothing is to promise proof
> To any shadow that there is no day

Which cannot be extinguished with some sword,
To want and weakness that the ancient crown. . . .

(*CP,* p. 370)

Perhaps the sestina form itself, with all those rhyme words relentlessly reappearing to limit the possibilities for every line, urges its repetitious sobriety on Sebastian.

Two other Poetic performances are interesting for different reasons. Miranda's villanelle, sometimes said to be a charming song of touching innocence, is nothing of the sort. The language in this intricate contrivance is hardly that of an innocent whose discourse falls accidentally into poetry: "her venomous body / Melted into light" (*CP*, p. 373). Nor is the speech at all straightforward ("My Dear One is mine as mirrors are lonely") or unself-conscious and unliterary ("As the poor and sad are real to the good king" *CP,* p. 372). The poem seems completely successful, but the speaker is not Shakespeare's Miranda by a long way, or an ingenuous country lass stumbling on the world. It is Auden as Poet, a highly learned, highly proficient, highly articulate Poet, putting on an extremely skillful exhibition in a game with very difficult rules. The Poet speaks not as Miranda, but as Miranda might speak could she analyze and conceptualize her emotions, realize her unrealized innocence, carefully silhouette herself against the wide world she does not know, and clearly articulate all these in an extremely sophisticated manner completely foreign to her. The entire poem is a wonderfully successful illusion. If Miranda really spoke in character she would sound much more like Trinculo than like the villanelle-speaking persona in her own poem. Trinculo's poem is something of an Auden anomaly, at least a very rare poetic species at this stage of his career. In Trinculo's speech Auden writes one of his very few unmocked, unparodied, plain-style poems in a manner similar to Blake or Frost. Trinculo is simple and ingenuous, a completely defenseless and open man, whose life (making the performance even more difficult for Auden) is one of pitiable suffering. All these features require a style and forbearance from mockery alien to the temperament Auden displays nearly everywhere in previous work. In no earlier poem has any neurotic speaker completely escaped his detached mockery or clinical scrutiny. But Trinculo is loved, not judged, pilloried, or even classified. No Antipoet scoffs at him. No Poet dissects his psyche or turns his fears into pompous inflations. The poem is written as though Auden's Poet had suddenly become a Blake. Auden's signature shows clearly ("a laughter shakes / The busy and devout"). But there is an unusual limpid simplicity:

> On clear days I can see
> Green acres far below,
> And the red roof where I
> Was little Trinculo.
>   (*CP*, p. 372)

Since other poems in this style, with a similar persona, begin to appear later, I will postpone discussion of them. It is enough to note here that Auden's success with Trinculo demonstrates his increasing technical mastery. That he should succeed so well with the unlikely Trinculo persona adds considerably to the dazzling achievement of his entire performance in *The Sea and the Mirror*.

For who would have thought that the creator of Trinculo's innocent sad song could also have produced Caliban? Caliban's speech is Auden's great chance to let Poet and Antipoet move completely away from their quietly harmonious middle style to surfeit themselves at their outer limits. By great good fortune he discovered a situation in which just such splendid indulgence is appropriate, so that the reader can cast aside puritanical critical scruples and dive in. The performance is everything. Transferred into dull homiletic prose, Caliban's thesis would scarcely hold our interest for half a page, certainly not for the thirty-some pages of his monologue. The speech itself, though in prose, is not much different from Auden's poetry. Its rhythms are like those in his syllabic verse, and its syntax and diction are those of his familiar Poet, allowed an elevation beyond his wildest dreams. At the same time the Antipoet practices every verbal trick in his vast repertoire. Grandeur and slapstick merge in one gigantic mock-heroic performance, the explosive start of the high-comic style soon to dominate Auden's poetry. And of course the performance itself carries a message at least as important as what Caliban talks about. The style of this remarkable Auden persona tells us a great deal about his creator—about his joyous delight in grandiose verbal oratory, about his awareness of his own skill and his own foolishness, about his belief in the value of such Art and his delight in the Life which makes it possible. Caliban talks explicitly about all these things, but what he says is scarcely important. *How* he says them so clearly carries its own message about Auden's values and beliefs.

The Sea and the Mirror is the culmination of the evolutionary line I have been tracing. All Auden's beliefs, his styles, voices, techniques come harmoniously together in this work. Not only do Poet and Antipoet merge, but form and content, Art and Life, philosophy and craft merge too. In *The Sea and the Mirror,* the speakers' subjects and the message of their performances are the same. Through much of the 1930's, while Poetic speakers might *say* that life was grim, its inhabitants sick, and its culture moribund, their performances, so often filled with an exuberant healthiness and worldly delight, sometimes denied what they were saying. While Antipoet speakers might *say* that Life was more important than Art, their delight in Artful performances belied what they said. Furthermore when Poet and Antipoet appeared together in many poems, they often unintentionally fought each other to a standstill, while the message of both speaker and performance collapsed around them helplessly filled with self-contradiction. In *The Sea and the Mirror* all these divergent forces meet, are fused together, and produce a single coherent, unified creation. What the speakers talk about and how they talk about it, their matter and their manner, carry the same message. Stated imperfectly, this message is that Art and Life are utterly unlike, that the Aesthetic is different in *kind* from the Ethical (and both are different from the Religious), yet each is necessary to the other. Prospero talks openly about this. Antonio, Stephano, Gonzalo, Alonso, Sebastian, Trinculo, and of course Caliban, do the same, while lesser figures (Ferdinand, Master, Boatswain, Miranda) talk about the relation of Art and Life without knowing it. And the manner of everyone carries the same message: that Art and Life, while unlike, are both valuable. All this is most clear in Caliban's address, of course. His very manner of speaking shows (1) that he values nothing more than an unashamed Artistic performance, as far from Lifelike speech in its open contrivance and indulgent artifice as the Poet can make it, (2) that he values non-Art at least as highly as Art, and from this point of view mocks his own Poetic exhibition with all his Antipoetic skill, and (3) that he unifies these contradictory values not by logically resolving their conflict, but by simply accepting their paradoxical relationship as a delightful part of human existence. In this first of Auden's high comic performances, where Poet and Antipoet careen far out from the middle, what the speaker says and what he shows by his performance are the same. After this all Auden's best comic poems carry Caliban's message about Art and Life, but their speakers, with this message securely embedded in their style, are free to talk about whatever they wish.

Whatever they talk about, most Auden speakers after Caliban are comic—either mildly so (when they speak in middle-style voices) or outrageously so. Their speeches create a comic poetry that ranges from the quietly meditative to gloriously mock-heroic slapstick. Chronologically, I should examine these speakers next, but since I consider Auden's comic poetry to be his most original and important achievement, I want to look at it separately in a final chapter. In the meantime I will follow the development of his speakers in those poems where Poet and Antipoet do not blend, or do not blend successfully, or blend to produce something new but not comic.

VIII

In *The Age of Anxiety* Poet and Antipoet move further from the center with very doubtful results. In this work Auden intentionally removes his Poet from the common speech of the middle style not by elevating his familiar *New Year Letter* voice but by returning again to his very first idiom, based on Anglo-Saxon. At the same time the Antipoet, whether this is intentional or not, clowns vigorously in the speech of all the characters. Buffeted by these two voices, the characters barely manage to speak distinctively, if at all. In spite of the Anglo-Saxon line, Malin sometimes speaks in the middle-style voice of Prospero:

> In peace or war,
> Married or single, he muddles on,
> Offending, fumbling, falling over,
> And then, rather suddenly, there he is
> Standing up, an astonished victor. . . .
> (*AA*, p. 41)

Rosetta, usually sad and solemn, though far less simple than Trinculo, on occasion moves in the direction of his forlorn simplicity:

> I see in my mind a besieged island,
> That island in arms where my home once was.
> Round green gardens. . . .
> (*AA*, p. 16)

Quant, on the other hand, is often nearly pure Antipoet, parodying and mocking his own failures and pretensions, and generally playing the colloquial clown. Describing his own sexual antics on "Venus Island," he recalls how he

> . . . legged it over
> A concrete wall, was cold sober as,
> Pushing through brambles, I peeked out at
> Her fascination.
>   (*AA*, p. 36)

The distinctiveness of Emble's speech, if it exists, eludes me, and this very elusiveness is one of the big problems in *The Age of Anxiety*. All four characters, their distinctive voices blurred by the extremes of Poet and Antipoet, lose most of their individuality. Rosetta sometimes speaks like Quant:

> . . . unicorn herds
> Galumphed through lilies . . .
> . . . courteous griffins
> Waltzed with wyverns. . . .
>   (*AA*, p. 49)

Quant sounds like Malin:

> The soldiers' fear
> And the shots will cease in a short while,
> More ruined regions surrender. . . .
>   (*AA*, p. 19)

Emble sounds like Rosetta:

> I've lost the key to
> The garden gate. How green it was there,
> How large long ago when I looked out. . . .
>   (*AA*, p. 50)

Auden's Poet and Antipoet, instead of creating the characters, often shove them off the stage and take over the spotlight to perform themselves, out of costume. In other words Auden keeps slipping off the masks of his characters to speak himself. Instead of four characters we find two voices, those of Poet and Antipoet, so dominant they threaten to become characters themselves. As a result the four alleged personalities often subside into mere names stuck in the margins of a long narrative poem told in two voices.

The characters collapse into nonentities mainly because of the Anglo-Saxon style. At the outset, the very words and syntax the personalities are supposed to be made of are clearly part of an audacious performance put on by Auden's Poet, not by the characters. The overwhelming demands of the Anglo-Saxon line (for rhymed consonants and four stresses) create a situation filled with possible triumphs for the Poet, but defeat for characters struggling to become individuals. To triumph as narrative poet, Auden must somehow run a plausibly modern speech across an archaic, patterned line. To triumph as a dramatist, he must make this modern speech somehow create different personalities for the characters. Success with either would be an artistic tour de force—deliberately setting up nearly impossible conditions and triumphing in spite of them. Such triumphs are surely aesthetically legitimate. Much of our aesthetic delight, as Auden often says, comes from watching the poet win the game in spite of very difficult self-imposed rules. But in *The Age of Anxiety* the very difficulty of the game draws so much attention to the artist playing it that the characters never have much chance to be themselves—even if their speech is somehow made distinctive. And it is not very distinctive. Fascinated, the reader seldom stops watching Auden get across those tricky hurdles, time after time coming up (to our grinning delight) with a word that really does contain the right consonant, perhaps tucked away in its middle somewhere. That Auden puts on a dazzling show, displaying a nearly incredible skill, is no trivial thing. The performance is genuine art, but the characters, so upstaged by the creator himself, fade into irrelevance.

That Auden should return, after nearly fifteen years, to the Anglo-Saxon style he favored as a beginner probably shows his increasing interest in moving his Poet and Antipoet further away from the center. Caliban had spoken an exaggerated, ornate idiom, developed from late seventeenth-century English (perfected by the time of Samuel Johnson and carried into mannerism by Henry James). Anglo-Saxon, something Auden always admired, offered the other English speech tradition furthest from common twentieth-century colloquial discourse. Since he was always looking for ways to escape the middle style once he learned it, it is not surprising that Auden remembered his earliest Poetic idiom. But the Antipoet, also eager to move away from middle-style restrictions, causes nearly as much trouble in *The Age of Anxiety* as the Poet—perhaps in the long run even more. If differentiated characters seldom show through the Poet's Anglo-Saxon idiom, their identity is further weakened by the frequent appearance of the Antipoet, whose joking and verbal play drowns out what little individuality the characters' voices may have snatched from the Poet. Remembering that in the 1930's any high Poetic performance was likely to provoke the burlesque mockeries of the Antipoet, we note with interest in *The Age of Anxiety* that an Anglo-Saxon-speaking Poet, something like Auden's earliest Poets, calls forth an Antipoet very much like the one in *The Orators,* a type of Antipoetic speaker who had nearly disappeared fifteen years before. One of Quant's descriptions, with its hints of private salacious delights and bawdy relish, might fit neatly into the "days of attack" in "The Airman's Journal":

> . . . lightning at noonday
> Swiftly stooping to the summer-house
> Engraves its disgust on engrossed flesh,
>
> . . . .
>
> And caustic Keith grows kind and silly
> Or Dainty Daisy dirties herself.
>
> (*AA,* pp. 40–41)

This is the Auden of *The Orators,* hidden for so long, but surely supplying much of the underground energy that drives the sedate and mature poet. What farcical possibilities that Anglo-Saxon style had offered more than fifteen years before. And none of them had disappeared by 1947. Even when most solemn, the style requires such tempting clever dexterity. What chance for jokes, steering among all those consonantal collocations and thudding stresses. And how queer solemnity sounds in lines so governed by alliterative demands. What pretensions to spoof then: twentieth-century people, half drunk in a New York bar, affecting the stilted idiom of a preliterate German tribe—and all of them at times sad, moping, lamenting, and lonely. And however faintly, all discernibly sick. For the Antipoet *The Age of Anxiety* must have seemed a paradise of possibilities. Things to burlesque and mock lay everywhere, and as usual little escaped him. When his voice and antics appear under the characters' names, they all sound alike. Since between the voices of Auden's Poet and Antipoet very little speech is left that characters can call their own, their existence, feeble at best, is always sporadic.

The Antipoet's clowning, if not as all-pervasive as the Poet's Anglo-Saxon idiom, in the end may be more destructive. The problem here is the old one: the total meaning of *The Age of Anxiety,* unlike that of Prospero's speech or Caliban's, or even *New Year Letter,* does not depend on self-mockery. In *The Age of Anxiety* the mockery of the Antipoet cannot be persistently turned against the Poet without destroying his message. It is difficult for Emble to convince us that the world is full of dread and despair so intense that

> . . . a wish gestates
> For explosive pain . . .
> . . . .
> The Night of the Knock . . .
>
> (*AA,* p. 40),

when for illustration he offers "Here a dean sits / Making bedroom eyes at a beef steak," or "girls . . . / . . . turn by degrees / To cold fish . . ." (*AA,* pp. 39–40). What are we to think when such sober analyses are mocked by their examples?

> Will nightfall bring us
> Some awful order—Keep a hardware store
> In a small town. . . . Teach science for life to
> Progressive girls—?
>
> (*AA,* p. 42)

Are we to believe the Poet's solemn diagnosis of a world grim with anxiety, or the Antipoet's healthy mockery of such a notion? In *The Age of Anxiety* the answer to this is never clear. The work remains confused like those early poems where Auden's Poet and Antipoet contradict each other. There is, of course, some appropriate mock-heroic: all of Part V (the Masque), some of The Seven Stages, and a good many of Quant's speeches throughout. In some of these places speakers purposely laugh at themselves by elevating their style and mocking it. Like other Auden speakers, they can become attractively humble by burlesquing themselves. Or clowning can even show love, as it does in Part V, where the farcical behavior of Malin and Quant is a gesture of their affection for Rosetta and Emble. Their horseplay says, in effect, that love, though absurd and ephemeral, is worth while. But elsewhere the joking, clowning, and mockery are often inappropriate. They blur character and reverse the message. Searching for ways to move outward from a middle-style, Auden fell into his old troubles. The *Age of Anxiety* begins as one kind of thing and slowly changes. It starts out to be a rather solemn Poetic perform-ance. By the end the message is carried properly enough in self-mocking speeches and the relaxed middle-style voices of Malin and Rosetta. But in between, where this transformation is taking place, Auden's Poet and Antipoet are at odds again. Damaged by the old struggles of Poet and Antipoet, *The Age of Anxiety* remains inconsistent.

Most of the poems in Auden's next two volumes, *Nones* (1951) and *The Shield of Achilles,* (1955) are comic and will be discussed in a later chapter. Both volumes show *The Age of Anxiety* to have been an experimental venture, not a decrease in Auden's powers. Having faltered there, Auden dropped the experiment with Anglo-Saxon idiom. Not a single poem in *Nones* goes wrong because of the clash between Poet and Antipoet. The speakers are clear descendants of *New Year Letter,* and almost all of them range outward from a familiar middle style toward the high comic. No matter how "comic" is defined, not more than five or six poems in *Nones* can be called noncomic, whether their speakers hover subdued near the middle style of Prospero or move off toward Caliban. The Poet never appears entirely alone, except perhaps in one song (though he dominates "Memorial for a City," *SA,* p. 35), and the Antipoet, very mild, appears by himself only two or three times. Blends of Poet and Antipoet are everywhere, and Auden's unification of both in single personae is nearly complete. Weak poems no longer owe their weakness to difficulties with persona. But in fact there are very few weak poems. Of the thirty-one selections in *Nones* seven or eight seem to me inconsequential ("One Circumlocution," "Their Lonely Betters," "In Schrafft's," "Nursery Rhyme," "The Chimeras," "Numbers and Faces," "Footnotes to Doctor Sheldon," perhaps "The Love Feast"). But none of these is seriously flawed. In short, the volume is a great success, far better than *Another Time* and even more distinctively Auden's than *Look, Stranger!* Success is carried almost entirely by Auden's having learned to unite Poet and Antipoet in single personae and having perfected a style for them to speak.

The Shield of Achilles, if anything, is even better than *Nones,* mainly because as Poet and Antipoet move farther away from a mild middle style the comic poems become more daring and exciting. "Bucolics" and "The Willow-Wren and the Stare" are surpassed by nothing Auden ever wrote. Of the twenty-two selections in *The Shield of Achilles,* eleven are definitely comic. Among the others only one (the title poem) is a significant performance by the Poet, who with solemn mien sings of grief, suffering, and sin, while the Antipoet with his mockery and jokes is completely absent. But though he is everywhere solemn, even this speaker never uses a very high style, which is noteworthy in the light of Auden's perennial attempt to discover a speech suitable for his Poetic voice. At this stage in his career Auden uses very high formal manner, elegant syntax, and eighteenth-century diction almost exclusively for comedy, for mock-heroic. Even the old middle style of Prospero and *New Year Letter* is made more comic by raising the Poet and lowering the Antipoet. What style, then, can the solo Poet speak? Alonso's brilliant declamation, Auden's best Poetic creation in the 1940's, could not be used very often. It might be dazzlingly appropriate for an aging Shakesperian courtier but not for an aging twentieth-century New Yorker. And a highflying Anglo-Saxon style had been tried and had come to grief in *The Age of Anxiety*.

In "The Shield of Achilles" Auden tries something else, something very rare for him, but one of the few alternatives heretofore nearly unexploited: simplicity. The speaker in "The Shield of Achilles" remains everywhere sober, but avoids both high elevation and the low conversational sobriety of meditative verse. He still declaims, but now with the dignity of simplicity:

> A crowd of ordinary decent folk
> Watched from without and neither moved nor spoke
> As three pale figures were led forth and bound. . . .
> (*SA*, p. 36)

He also does something equally rare for an Auden speaker. He expresses emotion directly, with even greater simplicity. For this Auden creates a songlike style:

> Men and women in a dance
> Moving their sweet limbs
> Quick, quick, to music. . . .
> (*SA*, p. 37)

An even less formal Poet speaks in "Fleet Visit," a thoroughly sober poem, without mockery or joking, yet everywhere made of colloquial idiom: "They look a bit lost, set down / In this unamerican place . . ." (*SA*, p. 38). Both poems, new attempts by Auden to find appropriate speech for his solo Poet, signal a change made even more obvious

(though perhaps less successful) in *Homage to Clio,* and further discussion of it can be postponed until examination of that volume. Of the nine
remaining poems in *The Shield of Achilles,* three are extremely slight and
can be forgotten ("A Sanguine Thought," "In Memorium L.K-A," and
"Epitaph for the Unknown Soldier"). One ("A Permanent Way") is a
middle-style noncomic poem, the speaker faintly self-mocking, but essentially content with himself and his world ("But, forcibly held to my
tracks, / I can safely relax and dream / Of a love and livelihood . . . ,"
SA, p. 48). Two selections are songs, and one of these, "Nocturne I,"
contains the rare instance of Poet and Antipoet in explicit battle cited at
the beginning of this chapter. "Hunting Season," a slight poem in tight
rhymed stanzas, resembles the speeches of Auden's Poet in *Look,
Stranger!* The remaining selection, "Horae Canonicae," one of Auden's
best works—certainly his best religious work, and a masterful display of
skill—is nevertheless a combination of Poetic and Antipoetic voices
examined elsewhere and can be passed over here. There is no significant
personae development in *The Shield of Achilles.* The comic poems
merely get better.

  Homage to Clio (1960) is reminiscent of *Another Time* in many
ways. A large volume (83 pages), it contains little that is new, and
nothing old that had not been done better before. It is rather a hodge-
podge of odds and ends—limericks, clerihews, thirteen pages of prose,
and some inconsequential poems of miscellaneous sorts likely to be denied
entry to the final Auden *Collected Poems.* As a consequence of all this,
Auden appears to have declined from the brilliance of *Nones* and *The
Shield of Achilles.* Though examination of individual poems can turn up
special faults in this one or that, no single widespread flaw can be isolated.
The volume simply shows, generally, a decrease of the high-spirited
inventiveness and exciting verbal skill that made the two former volumes
outstanding successes. Many poems obviously start out to be high comic on
the order of the "Bucolics" and "The Willow-Wren and the Stare"
("Merax and Mullen," for instance, "The Sabbath," and others). Each of
these begins with a persona, a voice, and a style like those in the earlier
comic poems. But the heights remain inaccessible, as though inspiration,
creative joy—or whatever it is that gives life to language—had failed to
come, and Auden either pushed grimly through or stopped short ("On
Installing an American Kitchen in Lower Austria" is the great excep-

tion). Often he settles for lesser and easier things—very light verse such as "T the Great," the limericks and clerihews, and traditional rhymed sonnets (sonnets appear again for the first time in ten years or more). These forms may have served temporarily as props for flagging powers. But powers do not flag in the next volume, *About the House,* (1965) and so the critic must look elsewhere to account for some of the less exciting poems in *Homage to Clio.*

Critics are prone, in any case, to mistake style changes for "flagging powers." The disappointing flatness in *Homage to Clio* is not everywhere a sign that Auden aimed at his old brilliance and missed. In a few poems he clearly tries to do something different. And that difference is surely part of his long-time unsuccessful search for a satisfactory Poetic voice. Auden tries to make a low, plain Poetic voice in *Homage to Clio,* and after the verbal fireworks in *Nones* and *The Shield of Achilles,* this plain speaker could only seem flat by comparison even if successful, and he is not really very successful.

Even *Nones* had begun to show that Auden's middle-style and high comic speakers were changing slightly. Occasionally, Auden's feeling that life is a blessing to be celebrated had led him to make poems where sentiment and love began to push aside the mockery and laughter—just as, on occasion, Prospero's middle-style joking sometimes gave way to the expansive love always implicit in it. "Not in Baedeker" was one of these. Affectionate joking about old lead mines in the first two stanzas changes, at the end, to affection without much joking. Nostalgia and sentiment come quickly forward as the speaker recalls his youthful visit to this special landscape (*N,* pp. 41–42). "Precious Five" had even less joking and more straightforward love, for the earth, for men, and for the marvelous delights of the senses (*N,* p. 67). Something of the same thing appears in the title poem from *Homage to Clio,* where a Prospero-like speaker passes easily from affectionate mockery to strong love for the whole record of history, men and the earth moving through time:

> . . . Clio,
> Muse of Time, but for whose merciful silence
>   Only the first step would count . . .
>
> . . . .
> . . . forgive our noises. . . .
>   (*HC,* pp. 5–6)

The same thing happens even more obviously in "Good-bye to the Mezzogiorno." Teasing and joking description of the most affectionate sort changes, at the end, to a love paean for the beloved land:

Go, I must, but I go grateful . . .
. . . and invoking
My sacred meridian names, *Pirandello,*
Croce, Vico, Vergo, Bellini,

To bless this region, its vendages, and those
Who call it home.
(*HC,* p. 82)

As Auden's poetry becomes more and more a celebration of sacred objects, telling of his love for the world and its inhabitants, the affection always latent in the middle-style poems rises more frequently to the surface. Love sometimes overwhelms the joking and wit while the dazzling display of verbal pyrotechnics subsides, though seldom entirely. In these cases, readers who fail to see what is happening—or who see but prefer high-spirited comedy to sentiment—may well feel that Auden has gone rather flat, that the verbal excitement has faded. (Poems falter for other reasons too, of course. "Secondary Epic" (*HC,* p. 26) and "The Sabbath" (*HC,* p. 12) are simply weak, but not from love.) If Auden's temperament continues to evolve in the direction evident from *New Year Letter* on, we can expect more poems like "Homage to Clio," "Metalogue to the Magic Flute," "First Things First," and most of the poems grouped under the heading "Thanksgiving for a Habitat" (*AH,* pp. 3–38). In these the overpowering message—bless what there is for being—begins to change the nature of the middle-style and high comic performances. The change, a curious one for Auden, occurs because the Poet in these blends of Poet and Antipoet begins to play a new role. Once the solemn observer of cultural sickness and human shortcomings, this Poet now solemnly begins to celebrate the joys of Life. Auden has mellowed some. During these celebrations his Antipoet can now sometimes sit unprovoked on the sidelines. And when the Poet, undisturbed, praises Life for its goodness, the comic and middle-style poems lose some of the excitement provided by Poet and Antipoet fighting a verbal duel. The blend of Poet and Antipoet in a single persona is still there, unifying the disparate parts of Auden's temperament, but the temperament itself has changed since the early 1930's. The parts are no longer so disparate. If this evolution were to continue to its ultimate limit it would mean, in the terms of my critical apparatus, that the Antipoet would disappear. Auden would believe solemnly, wholeheartedly, without reservation that Life is blessed and should be celebrated. Then the Poet would reign alone over the entire kingdom of his temperament. But there is not much chance that this will occur. Auden's Antipoet, his sense of human ridiculousness, his dislike of pretension, pomposity, and authority, and his genuine delight in clowning, are very much alive and are likely to remain so. Yet the path of Auden's development that leads straight to the comedy of self-mockery circles around in the distance in the direction of Yeats and Wordsworth as well—a most curious and interesting direction. Comic affirmations of love can easily enough become noncomic affirmations of love. Auden's anti-Romantic protests grow feebler. Perhaps their very strength was always a bit suspicious.

If Auden's temperamental changes alter the Poet in poems where both Poet and Antipoet appear in a single persona, solo Poetic performances should certainly show these changes even more clearly. We should expect the Poet to begin speaking directly about the goodness of Life, and he does. Early admirers of Auden as a stern social critic and leader of rebels would scarcely have believed that thirty years later he would have to guard against sentimentality. Yet guard against it he must. When present, the Antipoet is good protection. But when the Poet is alone how can he speak of his love, soberly and earnestly, without falling into sentimental gush? What persona can he assume? Auden has never found an answer, but from *Nones* on he is looking for one.

Let us suppose for a moment that even in the early 1930's, when he was most clinically pontifical on the one hand and farcical on the other, that Auden wished, on occasion, to write a straightforward, directly emotional poem. Even the coldest analyst or the most incurable prankster must have moments when he is swept by genuine feeling. Could Auden have put such emotion into a poem? He certainly could not create, without mocking it, a Shelleyan or Byronic persona to cry out his feelings. He seemed unable to write directly and soberly about his own life without laughing at his pretensions. Furthermore he had no style in which emotions could be straightforwardly expressed. What could he do? One possibility was to write songs or songlike poems. In these, strong traditions and conventions automatically create certain kinds of personae. Auden's earliest published song contains the following stanza:

> The wounded pride for which I weep
>   You cannot staunch, nor I
> Control the moments of your sleep
>   Nor hear the name you cry. . . .
>   (*LS*, p. 53)

Without its title (it is one of "Two Songs") this would in 1936 have been a very surprising poem. Could this be W. H. Auden, the unemotional, clinical analyst, the hardheaded satirist, the mocker of Romantic pretensions? Underneath could he be this sensitive plant? Emotional exposure such as this poem reveals produces great intimacy. Auden would be saying, in effect: "I, the complex, self-conscious poet, ordinarily hiding behind masks, embarrassed by self-exposure and sentiment, am dropping my disguises to lay myself completely open. My vulnerability is a sign of my trust. Even a faintly raised eyebrow, a slight twitch at the corner of the mouth, and I am undone." But with title affixed, of course, this poem is not W. H. Auden speaking. W. H. Auden, that ornate and complex stylist, is making a song. The emotions, simplicity, and exposed innocence are not his, but belong to the traditional persona in songs. The form itself, then, is another mask. I have no idea whether this early song was in fact a façade, protecting Auden's self from mockery, enabling him for once to cry out directly while pretending he was simply following a convention. I rather think it was not. I think he *was,* at this time, merely following convention, and did not contain within his temperament such simple Blakean innocence. But the convention lay there ready for use in case he ever became such a person, and by 1950, for a number of reasons, Blakean innocence had become much more congenial to him. His increasing conviction that life was blessed, and his increasing efforts to celebrate this blessedness in poetry, could now make the emotions of a Blake song seem attractive, whereas before he had often burlesqued such earnest simplicity. To a temperament burdened with contradiction and doubts, to a poet whose love emerged only by indirection from beneath masks and ornate stylistic complexities, simple professions of joy and love might seem to be both a moral and artistic triumph. Mired in complexity, anyone might long for the truths that only the simple dare utter. At any rate Auden makes a few such poems.

Here was a new and suitable style for his Poet. If he could only speak with simplicity and open innocence, he could (with luck) avoid sentimentality and self-conscious embarrassment—all the pitfalls of high oracular Poets. In *The Sea and the Mirror* such simplicity still lay behind a named persona, Trinculo, but in *The Shield of Achilles* the only protective mask is the title, "Nocturne II," and this mask (implying, "I've been trying my hand at making some simple night songs; here is number two") is not offered now as much of a defense against exposure. "Nocturne II" begins:

> Make this night lovable,
> Moon, and with eye single
> Looking down from up there,
> Bless me. . . .
>   (*SA,* p. 52)

Since there is no real pretense that this speaker is anyone other than himself, Auden comes closer here than in anything earlier to an unabashed emotional directness not undercut by self-mockery. For, of course, in these song-line poems of direct emotional simplicity the Antipoet is banished. The Poet, transformed from elevated rhetorician to guileless, humble innocent, speaks alone. Again in "Lauds," protected somewhat by the demanding form, this Poet sings out in emotion unparalleled for its intensity in anything Auden has written: "God bless the Realm, God bless the People; / God bless this green world temporal . . ." (*SA,* p. 84). Out of context, lying separately here on the page, these lines sound banal. Out of context, in fact, the entire poem is ineffectual, never rising from flat bare statements repeated over and over again without verbal excitement. But coming as it does at the end of a long sequence, where a complex persona struggles with the problem of evil, coming after twenty pages of middle-style and high comic self-deprecation, this simple poem at the end of "Horae Canonicae" becomes a magnificent cry, and just the moral and artistic achievement so unusual in Auden. After long struggles the speaker breaks through at the end to a triumphant innocence and simplicity: "God bless the Realm, God bless the People." It is a simplicity that must be won only after complexity to be worth anything. If "Lauds" is patterned by archaic Spanish rules, few readers will recognize this, but everyone can see that it is some kind of artificial song, made up of highly conventional diction and familiar phrases of the sort one used to see, spelled out in colored yarn, hanging on parlor walls. All this convention and tradition and familiarity protect Auden from the embarrassment he so obviously feels in displaying emotion—embarrassment at the immodesty. Without protection the speaker would be saying: See how I, more than most people, feel moved, suffer, cry out with joy. From behind the façade of convention and tradition he says, instead: See how I join those of the past, who in using old diction, old phrases, old song forms, have also felt strongly about life's blessedness. If the reader shares the speaker's glorious feeling of joy, so much the better. If, like Auden's Antipoet, the reader looks at this piece fishy-eyed, unmoved, scorning the weakness of such emotional exposure, Auden is protected. He can say: "It is not I, but the conventional song persona who speaks. I am making the poem."

Elsewhere in *The Shield of Achilles* Auden's Poet, though not exactly a song persona, shows a similar simplicity and directness, as in the title poem, where he examines the sickness of life, or in "Fleet Visit" (*SA*, p. 35), where he simply reports what he sees. In "Lauds," when simplicity demands more dignity than twentieth-century colloquial idiom generally provides, Auden uses a diction and phrasing rather like the Standard English purity of Blake or Housman. But in poems with much less intense emotion, the Poet can employ a more colloquial idiom without losing his soberness or all of his dignity and authority. When Auden's Poet, still striving for simplicity and directness, moves in this colloquial direction in *Homage to Clio,* unlikely as it may seem at first, he is reminiscent of Frost.

Asked for a quick judgment, almost anyone might pick Frost as the twentieth-century poet least like Auden in temperament and style. Neither the often learned subject matter of Auden's poems, his Christian world view, nor his elaborate and ornate speech resemble Frost's studious folk wisdom, dislike of cosmic speculation, and plain manner. Yet, peculiar as it is, Auden has moved toward Frost in several important ways. In the 1950's he began to celebrate life and its common items. (Though the common items of a cerebral city type are not always those that moved Frost, some are.) Then too, Auden shares with Frost an important common theme: "The earth's the right place for love." Furthermore Auden's sentiments in his later work begin to come through poems as seldom before. Many poems display a real *feeling* of love for men and the world (not just the *idea* of love), and in some, the sentiments of this once clinical poet get nearly out of hand. Auden's poems begin to show the struggle Frost also felt, called in one illustrative Frost poem "On the Heart's Beginning to Cloud the Mind." Just this struggle between heart and mind goes on openly in "Nocturne I," and less openly in many other places. But even more important, Auden moves toward Frost in striving for an ever plainer style for his Poet, so that the Antipoet may be safely left aside without danger of the Poet indulging in sentimentality or fantastic celebration. Auden had lowered his Poet from highfalutin Anglo-Saxon heights in *Look, Stranger!*. He had tried in "In Time of War" to make him speak in a low-pitched, flat style. In *Homage to Clio,* on occasion there is a new simplicity, an openness, almost ingenuousness, in the speaker, and now he sounds something like Frost.

This new persona shows up almost too imitatively in "An Island Cemetery," where we find perfect rhymes in each quatrain, regular four-foot lines, and reminiscences of Frost everywhere:

> Wherever our personalities go
> (And to tell the truth, we do not know),
> The solid structures they leave behind
> Are no discredit to our kind
>
> . . . .
>
> Considering what our motives are,
> We ought to thank our lucky star.
> (*HC,* pp. 58–59)

The same Poet appears in "Walks." The diction is extremely simple: "The road looks altogether new / Now that is done I meant to do." Striving for innocence, this speaker nearly falls into *A Child's Garden of Verses:* "Returning afterward, although / I meet my footsteps toe to toe. . . ." The entire experience here (with a rusticity, however faint, most unlike Auden), and the way its contents are developed and used, is very like the half-whimsical simplicity of Frost, pretending to find, with ingenuous surprise, some contentment in the orderly pattern of the smallest event: "It gets me home, this curving track / Without my having to turn back" (*HC,* p. 63). Both poems are close enough to Frost to be imitations. Others, where the Poet's simplicity recalls Frost only in a line or phrase, are not. But echoes turn up, showing that Auden draws on Frost, perhaps unconsciously, when he needs a plain line. Even in "The Old Man's Road" a phrase recalls Frost's "Directive" ("So cannot act as if they knew," *HC,* p. 62), and the style of that older bucolic poet turns up in "The More Loving One" (*HC,* p. 31), "Reflections in a Forest" (*HC,* p. 7), and in "First Things First" (*HC,* p. 56). Even country imagery begins to appear, not the rural allegorical masquerades of earlier poems, where every mountain and valley was an idea in disguise, but plain solid realistic country matters. Now we find bones planted "Like seeds in any farmer's field," sextons "digging up a crop" (*HC,* p. 58), the speaker taking a "stroll" on a "road" (*HC,* p. 63), and birds, trees, and hills that seem to be solid natural objects (as they still were not in "Bucolics," where the Frostian echoes were mostly good-natured parody).

Homage to Clio is a big book, and Auden's Frost-like personae appear in only a small part of it, so their appearance should not be exaggerated to make them sound like a major trend. But small though it is, this trend exists, and definitely is part of a larger and more important pattern, Auden's attempt to make a suitable speech for his Poet out of a plain, sometimes colloquial idiom whose main feature is simplicity. All this is almost totally foreign to his habits, skills, and temperament of thirty-five years, and its success is doubtful. When this plain Poet speaks, Auden must throw away nearly all his devices for making language lively, and he often succeeds only in being flat. Paradoxically his speakers seem more "sincere," personal, and emotional in the high comic poems where Poet and Antipoet perform with all the artifice at their command. Auden's folkish, unsophisticated, plain-speaking Poet with his small ironies, wistful observations, and mild playfulness, simply suppresses too much of the Auden temperament, as well as all his other voices. His greatest achievements remain those poems whose single speakers contain within themselves the whole complex range of his disparate inclinations—the things I have called Poet and Antipoet. Auden apparently senses this too, for in *About the House* all the poems of consequence are comic, their speakers again a blend of his Poetic and Antipoetic voices. The Frost-like persona disappears, and so does the solo Poet (except in the insignificant "Elegy for J. F. K" and some of the seventeen-syllable fragments that are scattered throughout). This volume shows Auden accepting his role as comic poet, and the comic poems are both more numerous and better than those in *Homage to Clio. About the House* is every bit as skillful as *Nones* or *The Shield of Achilles,* but the speakers have mellowed considerably. They have moved even further in the direction of love. The impulse to praise sacred objects is stronger than ever. Mockery grows more subdued, especially self-mockery. Sobriety is usually banished, but it is not so far off as before. This development, steady and predictable since *Nones,* suggests that Auden's Poet may return alone again in yet other attempts to find a suitable voice. As Auden's comic personae grow more serene, turning aside from the Frost-Blake byroad, the path of their development may yet lead them to veer off at a fork toward Horace rather than toward Yeats and Wordsworth.

IX

In tracing Auden's poetic development through his personae, I have purposely not referred to his expository prose. A brief coda here will explain why, and also indicate in general what the prose does and does not reveal about the poetry. What a poet *says* about poetry (his own or others) cannot be taken unexamined as a description of his own work, and this is especially so in Auden's case. Some poets have little insight into their own practices, or even into their own talents. And nearly every poet's critical prose, as Auden himself says (*DH,* pp. 39–40), is polemical, either a defense of what he thinks his practices are—or of what he would like them to be. But the relationship between the polemics and the poetry is seldom completely clear. A poet may argue against his own secret convictions to test their validity, or he may simply carry on a debate with himself in pursuit of truth. Or, under cover of an attack on others, he may be trying to rid himself of his own fondest weaknesses. A loudly anti-Romantic prose piece may very well announce the poet's internal war against his strongest Romantic inclinations. His insistence on the value of light verse and Art as entertainment, his preference for Dyer, Prior, and Firbank, may mask an ardent desire to sit alongside Milton, Wordsworth, and Yeats—and defend his inability to do so with claims that he never wanted to. In prose as in poetry we must look at what the speaker *shows* by his performance, as well as at what he *says*.

Auden's prose quite clearly shows the same temperamental split evident in the poetry. Prose statements by his Antipoet, then, certainly do not describe his Poet's verse practices. His Poetic performances are in reality more like the reverse of what his prose Antipoet advocates. Neither do his prose speakers agree among themselves. For instance, while the Antipoetic Auden extols the virtue of Art as delightful escape and entertainment in a number of essays,[6] Auden the Poetic moralist can deplore just such blithe transport: ". . . if the magical effect which, of

---

[6] See W. H. Auden, "John Skelton," *The Great Tudors,* ed. Katherine Garvin (London: Ivor Nicholson and Watson, 1935), pp. 53–67; introduction to *The Poet's Tongue,* ed. W. H. Auden and John Garrett (London: G. Bell and Sons, 1935); *The Oxford Book of Light Verse* (Oxford: Clarendon Press, 1938).

course, a work of art often has, be identified with its esthetic value, then the conclusions of Plato and Tolstoy that art is immoral seem to me to be irrefutable." [7] To the Antipoetic Auden the "silliest remark ever made about poets" is that they are "unacknowledged legislators of the world." [8] But according to the Poetic Auden, great art makes readers say to themselves, ". . . thanks to this poem, I shall feel differently." [9] Many essays claim, in the words of the Yeats elegy, that "poetry makes nothing happen" (CP, p. 50). In many others, with considerable ingenuity, Auden extracts from even the most unlikely literature (detective stories, fairy tales, Shakespeare) parables for our guidance. In fact Auden's incorrigible habit of discovering moral allegories in literature intended neither as moral nor allegorical, while a legitimate critical pastime perhaps, completely contradicts his repeated suspicion that Art can delight but not teach. Yet such contradictions, fundamental as they are, are only the beginning. On occasion Poetic and Antipoetic Auden have written essays so unlike not only in belief but in style that they seem the products of different authors. Perhaps readers have failed to notice this (if they have) because in adapting themselves to the persona of any given essay, they notice only the internal coherence of his personality and seldom stop to realize that the W. H. Auden in one place may be very different from the W. H. Auden of another. To take extreme examples: there is Auden the solemn pedagogue who wrote "The Good Life," an essay filled with categories and subcategories, grave pronouncements, and authoritative certainties delivered in balanced sentences: "If we regard the environment as static, then the problem is one of modifying our desires; if we take the organism as static one of modifying the environment. Religion and psychology begin with the first; science and politics with the second." [10] This Aristotelian Auden, with his formidably certain tone, his charts, lists, classifications, subclassifications, and impressive schemata of all sorts, dominates many Auden essays. A later and more sophisticated version reigns in most of *The Dyer's Hand,* where he condenses balanced sentences into epigrams: like an Aristotelian dictum

[7] W. H. Auden, "Kipling and Eliot," *New Republic* (Jan. 10, 1944), p. 56.

[8] W. H. Auden, "Squares and Oblongs," *Poets at Work* (New York: Harcourt Brace, 1948), p. 177.

[9] Auden, "Kipling and Eliot," p. 56.

[10] W. H. Auden, "The Good Life," *Christianity and the Social Revolution,* ed. John Lewis *et al.* (New York: Charles Scribner's Sons, 1936), p. 31.

with wit added, they first divide a subject into two parts, then make succinct or clever connections (preferably both). This Auden is the prose equivalent of the Poet. (In *The Dyer's Hand,* though, for the first time there is some self-mockery of this practice, and occasionally the playful artist wins out delightfully over the critic, and we find Auden more interested in the rhetorical performance than in the speaker's message.) In the latter half of "Making, Knowing and Judging," in a speech composed largely of awesome definitions, this Poetic Auden tells us that "To the Primary Imagination a sacred being is that which it is," while "To the Secondary Imagination a beautiful form is as it ought to be, an ugly form as it ought not to be" (*DH,* p. 56). Enamored of Art's high function, this Poetic speaker proclaims that poetry arises from a "passive awe provoked by sacred beings or events" (*DH,* p. 57). Beside such oracular pronouncements, Shelley's claim about unacknowledged legislation seems modest and pale.

Yet elsewhere, the Antipoet, that old foe of Pompositas and Authority, obviously quite a different sort of speaker, calls any kind of "passionate attachment . . . to persons, things, actions or beliefs" a "bore" (*DH,* p. 387). This speaker could hardly fail to discover some pristine examples in "Making, Knowing and Judging." Again, one Auden can write that poetry, "the only adequate medium for psychology," is concerned "with extending our knowledge of good and evil . . . perhaps making the necessity for action more clear." [11] Another Auden tells us that art, in a sense, is "beyond good and evil." [12] The extremely Antipoetic Auden who wrote the introduction to *Slick But Not Streamlined* would certainly think the pretentious solemnity of both statements equally ludicrous. If he could escape to the legendary isle of bliss, this speaker gleefully tells us, he would pack no Art at all in his travelling library. But he would be sure to take *Hymns Ancient and Modern, Lead and Zinc Ores of Northumberland and Alston Moor, Machinery for Metaliferous Mines, The Edinburgh School of Surgery, Mrs. Beeton's Book of Household Management* (1869), and similar worthy publications, among them an absolutely indispensable volume on Victorian plumbing, *Dangers to Health.*[13] This

[11] *The Poet's Tongue,* p. ix.

[12] W. H. Auden, "Mimesis and Allegory," *English Institute Annual,* 1940 (New York: Columbia University Press, 1941), p. 15.

[13] John Betjeman, *Slick But Not Streamlined* (Garden City, N. Y.: Doubleday, 1947), p. 15.

joking Antipoet would certainly make rude faces at the Auden in "Making, Knowing and Judging" who says poetry emerges from the "sacred encounters of [the] imagination" (*DH,* p. 59). This latter Auden would probably be jeered at, too, by the Auden who had "serious doubts" about the "poetic gift" of anyone who failed to enjoy "Minus times minus equals plus / The reason for this we need not discuss." What "sacred encounters of the imagination," sir, this Antipoetic Auden might maliciously ask, gave rise to *that* pleasant ditty—or to the Alka-Seltzer message that improves (loses "half its immodesty") by being tuned into poetry.[14] The point is, of course, without carrying matters further, that Auden's prose as well as his poetry reveals a split between what I have called his Poet and his Antipoet. Critics quote from the prose at their peril. Some Auden essays are written by a persona blended of both Poet and Antipoet (for instance, the first half of "Making, Knowing and Judging"). But in others the Poet dominates or is alone (and in the 1950's and 1960's he has become more Romantic than his counterpart in the poetry). In others the Antipoet modestly protests against Art being worth much, or frolics playfully with the subject at hand. If the Poet can occasionally grow rapturously solemn about poetry's awesome holiness (*DH,* p. 57), why not? The Antipoet still relishes the "delicious absurdity" of an "unintentionally funny line," where some Poet solemnly singing hymns to the English language appears ridiculous. In 1966 the two examples Auden cites ("Why should the aged eagle stretch his wings" and "Had De Valera eaten Parnell's heart") are the very ones that occasioned similar remarks nearly thirty years earlier in "Letter to Lord Byron." [15] Poet and Antipoet live on, in Auden's prose as in his verse.

[14] W. H. Auden and Norman Pearson, *Poets of the English Language* (New York: The Viking Press, 1950), III, xiii.

[15] See B. C. Bloomfield, *W. H. Auden: A Bibliography* (Charlottesville, Va.: University Press of Virginia, 1964), p. vii, and *LLB,* p. 233.

THREE

Style

I

"STYLE" IS how the persona speaks. Since in poetry no speaker exists without speech and no speech without speaker, "style" and "persona" describe the same thing. The two terms separate not objects but two ways of looking at the same object. The reader can describe the personality created by the only thing he can see, the speaker's speech, or describe the nature of the speech itself. While I have unavoidably used the word "style" many times in the preceding chapter, the emphasis there was on speakers. Here it will be on their speech.

A poet makes something with words as a painter makes something with paint. Everyone knows that a painting not only *is,* but is *about:* color, line, mass, spatial arrangements, and things of that sort. But there is still a good bit of resistance to talking this way about poetry. Poetry is not only *made out of* words, the analogous statement would go, but is *about* words—its message is a message about language. The difficulty is in inventing a way to talk about it. To begin with, we can think of language as the raw material a poet uses to construct something. Surveying the possibilities (our model may pretend), he can select from among such things as repeated sounds, strongly patterned rhythms, emotive diction, formal syntax, conceptual conceits, and dozens of other items. Open choice, of course, is a critical fiction. The poet's ability, temperament, and predispositions of various sorts rule out many options. And he does not really "choose" very often—by making a conscious survey of alternatives. Still, each poet does use some language resources and not others, and it is useful to think of him "choosing" these and rejecting the rest. There are no right or wrong selections. No resources are forbidden him, though fashion may rule out some in his own day. None are even intrinsically

better than others. The only requirement is that the poet must do something to turn ordinary words into art, a transformation that has often been
described loosely but usefully as giving language a "charge." Whatever it
is charged with (sound, emotion, ideas, significant form—nothing is ruled
out), verbal art must be charged. That is, its language must be more
"lively," more "exciting" than the verbal norm, more exciting than language in its natural state, as a "found" object lying strewn around
helter-skelter over the landscape of everyday discourse. If these terms are
inexact, they are probably better left that way. Every experienced reader
knows more or less what they mean. In the reader this verbal charge
causes that familiar feeling of exaltation—the aesthetic response. With
luck, the critic can describe something of what causes it.

Advancing into these areas, most critics will wish they had space for a
prolegomenon treating art in the abstract, to clarify and prop up their
approach—or just to establish a meaningful critical vocabulary. But
prolegomenon or no, throughout this chapter I must pause more than I
have done before to mention some general aesthetic matters without
which my description of Auden may be more puzzling than clarifying.
However elementary and pedagogical and oversimplified these observations may be when condensed, they cannot all be ignored if a man's
verbal art is to be described. In Auden's case, for instance, it seems useful
to point out at the beginning what everyone knows, that words have
visual and auditory properties, to either or both of which meaning may
adhere. Though some critics relegate sounds to a secondary role rather
like movie music, and others talk as though sound itself were always some
kind of narrow "meaning" in disguise (if not symbolic then mimetic,
corresponding to bird calls, lapping waves, or tram car clicks), I must at
least insist, if I am to describe Auden, that the sounds and visual configurations of words can exist independent of meanings that may become
attached to them (as anyone knows who looks at or hears completely
foreign languages), and that lookers and hearers may be pleasurably
stimulated by both sounds and visual objects apart from their meaning.[1]
If we can enjoy a pleasing taste—say, a candy bar—without its pleasure
coming from some "meaning" the candy bar has, we can surely get

[1] This is true even if "sound" in some way symbolizes the ongoing process of
life as Susanne Langer believes. If she is right (which I doubt), sounds may still
elicit pleasure apart from what they symbolize. In fact we may be delighted by
music while we hate the moving process of life.

pleasure from sounds and sights in the same way. Though with meaning added, true enough, the pleasure of any word or locution may be greatly increased. (But it may be diminished too. Every good reader knows that in some poems the words' meanings detract from the pleasure of their sounds, so that a poem may become better when the reader shuts out most of the meaning and lets the sound dominate.)

Poetry's visual possibilities may be passed over quickly in Auden's case. From time to time every art apparently grows uncertain about what it is and needs its outer limits explored, to determine what it is not. On such occasions painting may become three-dimensional and music, allegedly portraying gates of Kiev and other solid objects, may try to become visual. Though it is probably the most conservative of all the arts, poetry on occasion yearns to become visual as well as auditory, and has blossomed out at times with colored print, varying type sizes, and black and white patterns to please the eye. But from George Herbert to Charles Olson, most poets interested in type configurations have used visual devices mainly to emphasize sound. Auden (we may be thankful) departs in no way from conservative visual practice, and this linguistic potentiality (if it may be called "linguistic") need not be discussed.[2] But his auditory practice in complete contrast, deserves more attention than can be given it here. The sounds of any good poetry are so important and so particular to each poem that more than any other single element they deserve a volume of study to themselves. Short of that I can only indicate directions and sketch in patterns that should sometime be examined in detail.

What sort of large generalization can be made about the sounds a poet makes? Perhaps none about some poets, even good poets, whose style is highly varied. But Auden's habits do not vary much from poem to poem, and his manipulation of sounds, as obvious as Dylan Thomas', if in the opposite direction, contributes a good deal to the kind of thing his poetry is.

Most people who describe a poet as especially "musical" mean that his rhythms draw attention to vowel and consonant sounds repeated more than is usual in average speech—or if they are not repeated exactly, at least the syllable sounds make slow transitions from one to the next.

[2] "Encomium Balnei" (*AH,* p. 19) may be an exception. Yet its typographical peculiarities seem to follow the tradition of projective verse—using special printed arrangements to indicate tones of voice and speed. The sounding voice is more important to Auden than to most poets, but the exploded lines in this poem seem to me more a hindrance than a help.

Here, for instance, are such "musical" lines from Tennyson and Swinburne:

> They sat them down upon the yellow sand,
> Between the sun and moon upon the shore;
> And sweet it was to dream of Fatherland,
> Of child and wife, and slave; but evermore. . . .
>
> . . . .
>
> There is sweet music here that softer falls
> Than petals from blown roses on the grass
> > (Tennyson, "The Lotos-Eaters")
>
> I am weary of days and hours
> Blown buds of barren flowers,
> Desires and dreams and powers. . . .
>
> . . . .
>
> Pale beds of blowing rushes
> Where no leaf blooms or blushes,
> Save this whereout she crushes. . . .
> > (Swinburne, "The Garden of Proserpine")

Many twentieth-century poets (particularly Pound and Eliot) have struggled hard to escape the "music" of their predecessors, and in the climate of opinion caused by this a good many readers have come to think of "music" itself as something unworthy of serious, tough-minded modern poets. To be accurate, however, the repetition of identical or similar sounds is not "music," but only one kind of music. Equally musical, and equally distinctive, is a deviation from the average in the opposite direction. In short, sound becomes stylistically important whenever a poet moves in any direction away from the sounds of average discourse. The most obvious general directions to take are to make a language with either more than an average number of repeated sounds or rhythmical patterns or with less. If Dylan Thomas is the twentieth-century nonpareil of the repeated sound, Auden is somewhere near the opposite end of the line. He prefers collections of unlike sounds: "In Breughel's *Icarus*, for instance: how everything turns away" (*CP*, p. 3); "For this and for all enclosures like it the archetype" (*AH*, p. 8). The syllable sounds in these randomly chosen lines are like those in Eliot's quatrain poems, particularly "Sweeney among the Nightingales." Instead of being identical or similar (or giving the illusion of being so), the sounds, particularly vowel sounds, are abruptly unlike: I-car-us for in-stance: how. Pronouncing these, the mouth keeps changing shape, the tongue moving around to perform differently. All this is a matter of degree, of course. If a poem departs a great deal from the sound of average speech, or seems to do so, its sound becomes an important part of what the poem is, and a great many poets have leaned heavily on juxtaposed dissimilar sounds. But such masters of dissimilar sound as Shakespeare and Milton exploit similar sounds as well, under certain circumstances. Auden almost never does. Yet his Anglo-Saxon speech is of course some kind of exception, and makes further distinction necessary. Auden's Anglo-Saxon style repeats consonant but not vowel sounds. Vowel repetition alone or with repeated consonants moves in the direction of chant, where the mind succumbs to emotion, and the meaning of words disappears beneath the mounting excitement of recurring sounds. Whatever the psychological explanation for this, listeners and participants seem almost hypnotized by an emotional intensity that has little or nothing to do with the meaning of the repeated words. Nonsense syllables and unknown foreign languages will cause nearly the same effect, as anyone knows who has heard chants at football games or in cathedrals. Though poetry may never reach such extremes as these, it begins to elicit similar responses as it moves toward incantation. Auden never writes incantatory poetry except with tongue in cheek. His Anglo-Saxon style, though it has repeated consonants, is if anything less incantatory than his other verse. His early Anglo-Saxon manner is almost offensively harsh: " 'Is first baby, warm in mother, / Before born and is still mother . . .' " (*CP,* p. 64). The later, though less dissonant, is far removed from the sweet melopoeia of "The Lotos-Eaters." His antipathy for the verbal music of assonance seems to have been innate. Whatever he wrote, he avoided soothing repetition for serious purposes. As a thing to be laughed at or parodied, it turns up occasionally, showing that he thought of it as something embarrassing or pretentious (though the laughter may hide a suppressed longing). In "The Duet," for instance, the comic pomposities of a high style, openly mocked in the poem, prominently display not only parodied sentimentalities but also parodied sound repetition, exaggerated to caricature: *"Love lies delirious and a-dying, / The purlieus are shaken by his sharp cry . . ."* (*N,* p. 54). What is the point to be made about Auden's syllable music then? There is ultimately no point beyond what I have said. His type of sound—nonincantatory, nonemotive—is partly responsible for making his poetry what it is. To say that it *means* something in itself would be to translate our nonconceptual response to sound into a concept, thereby distorting everything. But it will become evident later that the act of *choosing* such a sound may be thought of as meaningful, part of a consistent pattern that reveals a temperament avoiding some of the common devices that make poetry emotive.

Arranged in patterns, syllabic sounds produce rhythms. Here is another enormous subject too complex to be examined in detail here. Auden's dazzling prosodic skill is acknowledged by everybody. Admirers talk about his mastery of nearly every metrical and stanzaic practice known to English poetry (and of several unknown), while detractors gleefully emphasize the same point as proof that Auden, the Good Gray Academic Poet, is a huge museum of outmoded prosody. Since more than anything else, rhythmical effects are peculiar to individual works, in one giant generalization I will pass over practices that may produce the most exciting effects in each poem: Auden's rhythmical skill, it seems to me, is almost completely traditional or an extension of practices introduced by his recent predecessors. Though his prosody is one of his great accomplishments, close analysis will show that he relies heavily on the rhythmical expectations established during centuries of English poetic development. His prosodic practices reveal what is obviously true of his temperament, that his own aesthetic excitement almost never comes from *avant-garde* art. Like most other admirers of past poetry, he clearly gets great pleasure from the skill with which a performer handles familiar technical devices. This has always been one of the most important sources of aesthetic delight in all the arts. Until expectations have been established by witnessing a great many similar performances, no reader can respond with excitement to an extraordinarily skillful exhibition. Auden's own habits show that he, like all good readers, responds aesthetically to a skillful performance quite apart from the performer's subject. This is part of what he means by poetry being a game. Like all the other arts it is a performing art, with the creator as performer. Every knowledgeable reader knows about the relative difficulty of certain practices (rules, Auden likes to call them), and will respond emotionally when a poet's skill makes difficulties seem easy. Even modern Romantic critics like Kenneth Rexroth or Karl Shapiro, while they deplore "rules," would surely understand and approve of Auden when he says, ". . . the formal structure of the poem *I Remember, I Remember* [by Phillip Larkin], in which the succession of five-line stanzas is regular but the rhyming is not, being used both within the stanza and as a link across the stanza break, gives me great pleasure as a device, irrespective of the poem's particular contents." [3] If that is not all art is, it is that as well. And just such a taste for prosodic technique for its own sake is, I think, the best general explanation of Auden's own practice.

Whatever its traditional roots, though, Auden's prosody conforms to the main stream of twentieth-century practice by freely using prose and speech rhythms. In his syllable-stress poems, his general practice is enough like that of his metrical predecessors to be passed over without comment. But his prose or speech rhythms deserve special attention, since they play a large part in creating one of his characteristic voices. Of course the pleasing struggle between metrical rhythms and those of speech and prose has always caused a good bit of the excitement in English poetry. And Auden's poetry contains all the varieties of this struggle: poems where syllable-stress rhythm dominates, poems where syllable-stress and speech rhythm are about equally powerful, poems where speech rhythms are played off against strong-stress patterns learned from Hopkins and Anglo-Saxon literature, and poems where speech or prose rhythms nearly obscure metrical patterns. In a great many poems, especially after 1940, foot and stress patterns succumb to their much stronger opponent. Speech or prose rhythms prevail, and no one exceeds Auden's virtuosity in running these across the most unlikely meters. One of the most unlikely, for instance, is in a playful monologue in *For the Time Being*. Here an extremely colloquial speech rhythm ("For having reasoned—'Woman is naturally pure / Since she has no moustache,'" *CP*, p. 425) flows through ten-line stanzas of intricately patterned four- and five-foot lines (4,5,5,4,5,5,5,4,5,5) rhyming abcacbddff. This rigorous stanza design in no way aids the colloquial speech. Quite the opposite. Its formidable demands make speech more difficult. Its creator is the poet who believes art to be partly a game. His aesthetic delight arises from self-imposed rules made increasingly difficult, and most knowledgeable readers will respond to this with a similar pleasure.

Whether accompanied by formal patterns or not, Auden's speech

[3] W. H. Auden, "Two Ways of Poetry," *The Mid Century* (October, 1960), p. 12.

rhythms nearly always have heavy stresses. Unlike Pound (who consciously explored the far reaches of rhythmical flatness),[4] Auden's speech rhythms usually have stresses as strong as (and sometimes stronger than) his metrical rhythms. Because of this it is not always possible to decide what formal pattern governs some of the later poems. Is Auden counting syllables, feet, or stresses? Some lines, for instance, in the acknowledged syllabic poem "In Praise of Limestone," are syllabic anomalies and seem to be governed by stresses. (Counting elided vowels as single syllables will not explain away all the syllabic deviations.) In contrast, foot and stress poems sometimes appear to be governed by syllable count. The cause of all this is not Auden's faulty ear, but that he hears something more pre-emptive than line pattern. Whatever their formal shape, many poems after 1940 contain an unmistakably similar voice, with its own strong speech rhythm. In various poems this same voice runs across lines that are technically six feet, five feet, four feet, three feet, even two feet, or syllabic. (It even appears in the prose included in poetry volumes.) The line unit, almost never dominant in these, often eludes the ear, and sometimes even analysis. In a given poem Auden may theoretically be writing thirteen-syllable lines, but he is mostly listening to a speech voice that sometimes may use fourteen or fifteen syllables or speak in six-stress units. The rhythms of this voice are so outstandingly distinctive that surely the voice itself can be singled out for identification. The voice rhythms are used by both Poet and Antipoet for all sorts of verse—high, low, or middle style—and I am tempted to guess that both voice and rhythms owe something originally to Marianne Moore. (Auden says he read her poetry for the first time in 1935, *DH*, p. 296.) Though short syllabic lines can often be heard (that is, the reader can hear or feel the proper number of syllables instead of stresses or feet) in long lines of the sort Miss Moore likes, the syllable count itself is often an intellectual rather than an auditory game. What the reader hears is not a repeated number of syllables but a distinctive speech rhythm. This is just what the reader hears in Auden's syllabic poems as well, and to my ear the voice in these poems sounds similar to that in Miss Moore's poetry, as though when he borrowed her prosody he also borrowed part of her voice

---

[4] See Pound's statement in *Literary Essays of Ezra Pound,* ed. T. S. Eliot (London: Faber and Faber, 1954), p. 12: ". . . there is verse libre with accent heavily marked as a drum-beat. . . . I think I have gone as far as can profitably be gone in the other direction (and probably too far)."

(perhaps the one is nearly the sole cause of the other). I say this only as a descriptive aid. When speech rhythms dominate in Auden they often create a distinctive voice. The voice first became distinctive in the late 1930's and early 1940's. Originally it sounded something like Miss Moore's poetic voice, and Auden used it in both syllabic and nonsyllabic poems and in prose. But no amount of abstract description can classify this voice as well as a few illustrations. Here is the voice:

> . . . to become a pimp
> Or deal in fake jewelery or ruin a fine tenor voice
>   For effects that bring down the house could happen. . . .
>   ("In Praise of Limestone," *N*, p. 12)

>   To manage the Flesh,
>   When angels of ice and stone
>   Stand over her day and night who make it so plain
> They detest any kind of growth, does not encourage. . . .
>   ("Mountains," *SA*, p. 18)

> To practise one's peculiar civic virtue was not
> So impossible after all; to cut our losses
> And bury our dead was really quite easy. . . .
>   (The Narrator in "For The Time Being," *CP*, p. 410)

> To break down Her defences
>   And profit from the vision
> That plain men can predict through an
>   Ascesis of their senses,
> With rack and screw I put Nature through
>   A thorough inquisition. . . .
>   (The First Wise Man in "For The Time Being," *CP*, p. 429)

> As long as there were any roads to amnesia and anaesthesia still to be explored, any rare wine or curiosity of cuisine as yet untested, any erotic variation as yet unimagined . . . there was still a hope. . . .
>   (Simeon in "For The Time Being," *CP*, p. 448).

The formal line patterns here (each different, the last prose) all quickly capitulate to the overpowering speech stresses of a voice nearly identical in each passage. This voice appears in a great many poems after 1940 and is an important and obtrusive feature of Auden's style, one created largely by rhythm. So powerful is this rhythm in creating a distinctive voice, that by the time of *Homage to Clio* it makes sense to say that in all of Auden the Grand Persona speaks in two distinct voices (used in variation by all his speakers), one created by dominant metrical, the other by dominant speech, rhythm. Poet and Antipoet make their speeches out of both. Despite the vast number of shared features these voices have (diction, imagery, and so forth) rhythm alone makes them very unlike. For instance:

> Within a shadowland of trees
> Whose lives are so uprightly led
> In nude august communities,
> To move about seems underbred. . . .
> ("Reflection in a Forest," *HC,* p. 7)

> Out of a gothic North, the pallid children
>   Of a potato, beer-or-whiskey
> Guilt culture, we behave like our fathers and come
>   Southward into a sunburnt otherwhere. . . .
>   ("Good-bye to the Mezzogiorno," *HC,* p. 79)

II

Most words have meanings as well as sounds, and unless a reader can shut off every organ but his auditory nerve, meanings will contribute their part to a poet's style. Since from the beginning the meaning of "meaning" has been the basic concern of dozens of intellectual disciplines, a mere literary critic might wish poetry were nothing but sounds and visual patterns, complex enough by themselves. But throughout this chapter some extremely important stylistic features in Auden's poetry will make the problem of "meaning" difficult to avoid. To begin with, a few basic axioms, clear enough for my purposes and vague enough to forestall appalled philosophers, aestheticians, linguists, philogists, and other interested parties, may be accepted by everyone. Let us assume first what nearly everyone has agreed on, that all human experiences affect the entire organism, both the "mind" and the "body," however we choose to define these. Every experience then will stimulate at least some intellectual response (however large or small) and some nonintellectual response (large or small). Like all other experiences, looking at a word will arouse in each reader both kinds of responses. Or, to describe the word rather than the reader, all words carry in them properties that can arouse feeling states as well as intellectual states in a reader. No words are entirely conceptual or entirely emotive; all are a mixture of the two. As long as a writer relies on a more or less even balance between the two, this distinction will be a useless critical tool. But Auden does not rely on a balance. His poetry, more than that of any important poet of our time, is made out of conceptual diction, words that by themselves, out of their context of phrase or line, produce in the reader not feeling states but intellectual responses. Now it should be remembered that according to my model all experiences contain both. In familiar terms, feelings and ideas are part of every experience, and either will give rise to the other. The very concepts in a totally conceptual poem will produce some feeling states in the reader. But the difference in degree can be enormous. If Dylan Thomas, for instance, relies almost entirely on feeling-state diction, Auden relies almost entirely on conceptual, and the artifacts made from these different language media are so dissimilar that in this case to call each "poetry" can be almost as confusing as helpful. Some critics, unable to respond to such unlike verbal objects, decide that if one is "poetry" the other cannot be, and Auden has suffered accordingly from the tastes of our age.

The problem can be described by recalling again that poetry or any verbal discourse relies either on sound or meaning for its effects (visual patterns having never played an important role). Meanings, of course, can become associated with anything, even with the sounds of individual syllables or letters, but by and large they do not do so. By themselves letter and syllable sounds usually mean nothing, or very little. They strike our sensibilities as pure sounds. Now if we examine the effect of these sounds and meanings separately, we can make a useful distinction: meanings alone easily arouse in the reader both feeling states and intellectual states, but syllable and letter sounds alone usually produce feeling states more often than intellectual states (or, more accurately, they produce an experience whose substance is more feeling state than anything else). One way of describing poetic art, then, is to say that it relies on three main properties contained in individual words:

1. The capacity of sounds (alone or made into rhythms) to produce feeling states.
2. The capacity of meanings to produce feeling states.
3. The capacity of meanings to produce intellectual states.

Despite poetic revolutions and critical protestations, twentieth-century tastes in these matters owe much to earlier practices. Nineteenth-century Romantic and Symbolist poetry relied so heavily on the second property that this has come to seem the poetic norm for many readers. For them this is what "poetry" is, and such readers usually find poetry that is heavily indebted to the third property dry, flat, shallow, "unmoving," or not "poetry" but more like prose. Like Ben Jonson or late seventeenth- and early eighteenth-century poets, Auden usually relies only moderately on the second property, and so has often written the sort of poetry many twentieth-century readers do not care for. But many older poets who used nonemotive diction also used highly concentrated and repetitive sounds. If their diction did not produce strong emotional responses in the reader, their syllable sounds did. This helps make them acceptable to the twentieth-century reader who expects to be emotionally "moved" by poetry in some direct fashion. Auden too is attentive to syllable sound, as I have said, but his syllable sounds—nonrepetitive, nonincantatory—are just the sort most readers find unemotive. Most Auden poems are not poetry moving toward song. And though many readers would not like to think they enjoy a poetry that is, the modern reader's ear, trained by listening to poetry up to its neck in French Symbolist and English Romantic inheritance, prefers just this sort of poem. Auden's poetry is a poetry moving toward talk. The reader must hear it not for the ecstasy of its sensual sound bath, but to catch the voice sounds that will tell him what the words mean and what sort of person the speaker is. Auden's conceptual diction and nonemotive syllable sounds, then, have worked against him, making his poetry seem "unpoetic" to some, and they have earned him a slow and grudging acceptance among many fine critics and readers who can clearly detect other of his excellent qualities. Even poets who rely for their effects primarily on the first and third properties mentioned—conceptual diction along with repetitive syllable sounds (as some eighteenth-century poets do)—have only slowly gained favor with modern readers, who much prefer poetry heavily indebted to the first and second properties, the media of much nineteenth- and twentieth-century poetry. Thus Auden's unusually strong reliance on the third property is unfashionable. This is despite a supposed taste, in our time, for "intellectual" poetry, a misconception largely self-generated by influential readers who pinned on Eliot the misleading label "classicist" and proceeded to read him as an "idea" poet. Perhaps no poetry ever written has been less "intellectual" in the sense of the third property than *The Waste Land,* a work made almost wholly of the first and second properties I have listed. It is an irony of our critical age that *The Waste Land,* a culmination of the Romantic-Symbolist tradition relying so heavily on properties one and two, should have been associated with the term "classical," while Auden's almost exclusive Augustan reliance on property number three should have confused many readers, who, having no labels or tastes left over for his sort of work, often wondered whether it was really "poetry" at all.[5] For Auden's words, taken individually, are almost without exception so highly conceptual that illustration seems almost unnecessary. From such very early examples as "neutralizing peace," "average disgrace," and "victorious wrestle" (*CP,* p. 179) to late examples such as "abhorrent dungeon" and "chaste Milady" (*AH,* p. 24), they are nearly all the same kind of thing.

Conceptual words made into sentences produce a kind of poetry sometimes called "poetry of direct statement." This phrase is almost impossible

---

[5] John Blair, *The Poetic Art of W. H. Auden* (Princeton: Princeton University Press, 1965) seems to come to similar conclusions. I think most twentieth-century criticism and the unexamined responses of most readers are essentially Romantic. The battles between critical schools in the twentieth century have usually been conflicts within a single tradition. The so-called "classicists" are usually only some sort of High Church Romantics. In the *Romantic Image* (London: Routledge and Kegan Paul, 1957), Frank Kermode has pointed out how Pater, Arthur Symons, Yeats, Eliot, and the New Critics are really votaries of the same faith. But this evidence about their avowed art theories is not as striking as the similarities of their tastes and unexamined critical responses to poetry. High Church Romanticism, one might say, is based on intellectually examined theology; the Low Church, on viscera. The former transcends ordinary experience (or "scientific" experience) by symbol, ambiguity, infinite suggestion, the Image, T. E. Hulme's curves, I. A. Richards' harmony. Low Church brethren transcend ordinary experience by trusting to the powers of spontaneity, the heart, the blood, the glands. Like Episcopalians and Baptist fundamentalists, the one finds transcendental reality in a highly learned theology, dignified tradition, and artifice; the other in instinct, spontaneous emotion, and naturalism. The first thinks of himself as "classical" because of his dignity, restraint, and formal skill. He thinks of his Low Church brother as a barbarian. The second looks upon his High Church colleague as effete, unreal, bloodless, bodiless, and given over to obsession with empty refinements of "style"—while he attempts to speak straight from the "self." At one end are Eliot and the New Critics; at the other Karl Shapiro, Kenneth Rexroth, Henry Miller, and Lawrence. But all would agree with Coleridge that great art comes from the Imagination. Almost no one ever thinks of questioning this. Both sides condemn the poetry of Fancy. Neither side is "classic" in the sense of being like British Augustan poets.

to define if its meaning is examined closely, but it refers generally to a sentence without figurative speech, symbols, allegories, metaphors, and other familiar rhetorical devices: "I know a retired dentist who only paints mountains" (*SA*, p. 17). If Auden did nothing but simply put his conceptual words together to make sentences, they would all be like this example, that is, "poetry of direct statement." How can a poet whose syllable sound is unemotive and whose diction is conceptual give his sentences the special charge, the linguistic liveliness or excitement, that will set them apart from the flat "direct" statement of ordinary discourse? He can of course do an endless variety of things. The remainder of this chapter will show only the most important things Auden does. At first I will maintain the useful fiction of describing words as individual entities, having properties apart from their context or usage setting. Of course words never exist in this pure state, so a sentence is never *merely* the sum of properties in its individual words. Two words put together become something different from the same two separated for analysis. All this will be taken up later.

Perhaps the most obvious way to give a "charge" to a bare sentence filled with conceptual words is to animate the concepts somehow, so they begin to have a life and feelings lacking in their essential selves. Auden's animating procedures are among the most distinctive features of his verse, and they have often been commented on.[6] The feeblest life begins when conceptual nouns become faintly personified by the mere loss of an article: "Not as that dream Napoleon, rumour's dread and centre . . ." (*CP*, p. 82). As yet this concept "rumour" lacks life enough to move, but already touched with the faintest suggestion of allegory, all it needs is another spoonful of vitality to begin acting. Auden's poems overflow with such concepts ("spacious days," "intransigent nature," "betraying smile"). Attach a verb to one and they begin to move across a landscape, blank and featureless though it may be:

> Let his thinning hair
> And his hauteur
> Give thanks. . . .
>   (*CP*, p. 17)

---

[6] Beginning in an important way with Randall Jarrell, "Changes of Attitude and Rhetoric in Auden's Poetry," *Southern Review*, VII (1941), 326–49 and most recently in Blair, *The Poetic Art of W. H. Auden.*

It is worth noting that the pressures of meaning are not responsible for this primitive allegorizing. Had Auden written, "He, with thinning hair and hauteur, gives thanks," meaning would have been essentially the same. These mild allegorical constructions are obviously native to Auden's temperament. They spill out as naturally as do Milton's Latinate sonorities. They occur everywhere, whether or not they enhance meaning, seem "fitting," or add anything of significance to the compositional texture of the artifact. But even when they accomplish nothing else, these small animations supply action and all sorts of verbal liveliness to words that by themselves are nothing but bodiless concepts. With active verbs their bodies begin to take shape ("presses of idleness issued more despair," LS, p. 42) and imply the existence of a landscape in which they act. Once that landscape is made explicit, by adding even the most humble and vague detail, these concepts come fully to life and move through an allegorical world: "Looking and loving our behaviours pass / The stones, the steels, and the polished glass . . ." (CP, p. 36). Here again the allegory is mostly just "poetic business," something to enliven bare conceptual discourse. The difference of meaning between "behaviours pass" and "we pass" is negligible. This sort of allegorical image flourishes everywhere in Auden's poetry regardless of type, whether love poem, satire, parody, or invocation; regardless of voices; regardless of whether Poet or Antipoet speaks. "Gone from the map the shore where childhood played," Auden will write, or "Islands of self through which I sailed all day" (CP, p. 115). As the first of these shows, Auden turns into concepts even words that might easily suggest solid three-dimensional objects we could taste, touch, see, or smell. Carefully removed from the sensual "real" world these are made to dance through an allegorical one: "The lilac bush like a conspirator / Shams dead upon the lawn" (CP, p. 83). If image is added to image, allegorical landscapes will simply grow more elaborately populated with actors, like this one from "Herman Melville": Terror

> . . . was the gale had blown him
> Past the Cape Horn of sensible success
> Which cries: "This rock is Eden. Shipwreck here."
> (CP, p. 146)

Expanded further they may take over entire stanzas, half a poem, whole poems, or even volumes, and in the early work they spread sketchily across several volumes. "Who will endure . . ." (*CP,* p. 176), a very early poem, is nothing more than a greatly expanded allegorical image. "In Praise of Limestone" (*N,* p. 11) is another, a masterpiece of its type, a giant allegorical landscape. Inside its big one little ones flourish briefly for a line or two, and even they may be made up of yet smaller allegorical images and single personified epithets. "In Praise of Limestone" shows how such language resources can be turned into art of the highest order.

Low-order art turns up too, bulging with allegory. If allegory seems one of Auden's most innate proclivities, it is also his last line of defense. When everything else fails he may burst out with a fantastic flourish of futile allegorizing, as though desperately trying to breathe a little life into a bit of dying verbiage. When he tries to simplify his Poetic voice, throwing out the highflying rhetoric that makes it lively, allegory is often the last device to go, and it sometimes remains stranded on the flat linguistic plain. "In Time of War" and poetry in the late 1930's suffer most from the attempts at allegorical resuscitation. "The Traveller" is a good example. Beginning with a typical line from this period ("Holding the distance up before his face"), the sonnet compulsively animates everything in reach ("harbours touch him . . . cities hold his feeling . . . earth has patience"), and transforms the extremely feeble substantive content of adjectives into capitalized nouns: "The One who loves Another," "the Expected," "The Soft, the Sweet, the Easily-Accepted" (*CP,* p. 55). Since these desperate allegorical maneuvers add no meaning worth mentioning and do not even prod the dead concepts into life, they add neither verbal excitement nor intellectual insight. What they add is an unfortunate glimpse of sweat on the author's brow. We see only the performer's strain, his *attempt* to pump life into anemic concepts. We do not see the life itself. Unsuccessful efforts of this sort carry a heavy penalty. When the poet is caught in the spotlight trying and failing, all his devices, a delight when they work, huddle exposed on the bare stage looking twice as large as usual.

Several other stylistic features seem to be related to Auden's allegorical methods of animation. Since his nouns are almost exclusively conceptual and generic, he relies heavily on attributive adjectives to animate them and give them the particularity absent in a language without so-called "concrete" diction. Adjectives are everywhere in abundance; the reader may open any Auden volume at random for illustration. The first poem in *Another Time* is an interesting case, since it shows how a completely

normal-sounding Auden poem can, on examination, prove to be made up
of an almost incredible number of adjectives. Beginning

> Wrapped in a yielding air, beside
> The flower's soundless hunger
> Close to the tree's clandestine tide
> (*AT*, p. 15),

the first stanza of forty words contains thirteen generally classed as
adjectives and nine nouns, a distribution roughly continued through the
remaining six stanzas. It is interesting to compare these figures to Josephine Miles's word count studies of eighteenth- and nineteenth-century
poetry. In this instance at least, Auden's adjective-noun ratio is even more
Augustan than the Augustans.[7] Of course adjectives do not crowd all
Auden poems as they do "Wrapped in a yielding air, beside. . . ." This
poem, in fact, appeared in the late 1930's when the vivifying machinery
got such a heavy workout, and weakly animated adjectives, capitalized or
personified by a preliminary "the," turned up too often: "He was the
Rich, the Bountiful, the Fearless" (*CP*, p. 321). Another and related
Auden device began to stick out noticeably at about the same time. This
one might be called the "Auden simile," since it is so common in his work
no other poet can possibly write even a faintly similar locution without
immediately revealing his debt: "Anxiety / Receives them like a grand
hotel" (*CP*, p. 330). The Auden simile is often another means of
animating concepts. It is almost always a miniature allegory, and it
frequently functions simply as an alternative to the attributive adjective.
Instead of saying war has a monumental simplicity, Auden writes, "Here
war is simple like a monument" (*CP*, p. 327); instead of writing that
boxlike museums store up learning, Auden prefers, "Museums stored his
learning like a box" (*CP*, p. 323). When he struggled hard to simplify
his Poetic voice in "In Time of War," Auden had to discard a syntax
capable of harboring a huge flotilla of attributive adjectives. The Auden

---

[7] In the first ten lines Auden uses seventeen adjectives and eleven nouns.
Selected eighteenth-century poets average twelve adjectives and nineteen nouns
every ten lines, selected nineteenth-century poets, ten and nine. See Josephine
Miles, *The Primary Language of Poetry in the 1740's and 1840's* (Berkeley and
Los Angeles: University of California Press, 1950). Since I have done no
extended word count in Auden I draw no conclusions, but I suspect such counting
might show something about his poetic affinities (although the count Miss Miles
does on Auden in her book on poets of the 1940's seems inconclusive).

simile replaced adjectives, and grew like a weed. At its worst it added nothing to meaning and only an embarrassing cleverness to animated concepts: "And paper watched his money like a spy" (*CP*, p. 323). But since 1940, when Auden has used it with much more restraint, the simile often works perfectly, as it does in Prospero's phrase "Familiar as a stocking" (*CP*, p. 356), mainly because Prospero uses it with faint comic detachment. As I have noted before, Auden's great poetic discovery was that a little self-mockery not only redeemed his most extravagant and questionable indulgences, but turned rather embarrassing liabilities into marvelous assets. What was pretentious before then became humility. What was unintentionally comic became intentionally so.

Closely related to the Auden simile is the short declarative statement that manages to be almost as distinctively Auden's as the notorious simile itself: "Wisdom is a beautiful bird," "Goodness existed," ". . . freedom was so wild" (*CP*, pp. 81, 146, 319). In a poetry made exclusively of conceptual diction, to describe means to classify. Descriptions do not trace the qualitative attributes of an object, getting the feel of its sensory surfaces. Instead they discover its logical essence, the verbal classification that sets it apart from alien data and determines its place in the chain of being. Auden's definitions, when still faintly descriptive, may classify by similitude, "rooks . . . / Like agile babies" (*CP*, p. 80), or by straight declarative statements: "For time is inches," "Touching is shaking hands" (*CP*, pp. 135, 19),

> Love by ambition
> Of definition
> Suffers partition . . .
>   (*CP*, p. 78),

> Between attention and attention
> The first and last decision
> Is mortal distraction. . . .
>   (*CP*, p. 22)

Out of these grew Auden's habit, especially strong in the late 1930's, of making statements followed by colons or implied colons, after which came lists or elaborations: "How prodigious the welcome was. Flowers took his hat / And bore him off"; "Goodness existed: that was the new knowledge" (*CP*, pp. 77, 146). Often effective, these rhetorical practices are partly forced on Auden by his almost entirely conceptual diction.

What for poets with emotive diction would become a "concrete" image or a sensory simile becomes a logical definition for a man limited to conceptual words. When used excessively, as they often are in the late 1930's, these declarative proclamations can seem peculiarly sententious and pontifical. When the Poet utters them, and pauses heavily at the end on period or colon, his voice seems to capitalize each word, as though as know-it-all and general Pronouncer, he wanted even his syntax to remind us that his speech was Very Important.

The practices I have described so far exist because the fundamental building blocks of Auden's poems, his words, lack sensory associations that produce feeling states in the reader. A large part of all English poetry depends on evocative diction for much of its effect, and without it Auden must use something else to give verbal excitement to what otherwise would be flat sentences of direct conceptual statement. Since the most obvious thing he does is to animate concepts, his poetry is filled with the moving, dancing ideas that animate allegories small as an epithet and large as a volume, and set in motion all the related verbal practices that attend them. This way of intensifying language has been very much out of fashion (at least in theory) since Coleridge labeled it Fancy and called it a lesser thing than Imagination, and Auden has suffered at the hands of critics who, knowingly or not, share this preference, probably more common now than in Coleridge's time. Auden himself has accurately described Fancy as a "conscious process" involving in its analogical method a "one to one correspondence . . . grasped by the reader's reason," while Imagination, he says, is a process emphasizing the "less conscious side of artistic creation . . . the symbolic rather than the decorative or descriptive value of images." A symbol "is an object or event . . . felt to be more important than the reason can immediately explain. . . ." [8] Whatever he may prefer in his theoretical prose, in poetry Auden employs the resources of Fancy: embellishment, decoration, invention, ornament. A great many twentieth-century readers respond to these words as Kenneth Rexroth does, when he says that "Bad poetry always suffers from the same defects: synthetic hallucination and artifice. Invention is not poetry. . . . Poetry is vision, the pure act of sensual communion and contemplation." [9] That

---

[8] W. H. Auden, *The Enchafèd Flood* (New York: Random House, 1950), pp. 61, 65.

[9] Kenneth Rexroth, introduction to *Selected Poems of D. H. Lawrence* (New York: New Directions, 1959), p. 11.

"invention" and "ornament" have such pejorative associations again shows how much twentieth-century readers are fashioned by the nineteenth-century tastes they so often deplore. For of course Dr. Johnson thought Rexroth's "bad poetry" the very best sort: " 'A work more truly poetical,' " he said of *Comus*, " 'is rarely found; allusions, images and descriptive epithets embellish almost every period with lavish decoration!' " [10] This is not the place to engage in lengthy polemics or to assess the caprices of changing fashions. But if some doubtful reader of Auden is put off by the very nature of his poetry (no one would claim it is everywhere successful, of course), he should recall that all poets must make their artifacts out of either conceptual or emotive diction, and there is no reason a priori to believe one better than the other. Nineteenth-century poets, of course, made much of their poetry out of feeling-state diction and other emotional devices. Their twentieth-century offspring (even in the act of rebelling against their elders) usually did too, and they sometimes developed this into what we loosely refer to as "symbolic" language. Symbolic language is mostly diction with a powerful capacity for eliciting feeling states in the reader. When he tries to describe these feeling states, the reader will discover (to the delight of symbol enthusiasts) that no language quite captures their special essence. "Meanings" seem to extend elusively and inexhaustibly in all directions, and readers so inclined can therefore extract from every symbolic grain of sand both the One and the Many. The curious paradox in all this is that though our own age prizes feeling-state poetry above all other kinds it persistently thinks of itself as highly intellectual and tough-minded. When an artifact arouses feeling states in them, most critics can hardly wait to translate these into intellectual conceptions. And though everyone knows that no conceptual description ever adequately describes or encompasses a feeling, some critics mistake this inevitable failure in the translation for a wondrous almost supernatural quality of the object itself, and believe they have stumbled on to something of great intellectual profundity. In literature conceptual fuzziness often passes for something orphic. The effort of trying to transform feelings into concepts may be exciting, of course, and even necessary. But the fact that concepts never quite resemble the feelings they try to describe cannot be taken as evidence that the cosmos is

[10] Quoted in Miles, *The Primary Language of Poetry in the 1740's and 1840's*, p. 236.

bejewelled with layer upon layer of awesome conceptual meaning. A feeling state caused by words may itself be quite simple. That an endless series of ingenious conceptual statements never exhausts its "meanings" does not show that the experience was mysteriously complex—only that it was not primarily conceptual. Paradoxically, when feeling states are mistaken for conceptual profundities, readers may condemn a nonemotive poetry for its intellectual shallowness precisely because it contains nothing but ideas. It is common to find commentators wistfully lamenting that "At some point in his [Auden's] development, mind triumphed over feeling," [11] or remarking sadly that his vices show only that "He would have made a very good Augustan poet." [12] The point is, I suppose, that if at a certain time a society prefers feelings to concepts that is its privilege, but such preferences can scarcely stand as universal criteria for what is good or bad in art. Even more relevant here, though, (since, as I will show, Auden often does evoke emotion with things other than individual words) is a misconception about the practice of all poets that makes readers condemn "ornament" and all the synonyms for Fancy. Whatever else it may be, poetry like all the other arts is a "made" thing, something that must be put together, fixed up, worked over, patched, rebuilt. If the end product resembles a divine voice or sibylline revelation, it is still a made-up performance, even if an oracular one, and a reader's delight in the performer's skill at putting on such a display is a genuine aesthetic response (perhaps *the* aesthetic response). Readers who do not enjoy skill, for whom an exhibition of craftsmanship seems a betrayal of the artist's sacred role, simply do not enjoy an artifact as an art object. Like everyone else Auden is a performer. He makes performances mainly out of conceptual diction, others make performances out of emotive diction, some poets, out of both. His distinction is not that he performs by ornamenting ordinary language to make it into art, but that he ornaments it with concepts. Others use feelings. Every poet ornaments with something. If a reader likes one kind of poetry more than the other, both are equally respectable. In Auden's performances an inventive Fancy often embellishes conceptual diction with the decoration of rhetorical ornament. Let the scandalous words be made healthy by exposure. Auden's practice is an honorable one.

---

[11] Cyril Connolly, "Losses and Gains," *London Times* (July 10, 1960).
[12] A. Alvarez, "The Slimmest Volume," *The Observer* (July 19, 1960).

III

But Auden's poetry certainly can arouse emotions in the reader. So far I have looked at the nature of his individual words, and how they are put together to make epithets, images, and allegorical phrases, clauses, sentences, and whole poems. But the linguistic assumptions useful for describing Auden's style so far must now be revised. If at times it is helpful to talk as though words have certain properties apart from their context and use-situation, this language model will certainly not describe everything. Auden's diction may be called highly conceptual only if words are thought to have some intrinsic nature of their own, but obviously readers can learn to associate any response with any word. Therefore, a word that may seem "intrinsically" dry as dust and as conceptual as x to some people, may set off emotional or intellectual fireworks in others. Or the sound of a voice may do it, or an old literary cliché, or a rhyme pattern, or a turn of phrase. The formal scheme of a villanelle can by itself move a man to tears. Anything can. It is true that many language associations are too private to be held up as "properties of the poem" rather than "properties of the reader." But thousands of others are public—wide as a culture, or a subculture, or the small group of people who read poetry. And poets have always manipulated these associations for artistic effect. They are *in* the poem as much as anything is and must be talked about, even if the talk needs to confine itself to vague finger-pointing and arm-waving gestures in the direction of something rather than precise descriptions.

Clearly language comes to have "properties" in the first place because an individual has learned to associate a particular word sound or word sight with some emotional and intellectual experience related to it. This, along with subsequent associations, is what the word will "mean" for him. Some associations will be private, peculiar to an individual, others, nearly universal in a given culture. Most will be a mixture of the two. And such meaningful associations will not be limited merely to the configuration of letters or sounds called "words." A reader may have learned to associate feeling states or intellectual states with all sorts of things: with separate letters (w may cause a reader to think of—even feel—wetness), with phrases, clauses, larger units of some sort, with subjects, forms (sonnets, for instance), or tones of voice. If in Auden's poetry neither syllable sounds nor conceptual diction, nor even rhetorical ornament, in themselves, arouse much emotion in the reader, here are dozens of other things that may. Experienced poetry readers will have a vast store of associations connected with hundreds of subjects and practices that have shown up in thousands of poems as well as in nonpoems. I have mentioned traditional forms. For the experienced reader the sonnet form is not just an interesting verbal mold separate from a poem's meaning. The form itself is a meaningful gesture (its very least message is, "I have chosen to align myself with a certain tradition"). This gesture may arouse feeling states in the reader that are independent of the words in the poem, perhaps even before the poem is read. The rather cautious traditionalism in many of Auden's selections, then, can be thought of as a *device* (whether he realizes it or not)—a stylistic device for stirring up feelings the reader associates with these practices. In fact, Auden's general adherence to metrical poetry, even when he scarcely uses the metrical stresses, sets off these emotional associations, even if faint. And they are not always so faint. In our age of prosodic experiment, there are readers who *feel* dislike for a poem simply because it rhymes, scans, or is laid out traditionally on the page. If Auden's poetry often aligns itself with a conservative past tradition, that alone will arouse emotion in some readers. Hostile readers, in fact, have been roused enough to condemn the alignment at some length.

"Subjects" can become stylistic devices too—for arousing emotions and intellectual associations. Mutability provides the best example. Since so many English poems have been directly or indirectly about some aspect of mutability, excellent readers will sometimes admit that poetry seems less "poetic" to them as its subject moves further from mutability (just as most readers feel, unconsciously, that a poem is especially "poetic" when its diction is elevated, its tone elegiac, and its rhythm metrical). Though they may feel a trifle guilty about it, some readers will even admit that the mere idea of mutability moves them—before they begin reading a poem about it. And a few can get choked up just thinking about Yeats, whose poetry contains all the paradigmatic features—elevated speech, meter, elegiac tone, mutability. To treat "subjects" as "style" may seem the ultimate defeat of all classification. Nevertheless, a brief survey of devices used to elicit emotions can scarcely ignore "subjects" as a stylistic device. In the 1930's Auden seldom wrote about mutability. He has no Lucy poems, no odes to nightingales, no darkling thrushes or crumbling brass. But he does have a few love poems. While these are not particularly nostalgic or filled with lament, they do gain some emotive charge from the subject itself, surrounded as it has been thousands of times with mutability and sentiment. Most of his subjects in the 1930's, though, are singularly unemotive in themselves. But in the 1940's and 1950's (as will become clear in the next chapter), his very subjects can arouse a good deal of emotion. Readers who might seldom be moved by the early descriptions of neurotics and sick civilization, or by the Antipoet's burlesques, can respond emotionally to the notion of man lost in a bewildering universe, though Auden's comic treatment of this familiar tragic theme has apparently befuddled many conditioned to regard comedy itself as emotionally and intellectually trivial. The point is, again, that if ideas can arouse feeling Auden's poems sometimes do just that. But until the 1950's and 1960's they probably do so less than most poetry of the past, and far less than some of the great mutability poets of the twentieth century—Eliot in *Four Quartets,* Pound in *Cathay,* Dylan Thomas in most places, and Yeats everywhere. Some critics, unable to feel strongly about either his subjects or his treatment of them, have concluded therefore that Auden is somehow suspiciously shallow.

Although it may seem to strain my classifications to the cracking point, there is a very real sense in which the persona is a stylistic device too. That is, if "style" is how the personae speak, a speaker may be said to "speak like a certain kind of personality," regardless of what he talks *about.* Whatever he says, this may be far less important in itself than the way he projects, by his manner, a special temperament of some sort, and this temperament may well be the most attractive and moving thing in the poem. In a Yeats poem, for instance, what moves us is not usually the speaker's ostensible subject, what he talks *about.* Few can care much about all those unknown people and places, about the forgotten political events in an insignificant country. What we care about is the speaker. While the speaker cares passionately about all sorts of subjects, we care only about passionate speakers. What moves him may not move us, but *he* moves us. On the whole, Auden's early speakers, as personalities, will elicit little emotional response from most readers, I think. (There are obvious exceptions, but many Poetic speakers are rather cold, clinical, and detached. The Antipoet often seems more attractive as a person.) But after 1940 the reverse is true. Speakers in Auden's middle-style or high comic poems, no matter what they talk about, fumble among the paradoxes of his comic view of existence. They see life as blessed on the one hand, ridiculous on the other. They know it to be both tragic and sinful, and yet that from afar both tragedy and sin seem comic folly. They know finally that the very attempt to see and accommodate all these conflicting forces accurately and honestly is the most comic folly of all. And they reveal all of this mostly by *how* they talk. Thus, looked at from one angle, the speakers themselves can be considered stylistic devices, things created by certain speech mannerisms, and these too can certainly arouse our emotions.

If a speaker is created, ultimately, by his own voice, the *sound* of that voice probably contributes most to his making. And no stylistic feature arouses more emotion in Auden's poetry than tone of voice—and the others do not contribute as much to Auden's uniqueness as this elusive auditory element does. Since "voice" is not a stylistic category firmly sanctioned by traditional criticism, some preliminary clarifying remarks may be useful. Outside of literature speakers often stir up emotions by nonverbal devices. We respond, for instance, to visual cues, to facial expression, gestures, dress, pallor, and so on. Though in written art no speaker possesses these, in most other ways speakers in print and in the flesh are similar. In real life situations the literal *sound* of a speaker's voice (its pitch, duration, tone color, stresses, and tempo) will make us react both emotionally and intellectually, regardless of whether his words are conceptual or emotive, in fact, regardless of whether we even listen to or understand his individual words at all. This common experience is easily enough explained. Just as everyone associates certain feeling states and intellectual states with meaningful sounds called "words," so do we associate emotions and ideas with many pure sounds themselves. Tone of voice alone (rise and fall, pace, and intensity) can turn declarative statements into questions or commands, petitions into threats, "tragic" to "comic," sadness to gaiety. This is an enormous power, and is one of poetry's greatest resources. Still, since the voice a poetry reader hears is in his own head, it is often thought to be suspiciously "private" (as though other responses were somehow less private) and ignored by many literary critics. But the critic of Auden can hardly avoid mentioning "voice." In nearly every context I have fallen back on the word to describe some distinctive element in a poem. If no poem by anybody comes into being until the reader hears the voice in it, voices are more than usually important in poetry as dramatic as Auden's, where so much meaning is carried by the *sound* of the speaking rather than by what is being talked about. Poetic and Antipoetic speakers might recite exactly the same sentence and indicate by their voice alone exactly opposite messages. "Styles" of voice, then, force themselves on a reader's attention in Auden's poetry and must be dealt with somehow, even if complexities can only be hinted at.

To do the job properly, a critic should probably try to describe directly the sounds he hears in his head (their pitch, duration, stresses, tone color, pace, and so on) or else describe the feeling states or intellectual states they arouse in him. But there is no satisfactory vocabulary for doing all this. Reading out loud might demonstrate even better what one hears, but until literary criticism is published on tape, this too is impossible. Luckily some sort of alternative exists. We can describe the cause rather than the effect, and since this seems to be outside our head, it has the added advantage of appearing to be more comfortingly public. Presumably, then, before reading a poem we and the poet have learned to associate certain printed word arrangements with certain voice sounds. When these or similar arrangements show up in the poem, we begin to hear a certain kind of voice. But the whole subject is still filled with descriptive difficulties, and I will venture no further than the most obvious matters that can hardly be overlooked. For example, since speakers in so many English poems talk about mutability, out of thousands of such poems have come hundreds of familiar kinds of locutions associated with loss, time passing, love faded, and lament. Put near the beginning of a poem, their mere presence can snap on a switch in the reader's head signalling: this poem is an emotive statement about loss and should be read in a voice whose tonal properties you associate with lament, loss, and so on. The poem's diction, it should be noted, may be entirely conceptual, the sentences either crammed with or completely free from ornament. These stylistic matters may have no effect on the emotive sounds of the voice. Even the flattest, barest, and most direct statement, uttered in a voice whose *sound* is emotive, can arouse a reader's most intense emotions. In Auden, emotive elegiac-mutability voices are created in poems that begin with statements like the following: "Taller today, we remember similar evenings" (*CP*, p. 113) or "Perhaps I always knew what they were saying" (*CP*, p. 99). Lines such as "Now from my window-sill I watch the night" (*CP*, p. 83) or "Out on the lawn I lie in bed" (*CP,* p. 96) will cause readers to hear a voice appropriate for a quiet, personal meditative poem with its usual quota of nostalgia and sentiment. Once the voice is established, part of our feeling states and intellectual states will be caused by the *sound* of the voice itself, as well as by the words it utters. Attributing such powers to the voice-making properties of phrases and clauses is not second guessing, caused by our previous knowledge of a poem's contents (in a well-known poem, of course, we know what voice to hear before we begin reading). Every experienced reader knows that he is often misled by the opening lines of an unfamiliar poem, that he often must revise his emotional set and the voice he hears before he has read half a dozen lines. Just such upsets, in fact, are one of the poet's most effective devices, playing off his own creation against our traditional expectations. Auden's poetry, depending as it does on such a variety of voices, contains a multitude of effects that simply cannot be described if it is assumed that words contain only the self-generating properties they seem to have apart from a speaker's voice.

From among the multitude, very few voice features can be isolated for investigation here. Though they are the easiest to illustrate, elegiac voices should not be overemphasized, since I have remarked before that Auden is seldom nostalgic or elegiac in the 1930's or 1940's, his Poet, almost never. (His middle-style voices often moved in that direction before 1940, and after when love replaces laughter many speakers use voices of this sort.) Perhaps the most important generalization to make about his voices is that most of them are oratorical, and this fact alone goes a long way toward describing the kind of thing the poetry is. In oratory especially, the sound of the voice flowing through sentences creates much of the emotion—rather than the meanings that come from individual words. If Auden's subjects, words, and rhetorical ornaments arouse little emotion, his oratorical voice can supply any amount. How is this accomplished? We associate certain emotions with certain tones of voice, certain tones of voice with certain diction and verbal constructions, and certain diction and verbal constructions with public speech, oratory. Once we see the diction and constructions we begin to hear an oratorical voice and the emotions flow.

Syntax, more than anything else, creates an oratorical voice. A 1939 poem opens with "Not as that . . . Napoleon, rumour's dread and centre, / Before whose riding all the crowds divide . . ." (*CP*, p. 82). This period runs on until the eighth line, a truly Miltonic postponement of subject and verb. Only slightly less imposing are the opening lines

> Will you turn a deaf ear
>
> . . . .
>
> Yet wear no ruffian badge
> Nor lie. . . .
>   (*CP,* p. 177)

By "oratorical" syntax I mean the syntax in just such lines as these. With their lengthy periods, declarative and declamatory questions, and such miscellaneous formulations as "Yet . . . Nor," such sentences are almost never used by two individuals speaking to each other, but only by speakers addressing much larger audiences. The syntax shows what even the meaning of the words may try to deny. For instance, one Auden speaker talks like this:

> And since our desire cannot take that route which is straightest,
> Let us choose the crooked, so implicating these acres,
> These millions in whom. . . .
>   (*LS,* p. 40)

Auden pretends that this is a lover speaking to his beloved, the "my darling" of a previous stanza. But we never doubt that these sonorities (astounding between two lovers) are meant for the ears of some vast public who will find such constructions appropriate. "Consider this and in our time," another speaker begins (*CP*, p. 27), clearly from the podium, and even in middle-style poems speakers usually adopt such oratorical voices. "Here on the cropped grass of the narrow ridge I stand" (*LS*, p. 42), though a traditional first line for English meditative poetry, is, however traditional, far too theatrical to be put to an individual in conversation or in a letter to a friend. Letter or conversation demand "I am standing here on the cropped grass of a narrow ridge"—at least. (Even "cropped" alone probably makes the sentence "literary" and oratorical.) One familiar generalization, then, is: the more periodic and inverted the syntax, the more consciously patterned, the higher the oratory.

A majority of Auden's poems have a voice at some level of oratory, whatever their subject or other stylistic feature. "To-day no longer occupied like that, I give,"; "Deaf to the Welsh wind now, I hear" (*LS*, p. 43). Whether appropriate to the subject or not, voices ringing out in these periods produce the emotional effects a poet with conceptual diction cannot get from his words alone, and the handy, and usually lengthy, inverted sentences make possible a wide variety of rhythmical complexity. Looked at this way, one of Auden's problems in the 1930's can be described as a syntax—or voice—problem. His oratorical syntax enabled him to create emotional voices and excellent rhythms, but its very existence automatically created a persona sometimes too sententious and formal for the occasion. If he wanted to bring his Poet down off the Parnassian peaks, Auden had to rebuild his syntax. The syntax of conversational speech generally runs to short sentences with a subject-verb-object arrangement or no clear grammatical arrangement, not to oratorical inversions and lengthy periods grammatically polished. Swinging from one extreme to the other, for a time in the late 1930's Auden's Poetic speakers came forth in those exaggerated short declarative statements I have already described. They reached a degree of compulsiveness in "In Time of War" that added another eccentric manner to that already mannered work:

> They wondered why the fruit had been forbidden;
> It taught them nothing new. They hid their pride,
>
> . . . .
>
> They knew exactly what to do outside.
>
> They left. . . .
>   (*CP,* p. 319)

Along with this new syntax came some of the choppy rhythms always threatened by short sentences with parallel structure. Auden was already a master of rhythms that could be made from oratorical speech, but he had not learned how to make this new style work. To get some kind of rhythmical flow across these maddeningly short and similar sentences, he began sticking them together with that weakest of connectives, "and." In the first 112 lines (eight sonnets), "and" turns up forty-four times at the head of a line. In *Another Time* he tried occasionally to remedy matters by pasting the oratorical "O" onto these nonoratorical sentences: "O in these quadrangles where Wisdom honours herself" (*CP,* p. 80). Sometimes that helped; sometimes it simply made the speech an incongruous mixture. But the excessively simple syntax began to fade. A higher oratory returns in *Another Time* and remains in the later poetry. Thus most of Auden's poetry could be described as fundamentally oratorical (the major cause, I suspect, of the peculiar belief that he is our most pedagogical poet).

But not all his poems, even the Poetic ones, have high oratory in them. Among the exceptions are those late poems where Auden again tries to develop a plain, nonoratorical voice:

> The sailors come ashore
> Out of their hollow ships,
> Mild-looking middle-class boys. . . .
> (SA, p. 38)

A poem that begins like this is certainly not a declamation from some high podium. But if it is not high oratory it is certainly not conversation either. It might accurately be called low oratory, part of the long tradition of poetic speech that presents the illusion of informality and conversation, but in reality always aims at a large audience from a public platform, which if low is always there.

Yet if much of his poetry is oratorical, Auden certainly knew how to write the syntax of face-to-face talk, informal and personal: "The fact is, I'm in Iceland"; "You must admit, when all is said and done"; "I don't know whether / You will agree, but"; "And then a lord—Good lord, you must be peppered [with fan mail]" (*LLB,* pp. 18, 20, 17). It must be clear by now that nonoratorical syntax and other colloquial features are the very things that often separate the Antipoet's voice from that of the Poet. I say "often" because while the Poet nearly always orates, the Antipoet does not always use the syntax of face-to-face talk. A good share of his syntax is oratorical too—parodied oratory. He mocks the Poet's style:

> For in my arms I hold
> The Flower of the Ages,
> And the first love of the world.
> (CP, p. 197)

> The didactic digit and dreaded voice
> Which imposed peace on the pullulating
> Primordial mess. Mourn for him now,
> Our lost dad. . . .
> (AA, p. 104)

I have remarked in various contexts that Auden never found a comfortable style for his Poetic voice. He dared not let it become too ornate. The

Antipoet would burlesque it. Neither could he seem to lower it with ease, even though he obviously had a knack for writing colloquial speech. Now we can speculate about the cause (the stylistic cause, at least) of Auden's problem. Apparently he could not separate certain kinds of speech from certain kinds of speakers. Colloquial voices seem to be so firmly part of Auden's joking, farcical sense of life's foolishness that he can seldom speak colloquially without being comic. In other words, the Poet cannot borrow the Antipoet's vernacular idiom without getting the rest of his mocking, comic behavior as well. However informal he may be, the Poet cannot maintain sobriety and speak conversationally at the same time, so Auden's Poetic voice, even at its least formal, fails to be completely informal and always sounds a bit stiff. On the other side, Auden's Anti-poetic self cannot speak formally without self-parody, self-mockery. Only when Poet and Antipoet are combined in the speakers of the middle-style and high comic poems can Auden successfully combine oratory with the most unbuttoned conversational syntax, sobriety with horseplay, and all with an emotive and intellectual profundity. These speakers mock themselves and their style, but their very self-contradictions and incongruities are the poem's intellectual and emotional message.

Voices, of course, are not made of syntax alone, and I have kept back diction and other matters so far only because the investigation of voice has turned discussion into a new area, that of usage. If words are things whose effect on us arises from associations with their past *use,* the notion of a usage tradition explains many things. All language either upsets or fulfills our expectations grown firm by thousands of previous linguistic experiences. For the poetry reader, many of the most important will have been poetry experiences. These upsets and fulfillments, then, will lend to any given poem emotive and intellectual meaning its words may not seem to have when they are artificially isolated from the language world. If these expectations are primarily "usage" expectations, the poet who makes things out of them must have certain special talents. First of all he must have an excellent ear. He must be able to *hear* the voices people use in different usage environments. Next he must have some special talent for arranging written words so that they create just the tone of voice he wants. Auden has both. His best poems nearly all succeed because he knows how to make voices by manipulating words we associate with special use-situations. This is his most unique talent. If Auden is in any way a poetic innovator in Pound's sense, a man who shows his followers how to do something they could scarcely do before, his innovation is in making poetry out of "special usage" words. This subject belongs in a chapter on style and will be introduced here. But as Auden's supreme language skill it will be examined and illustrated more fully in the next chapter, because more than anything else it creates his greatest achievement, his comic poems.

IV

By almost incredible coincidence Auden has been condemned for not doing at all just what I think he does best. Two poets have claimed that his work fails to be "new" precisely because he has no ear for speech usage. And since poets might seem to be more authoritative on these matters than anyone else, their accusations deserve examination before I go further. William Carlos Williams, himself fascinated by American speech usage, wrote in 1954 that Auden had come to the United States because of a language crisis in his poetry. According to Williams, Auden desperately needed a new idiom, and the United States offered something hopefully different. In America, Williams believed, "one might reasonably expect to find that instability in the language where innovation would be at home." Yet in the end Auden's search came to nothing, Williams decided. He failed to revitalize his poetic idiom with American usage and went on singing the old music of British literary speech.[13] Kenneth Rexroth, another poet with an ear for American idiom, apparently agreed. "W. H. Auden has spent years in America," he wrote in 1961, "and never learned a single phrase of American slang without sounding like a British music-hall Yank comic. . . ."[14] Surely both men's observations are partly right, but their conclusions wrong. Both Williams and Rexroth judge it a failure that Auden's speakers never make American idiom their own personal poetic language. Williams, of course, measures Auden against writers of his own sort, men who try to drop traditional meter, rhyme, and British literary usage, in order to fashion poems entirely in the American grain, out of the rhythms, syntax, diction, and voice tones of American nonliterary speech. True enough,

[13] *Selected Essays of William Carlos Williams* (New York: Random House, 1954), p. 288.

[14] Kenneth Rexroth, *Assays* (New York: New Directions, 1961), p. 234.

Auden does not do this. His speakers seldom for long talk like ordinary nonliterary Americans. But this is not because he cannot write colloquial speech, and certainly not because he has a defective ear. (In reality, Auden's later poetry—for all its artifice—sounds far more speechlike than Williams' own.) He does write colloquial speech, and if anything his ear is too good. Auden seems *always* to be standing back listening to his speakers talking. He watches their language, plays with it, makes rhetorical inventions of it, raises, lowers, mocks, and revels in it. Far from having no ear for speech, American or otherwise, Auden is so acutely conscious of every level of speech usage that he is incapable of speaking at all without realizing: Now I am talking like the Prime Minister, now like King Lear, now like a public relations man, now like an Oxford don, now like a music hall comedian. This is a marvelous gift, and it took him a long while to use all of it. I have already pointed out how in the 1930's he sometimes got amused and caustic watching his own performances roll out. Then he might begin to mock them, or, finding them such good fun, exaggerate their special features into caricature. While he attacked or played with usage levels in these performances, the persona switched back and forth from Poet to Antipoet, and the unwatched subject blandly floated along, inadvertently shifting from solemnity to burlesque. In the 1930's his hypersensitive ear may have been more a hindrance than a help. How could he become a Poet in the grand tradition of English poetry when his quizzical ear kept noticing in every sober speech certain usages that seemed ridiculous? Thus I suspect that Williams' intuitions were, in a sense, correct. Auden had for years been searching without much success for a suitable language—particularly for his Poet—and by the late 1930's seemed uncertain and lost. "In Time of War" and *Another Time* show this. But he seems to have found in America exactly what Williams thought he failed to discover, a new idiom that made innovation possible. As Rexroth notes, this new idiom is often handled comically. But the implied condemnation is misplaced. The truth is that Auden had never used *any* idiom without the detachment that at times makes all usage levels seem comic. But only after coming to the United States did he learn how to make excellent art out of this comic detachment.

Temporarily it will suffice to describe usage as a matter of levels. Certain kinds of words, phrases, syntax, and other verbal components

become almost exclusively associated with certain levels of speakers acting in certain levels of situations. Whenever such usage appears it elicits
associations attached to these levels. In short, a word's usage level is part
of its meaning. (In the next chapter usage descriptions will have to be
refined further. Words can obviously refer strongly to special use-situations without suggesting levels. The special vocabulary of trades and
professions does that, for instance.) Three levels will be enough to
introduce the subject, and in fact have been indispensable all along. The
"high," "middle," and "low" designations I have used nearly everywhere
in this and the previous chapter obviously refer in large part to a speaker's
prevailing usage levels. And as past discussion has suggested, individual
words and syntax are not the only things that become associated with
these. Phrases, clauses, sentences, poetic forms, stanza and rhyme patterns
all attach themselves to usage levels too. The kinds of people who have
used them and the kinds of situations they were used in are all part of
their meaning. By high usage I mean, roughly, the language of learned,
oratorical, formal, educated, conservative speakers on solemn, usually
public, occasions. By low, the opposite: speakers in intimate or conversational situations, informal, nonoratorical, keeping their learning and education (if any) rather in abeyance, employing slang and vogue words and
phrases. Middle usage is somewhere in between. These classifications may
seem comically vague to the linguist or sociologist, but they satisfy my
purposes here. In any case, illustrations are probably better than definitions. Auden's highest Poets use oratorical syntax and fill it with diction
such as "fortuitous shapes," "innocent / Unobservant offender," "malicious village" (CP, p. 100), "intolerant look," "nurtured in that fine
tradition," and "human ligaments could so / His southern gestures modify" (CP, p. 95). Voices at this high usage level, by their mere sound,
can make almost any locution emotive, and their high diction has the
virtue of putting special emphasis on syllable sounds as the multisyllabic
words roll off the tongue. Furthermore, the Poet's enormous vocabulary
enables him to arouse a reader's delight in the *mot juste,* where our
expectations, based on normal imprecision and drab inaccuracy, are upset
by the excitement of an absolutely right meaning. Auden's Antipoetic
voices, in contrast, speak either low usage or a parodied high idiom: "but
I should come a cropper," "I'm sure we hope it pays," "run to a two-bob
edition" (LLB, pp. 22–23);

> Queen of the Night and Empress of the Air;
> Tell how her fleet by nine king swans is led
>
> . . . .
> And Hippocampi follow in her wake . . .
> (SA, p. 45);

> . . . should contrive
> A heathen fetish from Virginity
> To soothe the spiritual petulance
>   Of worn-out rakes and maiden aunts. . . .
> (CP, p. 425)

Low-level usage never contains ornate periodic syntax or diction such as "subaltern mockery" and "archaic imagery" (*CP*, pp. 132, 133). High-level usage never contains expressions such as "Many were raggable, a few were waxy" (*LLB*, p. 206); "It's not a white lie, it's a whacking big 'un" (*LLB*, p. 50); " 'You can't change human nature, don't you know' " (*LLB*, p. 55); "Now let me see, where was I?" (*LLB*, p. 99). High-level usage may permit a few witticisms ("Wandering the cold streets tangled like old string," *CP*, p. 151), but not the unrestrained coarse joking of "your face as fat as a farmer's bum" (*O*, p. 62). In these examples some word or locution is so clearly associated with a certain usage level that if it appears in foreign surroundings the effect will be shocking (shocks, of course, can be both pleasurable and displeasing). Similar but considerably milder usage conventions govern poetic forms (sonnets are high), subjects (mutability is usually high), even meter and rhythms (anapestic meter is low). It is no surprise then that Auden's high Poets so often speak in strong metrical rhythms. The highest Poets in English poetry have almost always spoken a metrical speech. Of course, most low speakers in English poetry speak metrical lines too (though their rhythms are different from the high speakers'). But Auden's low Antipoetic speakers often associate meter itself and Poetic rhythms of all sorts with high-level usage. If they speak in metrical lines and Poetic rhythms, they are usually making comedy out of the usage level itself. Their metrical poems, in effect, are *mock*-metrical, and they often mock rhyme and stanza forms as well. "Letter to Lord Byron" is the largest example, but Auden's ballads nearly always do this too:

> "I'm going to find it,
> That's what I'm going to do."

Doreen squeezed his hand and said:
"Jim I believe in you."
(*AT*, p. 79)

Antipoetic voices then often parody anything associated with high usage levels. But the laughter of parody, as the next chapter will show, need not be contemptuous. After 1940, when Auden's Antipoetic speakers mock poetry, their laughter is usually the laughter of love. High usage is absurd but blessed.

The final stylistic device to be mentioned then, and the most important of them all, is incongruity. After 1950, with a few important exceptions, Auden's personae always speak in voices made up of more than one usage level. "Levels" mean "differences," "differences" mean "incongruities," and incongruities are usually comic. An artist who habitually makes his art out of different usage levels is born to be a comic artist. While he may struggle against this fate, may even avoid comedy entirely, he can do so only by suppressing part of his native talent. As a creator (the Romantic psychologist might say) he will remain unfulfilled if he never makes comedy. Since usage levels are by definition incongruous, whichever way Auden departs from normal usage, whether up or down, he is moving toward comedy. Lowered only slightly from normal usage, speech appears faintly amusing, a mild exaggeration of familiar loose syntax, vogue words, and cliché. But if the lowering continues, at some point the incongruity between a speaker's usage and average discourse will make his speech comic. Wit probably appears first, then (as the gap widens) what we think of as broad burlesque, slapstick, farce. Oddly enough, language slowly raised from normal usage will ultimately have the same effect. A very slight rise from average speech simply adds a sobriety and dignity to speech of the ordinary man. A further slight elevation increases the intelligence and learning of this honest speaker. But a few notches higher, and traces of pretentiousness will begin to mar his solemn, learned sincerity. A shade higher yet, and pomposity will set in. The speaker will seem to be something of a poseur. And beyond this, every further heightening will turn his usage into open comedy. The incongruous distance between very high and average usage, like that between average and very low, will strike the reader as funny. In usage too, the way up is the way down. Auden's very method of constructing poems, then, had a built-in comic predisposition. To become a comic artist all he had to do was realize (or submit to) this and exploit it. He could only escape his comic destiny by timidly refusing to develop fully his own linguistic practices. Simply let him try for more exciting heights, and at some point heights would burst into comedy. Daring low usage would turn comic even sooner. As I have pointed out, Auden began by being far from timid. He ventured boldly toward both heights and depths in the late 'twenties and early 'thirties and often fell headlong down from the one into the other. Then he turned cautious for awhile, borrowed some safe English poetic styles, and seldom strayed far from the middle plains toward either heights or depths. But different parts of his temperament clealry remained attracted to both extremes, and while he learned to tame both mountain-climbing Poet and depth-plunging Antipoet, he sometimes still purposely explored the peaks and abysses. On these expeditions he learned how to speak all sorts of high and low languages, and in the end made the greatest discovery of his career—how to speak all of them at once, and to make out of their incongruous usage levels a high art that in the very nature of its language carried a profound comic vision of life.

FOUR

Comedy

I

IF THE preceding chapters sometimes imply that Auden's poetry moves forward through the years as though pushed from behind by forces of comedy struggling to get to the front, this is because such a pattern seems descriptively useful, whatever may be the doubts about its questionable Hegelian causality. The pattern of Auden's poetic development does resemble an unfolding comic destiny—though combinations of chance, luck, and accident may have helped shape it. Nevertheless, beneath even this descriptive pattern lies a value judgment I have revealed before and should acknowledge again. I think that taken as a group Auden's comic poems are his best work. As I examine it, then, his career moves generally toward better and better art—like the career of Yeats, but unlike that of Wordsworth, Conrad, or Lawrence. This colors everything. Admittedly my analysis tries to account for this increasing success. Behind each observation is a general teleological question: what forces move the poetry toward its happy and successful comic culmination? Whatever answers emerge, their general pattern must resemble an upward spiral. Readers who find Auden's comic poems trivial or otherwise distasteful (and some do) will see his career as a descending spiral. For whatever their tastes, critics will agree that after 1950 his poetry is largely comic. Disappointed readers must search for reasons to explain the "dreadfully wrong-headed diffidence" that allows him to fritter away great talents "on the commonplace," as one writer put it,[1] just as Jarrell sought reasons for Auden's "decline" from Marx to Kierkegaard. Whatever else it does, each critic's analysis must at least support his evaluations.

[1] Robert Mazzocco, "The Poet at Home," *New York Review of Books* (Aug. 3, 1965), p. 7.

If Auden's poetry seems to be pushed toward comedy, Kierkegaard gave one big push. I have already shown how, by 1941, Auden's empirical humanism, developed under the tutelage of Marx and others, had begun its profound Kierkegaardian transformation. Both Marx and Kierkegaard had agreed that knowledge, values, tastes, names, politics, loves, even religions came out of man's own interaction with his environment. But what vanity, Kierkegaard added, to believe these offered any significant certainty to men adrift in the vastness of cosmic uncertainty. Admittedly we must all make up our own world from empirical observations, he said; we can do nothing else. But this thing made up, whatever its shape, is always ultimately wrong. Only God knows the truth about the make-up of the world, and we know nothing about Him or his plans. Compelled to grope about in this darkness, forced to act as though certain, knowing everything to be uncertain, men stumble helplessly through the blackness, every active moment a jumble of bruised shins, painful falls, and baffled cogitations about where they are and what they are doing. And as a final indignity, divine necessity compels us to search out and know this God, whom by definition we can never see, or hope to find, or even clearly think about. Trapped in such circumstances, anybody might wish occasionally (or ceaselessly) to escape. But no one can choose to evade life. We can choose only different ways of living. We can accept the folly of our predicament with resignation and despair or with joy at its divine blessing. In a rough way these two responses separate the tragic view of life from the comic. The one stresses the absurd suffering of man's Fall, the other the delightful absurdity of his foolish tumble. Characteristically, Kierkegaard rejected in principle neither the tragic nor the comic response, but insisted that both must be embraced at once. For life was both tragic and comic, he said.

Auden's comic proclivities were certainly obvious long before he read Kierkegaard. But he lived uneasily with them during the 1930's, since, as I have shown before, his own attitudes about Art and Life were sharply divided. As Poet he accepted the prevailing view that Art was solemn and good while Life was solemn and bad. This made comedy seem frivolous. But as Antipoet he thought all Art was comically absurd and inconsequential and that Life itself was probably comic too, though good. Obviously these temperamental contradictions were strikingly similar to Kierkegaard's philosophical paradoxes that made life seem both tragic and comic at the same time. But if Auden had been bothered by the contradictions in himself, Kierkegaard thrived on his. If anything they seemed to offer him one of the few pleasures in a generally bleak world, and instead of considering them symptoms of his weakness as a thinker, he took them to be a sign of strength. In a universe too large for man's puny comprehension, he implied, a philosophy without self-contradiction could only be wrong. If to mortal eyes the world always looked like a disorderly jumble, a neatly consistent philosophy would certainly reflect a very distorted and incomplete image of reality. Furthermore, if men themselves were equally unfathomable, a man displaying no incompatible impulses in himself, could scarcely be human. Only the muddle-headed were ever clear about anything. Temperamental contradictions and a comic view of life were respectable, Kierkegaard insisted. This was just what Auden needed to hear.

From Kierkegaard Auden could learn that his own conflicts could actually be considered a valuable unity. If Life was grandly and comically absurd, the case of his own split self was nothing worse than an interesting example. All men bumbled around foolishly, tripping over half-truths and inconsistencies; to be human was to be comically absurd. Almost immediately after reading this in Kierkegaard Auden started making poems that endowed single speakers with the contradictory parts of his own temperament, and now these conflicting forces no longer destroyed each other. Instead they showed the speaker to be especially human, demonstrated the absurdity of Life and Art, and began to reveal the goodness of everything. Auden's comic poetry was under way, and, far from being frivolous, it could now contain the most sweeping and profound vision of human existence. Comic poets did not have to huddle self-consciously at the base of Parnassus. They might be awarded a place at the very top.

Yet I have said before that ideas or philosophies probably should never be considered necessary or sufficient causes of art. Had he never heard of Kierkegaard, Auden might have developed in much the same direction, since his own inclinations and stylistic habits, even without the intellectual support of Kierkegaard, led toward comedy. As long as he maintained his Antipoet, comedy was inevitable, Kierkegaard or no. And as long as he maintained his Poet, the clash between Poet and Antipoet made comedy certain in any poem that contained the whole Auden—both sides of his temperament. If Kierkegaard helped him accept his comic tendencies, these same tendencies undoubtedly helped him accept Kierke-

gaard. Whatever their relative importance, temperament and philosophical sources joined forces to turn Auden into a comic poet.

II

Comedy is a vague word, not always synonymous with funny, or with
any other easily identified essence. It will not do simply to pin a comic
label on certain Auden poems, then, without some more careful description of what this term is meant to describe in his work. One immediate
difficulty is that the word comedy itself may refer to either manner or
matter. Some writers have a vision of life that can be called comic but no
comic style. Others have what is generally considered a comic style but no
view of life worth mentioning. Some writers have both a comic vision and
a comic style. From the very beginning Auden had produced stylistic
comedy, mainly by incongruous usage, but after 1945 his best comic
poems contain in addition a very large vision of human existence. To
consider the matter of comic vision first: the entire subject is frequently
confused by the many uses to which the words "comic" and "tragic" can
be put. The word tragic in "a tragic shortage of animal fats" can claim
some etymological kinship to the same word in "Greek tragic theater,"
but the relationship is remote. Yet the terms tragic and comic in the
almost technical cliché "tragic (or comic) view of life" have a fairly
definite meaning, and it is a meaning useful in discussing Auden. Both the
tragic and the comic view begin with a common fact. Men, imperfect,
perpetually fall. Looked at from up close these falls seem painful and
disastrous, even if ennobling. This is the tragic view of life. Seen from
farther off the same falls seem less painful, from very far off, even
amusing. This is the comic view. In short, the comic view of life begins at
that point where pain and suffering become less important than something else—serenity, contentment, bemusement, laughter, even amused
contempt. The difference between the comic and the tragic view of life is
largely a matter of distance, then ("distance" being a metaphor whose
dissection is best left to the psychologist). Pain, injustice, error, evil—the
inevitable suffering attendant upon imperfect human existence—observed
sub specie aeternitatis may seem but insignificant ripples in the serenity of
time.[2] From this distance all folly seems benignly absurd. This would

[2] Of course these sketchy guidelines will not pass as a definitive treatise on
comedy and tragedy. Tragedy has its form of "serenity" too. Tragic serenity is

seem to be a sweeping and profound insight, yet many people feel that comedy is at best a second-rate vision, shallow, trite, and frivolous. Their conviction rises partly, I suspect, because of a striking similarity between two kinds of art bearing the comic label. One is called comic because it fails to notice the existence of suffering. The other is comic because in its very large vision suffering is only one thing among many other kinds of things. The first sort ignores pain; the second sees beyond it. If there is some justification for considering the one "light" comedy, the other might reasonably be defended as man's largest and most profound philosophical vision. At any rate this second kind of comedy encompasses more than tragedy, which is subsumed within it, and it is the substance of some very great art. Auden has written some "light" comic poems, but he has made many of the other sort too.

For my purposes then the tragic vision may be said to emphasize the pain of human folly, the comic its nonpainful absurdity or its benign insignificance (the first comedy will be mainly "funny," the second mainly "serene"). Yet pain may receive very different amounts of emphasis in works that remain fundamentally comic. In the black comedy of despair, pain becomes so prominent that it nearly always threatens to overpower serenity or benign ludicrosity. The bitter comedy of Swift is such a case; a seemingly malign or pointless cosmos, fortuitous calamity, and painful human folly create the bitterness, anger, and despair that sometimes overwhelm Swift's sense of the benignly ludicrous. Kafka too emphasises suffering, painful absurdity. In these writers the tragic facts of life, always included in profound comic visions, are especially visible, and they sometimes rise up to obliterate their comedy. Kafka, for instance, detaches himself from pain only with difficulty. Distance for him is a heroic achievement won after great struggle, and frequently lost again.

---

apparently caused by a suffering so intense the individual becomes distant even from his tortured self and his pain. Tragic serenity is the peace caused by surfeit of pain, comic serenity the peace caused by surfeit of pleasure, or contentment, or love. Both put a considerable "distance" between observer and the hurly-burly world of pleasure and pain. The quality of the tragically serene experience probably differs from the comically serene, but it is possible that at some point the distance between the two ceases to be a useful distinction to make. The classification model breaks down, and tragic and comic remain words to describe two different roads to a similar destination, the detachment from life that enables men to view it from some distance with serenity.

Suffering is rather strong in Chekhov too, as it is in the modern theater of the absurd, some of which is not comic at all. Chekhov and Kafka in fact nearly always hover near that middle distance from which life seems about equally tragic and comic, and their emphasis flickers from one to the other. Writers of this sort produce works with a familiar, but peculiar, optical illusion, in which the same actions can appear either funny or sad (ludicrous or terrifying) or both at once. A second reading of such authors often reverses our first responses. Scenes that originally seemed funny now seem solemnly pitiful or painful. For of course the very scene that moves us to weep for a fallen man suffering can move us to laugh at his awkward sprawl, and there are artists whose inclination is to keep us right on the emotional line separating the two. Chekhov and Kafka are on occasion masters of this art. *The Tempest,* on the other hand, reduces suffering to a mere verbal report and forgives everyone (even Antonio) for his folly. Shakespeare observes evil and pain—indeed all human events—from the distance of eternity where existence, though endlessly attractive, appears no more substantial than the distant rack of clouds, and man's temporal absurdity an ephemeral thing to be cherished for its fragility.

I have suggested throughout these chapters that Auden's earliest comedy seemed to come from his innate hypersensitive inclination to see the ludicrous side of nearly everything, and from a native delight in various kinds of comic styles. Although style always carries with it some philosophical message, Auden's early comic poems did not produce a consistent —or at least persistent—comic vision of life. Some of his comedy even turned up inappropriately in poems that began with a tragic vision. In any case Auden's vision was unformed and beset with the contradictions I have described as conflict between Poet and Antipoet. But after 1940 his poetry became increasingly comic in the sense of having both a comic vision of life as well as a comic style. The philosophy of acceptance described in Chapter One, and the feeling that life is a blessing to be celebrated, develop as part of his rapidly expanding comic view of existence. In most poems from *Nones* on, life with its perpetual follies nearly always seems more amusing than painful, and frequently appears delightfully absurd or gloriously farcical. This comic vision is often explicit. "Ischia," for example, places human suffering within a larger comic view. The last four stanzas state clearly enough that for each individual "all is never well." "Pain," "darkness," "outcry" are inevitable. But these are observed from a distance that emphasizes all of humanity rather than individuals. From this vantage point, suffering by its very universality loses most of its importance. Since no one can escape pain ("Nothing is free, whatever you charge shall be paid") the certainty of human torment becomes a fact so obvious it scarcely warrants more than a perfunctory glance. Though when observed close up, "all is never well," from a distance life appears, like Ischia itself, absurd, silly, splendidly blessed (*N*, pp. 22–23). The same judgments are reasserted in "Pleasure Island." Suffering is, of course, inescapable. "Miss Lovely, life and soul of the party," is destined to awake, as we all must, to find that "Whatever—O God!—she is in for / Is about to begin . . ." (*N*, pp. 25–26). Yet looked at from somewhat further off, human folly, spread out on the sun-drenched Ischian beach, becomes funny and serene. The comic vision in these and many other poems is that stated succinctly and explicitly in "Tonight at Seven-Thirty":

> for the funniest
> mortals and the kindest are those who are most aware
> of the baffle of being, don't kid themselves our care
> is consolable, but believe a laugh is
> less heartless than tears.
>   (*AH*, pp. 30–31)

No one should confuse the colloquial style here with triviality. This easy statement conveys the wide scope and profound dimensions of Auden's comic view of life. Since human folly and imperfection are inevitable and inescapably absurd, life is both tragic (inconsolable) and comic ("a laugh"). But if neither can be denied by the man of integrity and perception, the wise laugh at man's uncertainty ("the baffle of being") and the good (the least heartless) love him for his absurdity.

Auden's best comedy, like that of Chekhov and Kafka, contains the tragic within it. But there is far less emphasis on suffering in his than in theirs. He never writes black comedy, the self-tormenting laughter of a suffering writer shocked or tortured by human folly. And he does not often hover near the line where the tragic and the comic are emphasized about equally. When pain does emerge in his comedies no bitterness, contempt, anger, or horror lurks amid a desperate gaiety. Instead the speaker usually turns quiet, wistful, almost sad—as he does in "Ode to Gaea," where the world is looked at from an airplane. Even this slight distance reveals that men are ridiculously insignificant compared to the large expanse of indifferent earth. At first the absurdity of both earth and men, and their preposterously disproportionate size and permanence, elicit from the observer a lot of joking and wit. But the catalogue of comic foolishness thins out toward the end. The amiable joking turns melancholy. Laughter fades before extremely painful and recent folly (such as "the Second Assault"), and the speaker, almost openly sad, longs more wistfully than usual for a Good Place removed from pain and grossness, where "verse by Praed," "arias by Rossini," and "entrées by Carême" might bless the unflawed existence of everyone (*SA*, p. 58). The comic view flickers feebly here for a moment, but nevertheless prevails. Wit and banter never stop entirely, and at the very end painful facts fade in importance within the speaker's large vision. Looked at from the distance of time, man's perpetual bungling appears inconsequential. The earth obviously endures, essentially unchanged by human follies. But closer to the tragic this time, the speaker's wistfulness has not been entirely mock, as it usually is. For once genuinely hurt, he has looked with real longing at the distant prospect of a Good Place, stretching impossible and unreal in the hopeless future.

If Auden's comedy is only rarely threatened by tragedy, then, occasionally a poem will drift toward the hierarchy of tragic emotions, beginning with wistfulness and nostalgia and moving on toward sadness and pain. But Auden's comic vision cannot be adequately described merely by distinguishing it from the tragic or by noting the balance of comic and tragic within it. It is worth while going at least one step further—to distinguish between two types of comic vision, both of which show up in differing combinations in Auden's work. When the tragic facts of life recede in importance, life stands forth as ludicrous and good. All comedy will affirm this. But heavy emphasis on the ludicrous will create one sort of comic vision, emphasis on the goodness another. The first will be "funny" comedy, comedy of laughter. The second will be serene. In extreme cases these two will have very different surface appearances. One sort may elicit no laughter at all, while the other can be filled with a ceaseless madcap hilarity.

In the 1940's Auden's comedy was not very serene. Acceptance of men and life was still mixed in with a fairly strong emphasis on the unpleasantness of human suffering. Life was blessed, the long works indicated, but they gave more space to pain. From *Nones* on, though, as the tragic receded from Auden's comic vision, life began to seem both funnier and more lovable, and as the love grew so did the serenity. If the earlier work stressed the absurdity of a loved existence, the later stresses love for an absurd one. In many poems both love and funny absurdity go almost evenly balanced, but not always. Occasionally there is absurdity without love, or satire, the laughter of disapproval, though satirical laughter is rare in Auden after 1945. More often, when there is an unbalance it is of the opposite sort, love without laughter, the opposite of comic satire: comic serenity. Life is loved for its blessedness and does not seem particularly funny. Some very great works, among them *The Tempest,* contain this sort of comic vision, but serenity carries with it a danger. A thin line divides the serene simplicity of profound and noble minds from that of the simple-minded. When Auden's laughter subsides beneath the weighty eminence of his love, he can come perilously close to sentimentality, and occasionally we are not certain that his speaker is not unintentionally absurd ("Precious Five" is an equivocal case). When pain and suffering are nearly invisible, and human absurdity is no longer visibly funny, love can easily begin to cherish and celebrate a world that never was. Luckily this seldom happens, since Auden's love almost never banishes laughter for an entire poem. Usually it comes forward only for a moment out of the comedy in which each plays its harmonious part. It does this in "For Friends Only," where the speaker's implicit love for his impending visitors emerges just briefly into the open, to obscure playfulness and mockery: "within the circle of our affection / Also you have no double" (*AH,* p. 28). Usually even explicit declarations of love are mixed together with laughter: "only a villain will omit to thank Our Lady or / her henwife, Dame Kind" for the "joy in beginning / for which our species was created . . ." (*AH,* p. 34).

So far I have written only of comic matter—Auden's comic philosophy or vision of life. But this has left aside the subject of his comic style. *The Tempest* is a good example of how the two can be separated. In *The Tempest,* for instance, Trinculo's manner is funny while Prospero's is not. Prospero's vision is serene; Trinculo's is not. The manner of one, the matter of the other, is comic. The message of both is the same: seen *sub specie aeternitatis* men are absurd but all is well. Trinculo's message comes almost entirely from *how* he speaks. Prospero's comes almost entirely from what he talks *about* (almost: Prospero's serenity shows in his serene style as well, of course). In this chapter so far quotations illustrating Auden's comic view have shown speakers talking explicitly about a comic philosophy of life. But far more often their comic message comes implicitly from the style itself. If Trinculo is a foolish and funny Antipoetic speaker and Prospero a wise and serious Poetic one with a philosophical message, the speakers in most of Auden's comic poems are rather like men with the wisdom of Prospero and the manner of Trinculo. Unused to such art, unfortunately, some readers have overlooked his wisdom and mistaken the comic Auden for a shallow clown.

III

Style and content may work at cross-purposes in comic art as in anything else. Theoretically a speaker may tell us about his comic view of life in a voice filled with the sounds and rhythms and even the vocabulary of suffering, pain, despair, and defeat. Or, telling us about the pain attendant upon all existence, he may use a style full of wit and playfulness. In either case the implicit message from the style may well overpower the explicit message of the content. This is exactly what happens in a number of Auden's early poems, as I have shown. I have insisted throughout, then, that it is impossible to think of style as merely the *method* of communicating something. The style is part of the message, and in Auden's comic poems it is usually the most important part. I have already cited Auden's Caliban as a clear illustration of this. After Caliban no speakers talk about their comic vision so directly or at anywhere near such great length. But their manner carries a comic view of life very much like his, whatever they talk about, whether it is the earth, Dame Kind, mountains, Ischia, ears, kitchens, or bathrooms.

Whatever his final place among the modern poets since Wordsworth, there can no longer be any doubt, I think, that in his comic style, developed and perfected since *New Year Letter,* Auden has created a poetic language of striking originality and skill. In retrospect this achievement may well appear as revolutionary as the language of Pound, Eliot, or Wordsworth himself, certainly more of an innovation than Yeats's idiom. (Innovation is not synonymous with excellence, of course; Yeats is probably the best English poet since Milton.) Furthermore Auden's comic speech is constructed almost entirely out of a language resource probably never before so fully exploited in English poetry—out of the associations attached to words from the way they are used in special situations. Pound (perhaps the most brilliantly perceptive and maddeningly slapdash of all twentieth-century critics) called this sort of poetry "logopoeia." In his view logopoeia was one of three major "kinds" of poetry, yet so rare and recent that LaForgue seemed almost to have invented it.[3] The arbitrariness of Pound's triple division (melopoeia, phanopoeia, logopoeia) does not diminish the neatness of his excellent insight. He defined logopoeia as " 'the dance of the intellect among words', that is to say, it employs words not only for their direct meaning, but *it takes count in a special way of habits of usage,* of the context we *expect* to find with the word, its usual concomitants, of its known acceptances, and of ironical play." [4] Pound himself, perhaps poetry's most deliberate experimenter, wrote a number of logopoeia poems, but his main talents lay elsewhere, as did those of Eliot, who also made passages that owe much of their verbal excitement to usage levels. Yeats, on the other hand, was not attracted by this sort of art. Indeed, though the point is not one of great importance, probably no poet in English equals Auden's ability to make poetry out of "habits of usage."

Ultimately "meaning" and "usage" are the same, since how a word is used, when and where and by whom, is what it means. The distinction between the terms is a matter of degree—does the environment in which a word is used add to it something of great or little importance? About most words cluster some associations that survive relatively unchanged in any environment. Other associations will change violently—even appear or disappear—from one situation to the next. The former we generally assign to a word's meaning, the latter to its usage. The very notion of usage then becomes important only when a word's associations change greatly as its environment is changed. For example, the words "line" and "lay" have certain associations adhering to them in almost all usage situations. In "Lay your sleeping head, my love . . ." (*CP,* p. 208) or "Upon this line between adventure . . ." (*CP,* p. 151), these constant, nearly universal associations are most important, and the usage environment nearly irrelevent. But in "a clever line. / Or a good lay" (*N,* p. 11) the usage environment is most important and the universal associations

---

[3] *Literary Essays of Ezra Pound,* ed. T. S. Eliot (London: Faber and Faber, 1954), pp. 25, 33. Pound admits, of course, the prevalence of logopoeia in the late seventeenth and eighteenth centuries, though he probably underestimates its importance there. And of course he thought he detected it in Propertius, as his imitation of that poet shows.

[4] Pound, *Literary Essays,* p. 25. My italics.

attached to the words almost irrelevant, even misleading. In the latter case the reader must know what kind of people use these words in what kind of circumstances.

Auden's comic style depends almost entirely on the incongruity caused by jamming together usage associations ordinarily separated. The variety of possible clashes is enormous. "Incongruous" means our expectations are being rather violently upset ("delight," "amusement," "surprise" denote lesser upsets), and endless hypothetical upsets can be imagined. It is not saying much, then, to remark that all these fall into three classifications, but it is a helpful beginning. Verbal incongruities arise either from manner, matter, or tone of voice. That is, style may clash with style, subject with subject, either with the other, or the whole verbal object with the tone of voice uttering it. Within these general categories are an almost infinite variety of particular incongruous practices. Solemn subjects (theology) may be placed next to very dissimilar solemn subjects (botany). That will make comedy. So will a solemn subject placed next to a similar but unsolemn subject (Dame Kind, Coarse Old Party). Syntax can be made to clash with syntax, syntax with subject, syntax with diction, diction with diction, diction with subject. Sense can be played off against nonsense (neologisms, for instance), meter against subject, syntax, diction. Syllable sounds can clash with anything (funny sounds against solemn subjects, diction, syntax). Voice may clash with everything (certain tones of voice can contrast ludicrously with any kind of subject, syntax, diction). Since any attempt to define and illustrate even a large sampling of Auden's comic devices would surely be stupefying, I will instead suggest the kind of thing he does and examine and illustrate only a few of his more obvious practices.

By somehow making incongruous either his manner, his matter, or both, Auden mocks each. His most general comic procedure, then, should probably be labeled "mockery." Subject and style are burlesqued, caricatured, parodied. Mimicry is therefore one of his great talents. He copies familiar usage, but out of context to make it absurd. Yet, as I have said before, the comic style does not usually satirize; it celebrates. While he may mock the thing celebrated, himself as celebrator, the notion of celebrating, and the manner of celebration, in the end his praise is genuine and his mockery a gesture of love. His dominant form, then, (if a construction with no rules can be called a "form") is the ode, the poem of praise; and sometimes mockery begins by making the form itself incongruous. The ode's conventional trappings, used ordinarily for high solemn occasions, will be placed in absurdly unfamiliar surroundings. Thus the opening invocation in "Dame Kind" ("Steatopygous, sow dugged and owl headed," *HC*, p. 53) and the epic parenthesis in "Winds" ("Across what brigs of dread, / Down what gloomy galleries . . . ," *SA*, p. 11) turn foolish in unlikely contexts, as of course do the inverted syntax, high-flown diction, and other features of grand-manner epopee. So too Auden parodies pastorals, epics, love songs, ballads, and (a favorite) the nineteenth-century meditative poem. Stuffed with inappropriate style or subject, all these forms are made to look benignly absurd. But if these are poetic "forms," their conventions are not very rigid, calling usually for only a certain type of subject, syntax, and diction. Auden's mockery of such things will show up abundantly throughout subsequent discussion and need not be given special examination here. But in some poems he mocks much more definite poetic forms. In " 'The Truest Poetry Is the Most Feigning' " (*SA*, p. 44) or "Metalogue to *The Magic Flute*" (*HC*, p. 69), for example, he laughs at a very rigid formal convention, the rhyme scheme of heroic couplets. The unintentional absurdity of excess rhyme is made intentional. Rhymes are raucously flaunted and burdened with the silliness of unlike subjects and awkward sounds. "Do" is forced to rhyme with "hullabaloo," "love me" with "cosí-cosí," "sorts" with "thoughts," "lily-breasted" with "lion-chested" (*SA*, pp. 44–45), "enjoys" with "twelve-tone Boys," "knees" with "*B*'s," "barbaric dark" with "Bronze-Age Matriarch," "be" with "Ph.D," "feel" with "glockenspiel," and so on (*HC*, pp. 70–71). In a larger sense these mocked couplets are only part of Auden's practice of mocking any sort of rhyme. In a variety of poems he laughs at the custom of ending lines with similar sounds by forcing together dissimilar sounds or similar sounds with incongruous meanings: "sea" and "agape," "jobs" and "Hobbes" (*SA*, p. 23), "mysterious" and *"partibus infidelibus"* (*SA*, p. 55), "sense has jelled" and "jet-or-prop-propelled," "infra dig" and *"analeptic swig"* (*AH*, pp. 51, 53).

Among its other functions, rhyme organizes with its repeated sounds, and Auden likes to parody organizational devices, logical as well as auditory. He especially enjoys playing with topic sentences, purpose statements, transitional locutions, and all the special devices that help hold verbal collections together. Both philosophical and rhetorical structure can be made absurd by tinkering with these vital parts. Sometimes they

turn comic simply by being shoved ingenuously forward, as though some
novice were proudly displaying his skill by calling attention to the
ponderous link pins joining his compositional chunks. They stick out
most crudely in the odes, where the speaker, waggishly pretending to
write an earnest celebration, organizes his speech around an awkward list
of praiseworthy attributes. It is as though he had originally sat down,
pencil thoughtfully in mouth, to think up a list of praiseworthy items,
and were now transferring them mechanically to verse. As part of the
joke, the organizational list not only will contain wildly clashing subjects,
but will itself be a logical mess, a mixed-up collection of unsorted items,
arranged neither by chronology nor by levels of importance, nor by anything else. "Streams" is a particularly good example. The structural list of
mock-attributes juts out with more than usual logical disarray, as though
a tyro organizer had, blindfolded, pulled his absurd bunch of attributes
one by one out of a bag. The following sentences introduce, each for
rhetorical development, the seven virtues of streams: "But you in your
bearing are always immaculate," "Nobody suspects you of mocking him,"
"nowhere are you disliked," "At home in all sections," "How could we
love the absent one if you did not keep / Coming from a distance,"
"Growth cannot add to your song," "And not even man can spoil you"
(SA, pp. 28–29). Their unexpected triviality and irrelevance make these
unsorted items especially incongruous. Who would think of streams as
particularly beneficial because separated lovers can sail up them? But the
abruptness of the transitions from one subject to its unlike next is also
comic. By definition an "abrupt" transition is an incongruous one, indicating usually that dissimilar subjects have been jammed together. Abruptness probably cannot be illustrated out of the context that makes something abrupt, but a glance at "Woods" (SA, p. 14) or "Lakes" (SA, p.
11) will show particularly well what I mean. Nearly every stanza in
"Woods" is one item in a list of definitions and features to be praised, and
the connections between these items have been purposely left out to make
the whole panegyric proceed by a series of awkward jerks. "Lakes" is
similar. The poem might well have been titled "Some Beneficial Attributes of Lakes," since most stanza breaks mark off the attributes. Without
smooth transitions between the bald list of items the whole poem moves
forward by comic stops and starts. If these large devices cannot be
conveniently illustrated, their incongruous effects can be shown in miniature in smaller lists that work the same way. For instance:

> Nobody I know would like to be buried
>   with a silver cocktail shaker,
> a transistor radio and a strangled
>   daily help. . . .
>   (*AH*, p. 5)

Abruptness can be emphasized in these small units too:

> Winds make weather; weather
> Is what nasty people are
>   Nasty about and the nice
> Show a common joy in observing. . . .
>   (*SA*, p. 11)

This last example reveals another common feature of the Auden comic list. Each item is generally a definition, defining the essence or the virtue of the thing praised. But now Auden is mocking his own lifelong defining habits. Again comedy arises from the unexpected irrelevance or triviality or farfetchedness of the subject itself, or its definition. Islands are "the shore / Of a lake turned inside out" (*SA*, p. 24); Winds "what nasty people are / Nasty about" (*SA*, p. 11); Woods "a hotel / That wants no details and surrenders none" (*SA*, p. 14); Lakes the space "an average father, walking slowly," can "circumvent . . . in an afternoon" or a body of water "any healthy mother [can] . . . halloo the children / Back to her bedtime from their games across" (*SA*, p. 20). All these cases upset the way definitions, lists, and structural guideposts are ordinarily used. Their new usage is unexpected, incongruous, comic.

One of Auden's most common practices shows up in these tongue-in-cheek definitions—something that might be called "attributed absurdity." The speaker first attributes absurd behavior to somebody else (whether justly or not makes no difference), and then mimics his victim's alleged silliness. The speaker himself acts foolishly, but the person he imitates is the fool. This is a familiar comic practice, in and out of literature, and most audiences can immediately distinguish between a mimic's behavior and that of his alleged victim, and easily recognize which foolishness genuinely belongs to the victim and which functions simply as the mimic's attack or commentary on him. Yet the analysis of such subtleties requires rather elaborate exposition. But one characteristic of Auden's practice can be set down immediately. His mimicry is seldom contemptuous. The mimicry of attributed absurdity can produce vicious satire, since its allegations may be completely false (and are more insulting if they are), and since, implicit rather than explicit, they are almost impossible to refute or deny. The abused victim, whose real behavior may not resemble the mimic's at all, can only grapple ineffectually with implications, and any earnest refutation ("I never *did* speak in that absurd fashion") will only make him appear sillier. But since Auden generally loves rather than hates, abuses, or contemns, his mimicry of absurd attributes ultimately implies, usually, affection. His mockery can be very complicated therefore—carrying approval and disapproval at the same time, and various degrees of each. "The Duet" is a good preliminary example because it is least complicated. Here the primary speaker not only attributes absurdity by mimicking others, but two others actually appear in person to speak the styles being mimicked. All three are absurd, but in slightly different ways. The tragic view of life, pompous, pretentious, and shortsighted, shows through the preposterous style of an agonized rich lady: *"The spreading ache bechills the rampant glow"* (N, p. 54). Her foil, the scrunty beggar, celebrates life's blessedness no less absurdly:

> *The windows have opened, a royal wine*
> *Is poured out for the subtle pudding,*
> *Light industry is humming in the wood. . . .*
> (N, p. 55)

The narrator, the main comic speaker, is absurd too: "For still his scrannel musicmaking / In tipsy joy across the gliddered lake" (N, p. 54). In context these comic styles are slightly different. Auden's approval shows in the beggar's joyously ludicrous speech, while the lady's slightly less forgivable style carries his mild disapproval. But the narrator himself, self-consciously mocking his own utterances, shows by his manner that if the mocked are foolish so is the mocker—for all men are ultimately absurd, though some are more acceptable than others.

"The Duet" has three speakers. In most comic poems a single speaker takes all the voices himself. Victims do not display their own absurdity. Instead a speaker *attributes* foolishness to them by his mimicry, and, by passing rapidly back and forth from one voice to another, he can register approval and disapproval of both victims and himself. "Under Sirius" is a simple case of this. The victim here is a poet, Fortunatas. Fortunatas never speaks, but many usage incongruities in the poem are caused by the speaker's switching back and forth from his own voice to the mimicked voice of Fortunatas. Fortunatas' style, the speaker implies, is an inept mixture of pedestrian cliché and overblown preciosities, and his mimicry holds these out fastidiously at arm's length, as though each were almost unbelievably banal and pretentious. "Only you, good Lord, would use such tasteless inelegancies and gauche locutions," the speaker's manner implies; "I mimic these to show the comedy of your behavior." For instance:

> All day, you tell us, you wish
> Some earthquake would *astonish*
> Or the *wind of the Comforter's wing*
> Unlock the prisons and *translate*
> The slipshod gathering.

My italics simply heighten attributions the speaker would not deign to emphasize so crudely. He continues with amusement,

> . . . And last night, you say, you dreamed of that bright blue morning,
>
> . . . .
>
> When, serene in their ivory vessels
> The three wise Maries come,
> Sossing through seamless waters, piloted in
> By sea-horse and fluent dolphin. . . .
>
> (*N*, p. 39)

Fortunatas is flattened under the crush of this attributed absurdity. Here is your own preposterous manner, the speaker implies: "bright blue morning," a laughably low-brow cliché; "three wise Maries," your search for the *mot juste* ending ineptly with this stock epithet; "Sossing," your sudden ridiculous leap to the rare; "seamless waters," now a lunge toward fine writing; "piloted in," an abysmal tumble to the breezy colloquial; "fluent dolphin," up again to the absurdly triumphant *bon mot*. And yet throughout, drawing back into his own voice, the speaker tempers disapproval with his own clownish manner. Laughter at Fortunatas is so nearly balanced by laughter at himself that his mimicry is mostly affectionate. "Look what fools we both are," the performance implies. Disapproval then, the degree of satire, is controlled by the balance between the speaker's own absurdity and that of the victim he mimics.

Usually the balance is about equal, but not always. The individual mimicked in "A Household" is, in the balance, genuinely unpleasant, and the speaker's mimicry helps establish this. Even before the victim's unsavory domestic shambles appear, the speaker attributes foolishness to him by copying his clichéd speech. He is, we are made to understand, the worst sort of parental bore, habitually lapsing into sentimental stories

> . . . of that young scamp his heir,
> Of . . . thrashings
> Endured without a sound to save a chum;
>
> Or [of] . . .
> His saintly mother . . .
> A grand old lady pouring out the tea.
> (N, p. 52)

Though no disapproval is explicit in this, it is implicit in the mimicry. "Scamp," "chum," "saintly mother," and "grand old lady" are absurd locutions attributed to the man disapproved. "We know what to think of men who speak like *that*," the speaker implies. Whether the victim really speaks that way is irrelevant. By claiming he does, the speaker scoffs at him. "Your character is so rotten," the speaker says in effect, "I can reveal it by attributing to you a corrupt style, whatever your real one is."

Because their techniques are so clear, "The Duet," "Under Sirius," and "A Household" are good illustrations of how mimicking speakers make comedy out of attributed absurdity. But they do not begin to indicate the enormous scope and subtlety of Auden's practice. These three poems have clearly visible victims, but most do not. Since Auden is usually far less interested in attacking someone than in making comedy out of usage, victims materialize, when they do, almost inadvertently. If there can be no "usage" without a "user," when speakers draw usage from a dozen areas, a dozen implied *users* automatically spring into existence willy-nilly. Sometimes Auden may wish to laugh at these. But more often he wants only their incongruous language, not the people who speak it. His widespread mimicry, then, is much less an indication of his satirical and moral judgment about the mocked stylist than a symptom of his fascination with language. His comic speakers simply take an endless self-consciousness delight in usage variety. As a result, they might be described as never for long speaking in anything that could be called voices of their own. Instead, they constantly flicker back and forth from a parody of one voice to a parody of another. Yet in a sense it would be more accurate to call these parodied voices their "own." Each speaker's native voice is simply a collection of mimicked voices and styles, each composed of borrowed special usage levels and contexts.

The variety of borrowings is very large, from the commonest street slang to the most pompous formality. Words like "mawk" and "hooey" will share space with locutions like "politically numinous" and "immanent / virtue" (*AH*, pp. 9, 11). Among such words as "protocol," "supererogatory" and "crenellated" will almost always be something on the level of "foul-mouth gets the cold / shoulder" (*AH*, p. 29). Slang phrases like "cheesy literature," "corny dramas" (*N*, p. 43), "has the hots," "Playing hard to get" (*N*, p. 18), "great-great-grandmother who got laid" (*AH*, p. 5) appear regularly among the most high-brow diction. And there are occasional vogue words such as "proof positive" (Mac-Neice's works "from *Poems* to *The Burning Perch* offer proof positive," *AH*, p. 10), the slogan of a well-known television tooth paste commercial, repeated in the 1960's until it became a national household joke. Diction is frequently played off against syntax and both are played off against subject matter. In "Woods" much of the comedy comes from a parody of eighteenth-century syntax: "But, flabbergasted, fled the useful flame . . . / And to abhor the licence of the grove . . . / Now here, now there, some loosened element" (*SA*, pp. 14–15). Auden's pervasive oratorical syntax, by nature formal, is in fact made incongruous almost everywhere in his comic poems. "Dame Kind" is only an extreme case of a widespread practice:

> Even there, as your blushes invoke its Guardian
> (whose true invocable
> Name is singular for each true heart
> and false to tell)
> To sacre your courtship. . . .
> (*HC*, p. 55)

Whole poems go on like this, if more mildly, while in its smallest manifestation the same kind of manner-matter contrast creates euphemistic epithets—or the reverse. In the eighteenth century, euphemism gave dignity to the vulgar. Today, when such misplaced innocence seems laughable, the incongruous distance between elegant words and their inelegant referents is comical rather than dignified: "venereal act" (*N*, p. 22), "spasmodic peck" (typing, *N*, p. 24), "lacustrine atmosphere" (*SA*,

p. 20), "amniotic mere" (womb, *SA*, p. 21), "Primal Scene" (sex act), "anomolous duchy" (mutual love, *HC*, p. 54), "ur-act of making" (bowel movement, *AH*, p. 17), "cold hydropathy" (cold bath, *AH*, p. 19), "filter-passing predator" (virus, *AH*, p. 7). The reverse euphemism —low term, high subject—produces the same effect: "smidge / of nitrogen" (human body, *AH*, p. 7), "Mrs. Nature" (*SA*, p. 28), "Ovid's charmer" (Cupid), "old grim She" (Dame Kind, *SA*, p. 26), "our First Dad" (Adam, *SA*, p. 11).

But manner and matter need not be unlike to make usage incongruity. Two highly dissimilar subjects alone will serve as well. Their incongruity can arise from at least two sources. First, since many subjects are ordinarily almost exclusively connected to certain usage environments, outside of these they will appear comical. Second, each subject, in its native usage context, will usually have some inherent solemnity level attached to it. Similar subjects with different solemnity levels will seem comic if placed side by side. So will wildly dissimilar subjects, whatever their usual degree of solemnity. "Agape," for instance, a fugitive from theological discourse, is usually a solemn matter. "Female pelvis," on the other hand, though a sober subject in medical environments perhaps, carries with it thoroughly unsolemn associations from the world of sexual humor. Removed from native context and set side by side, the incongruity of both their dissimilar subjects and their dissimilar solemnity levels makes them comic:

> Old saints on millstones float with cats
> > To islands out at sea,
> Whereon no female pelvis can
> > Threaten their agape.
> >   (*SA*, p. 23)

This is only an obvious example of one of Auden's most constant practices. His speakers are forever jamming together words ordinarily used only in very special environments, with widely varying degrees of solemnity. Dozens of highly technical terms and phrases are scattered throughout the poems: "gallery-grave" (anthropology), "carbon clock" (physics, *AH*, p. 3), "clone" (zoology), "Arachnids" (zoology, *AH*, p. 6), "nanosecond" (physics), "c.c." (chemistry), "giga" (physics, *AH*, p. 7), "Pliocene" (geology), "arthropod," "teleost" (zoology, *SA*, p. 11), "tarn," "lacustrine" (geography, *SA*, pp. 19, 20), "Moraine, pot, oxbow, glint, sink, crater, piedmont, dimple" (*SA*, p. 22), "marls," "megalith," "armigers" (*SA,* pp. 28, 30), and so on. Wrenched from their verbal homes and thrown among alien fellows, each of these loses dignity and becomes incongruous and comic. When the jargon of psychology breaks foolishly into a strange verbal world in "Ischia," the high solemnity of both collapses:

> Changes of heart should also occasion song, like his
> Who, turning back from the crusaders' harbour, broke
> With our aggressive habit
> Once and for all and was the first
> To see all penniless creatures as his siblings. . . .
>
> (*N,* p. 21)

The same thing happens when the terminology of natural science is thrust absurdly into the vocabulary of informal chatter in "Thanksgiving for a Habitat":

> . . . unless at the nod
> of some jittery commander
>
> I be translated in a nano-second
> to a c.c. of poisonous nothing
> in a giga-death. . . .
> (*AH,* p. 7)

In "Winds" the nomenclature of geology and zoology intrudes awkwardly into the unscientific vocabulary of an impassioned and inflated ode:

> Recall to Metropolis
> That Pliocene Friday when,
> At His holy insufflation
> (Had He picked a teleost
> Or an arthropod to inspire,
> Would our death also have come?). . . .
> (*SA,* p. 11)

"Teleost" and "arthropod" may be sober words in their proper zoological usage-world, but cast adrift among the high-literary vocabulary of heroic poetry, they are absurd. In the same way, the Latin classifications of familiar animals often strike the layman as ridiculous. There are, for instance, "Arachnids" in Auden's garden (*AH,* p. 6) and (at the opposite usage level) "creepy-crawlies" in his cellar, (*AH,* p. 14).

Even most educated readers will not know the precise meaning of "teleost," "arthropod," and "arachnid." Everyday terms for the zoologist, these hover on the edge of the nonsensical for the average man, who knows they are not really nonsense inventions, but probably knows little more. But if they are not neologisms, Auden vigorously exploits what neologistic potential they have. The neologism is surely the Ideal Form of incongruous usage, the paradigm of all diction floundering foolishly out of its native territory. At home in no linguistic environment, it is always out of place. Strictly speaking there may be no full-blooded neologisms in Auden's poetry, but a great many rare and archaic words might as well be. They produce the same effect. Paradoxically, these esoteric terms can have a scrupulously correct meaning and be totally inappropriate at the same time. Their meaning is all right, their usage all wrong. It is as though some glint-eyed poet, driven mad in his fanatical search for the *mot juste,* had discovered words with meanings *juste* beyond his wildest dreams, but in their almost pristine desuetude, absolutely unintelligible to anyone. Since parody, mimicry, and caricature move in the direction of nonsense anyway as they become more extreme and farcical, sometimes Auden's neologistic discoveries can be considered the final glory of passages already working their clowning way more splendidly closer to gibberish. "Music Is International," for instance, a poem full of verbal high jinks, moves ever more sluggishly forward through a thickening morass of Latinate diction to sink finally into sheer nonsense (for anyone without the unabridged *Oxford English Dictionary*):

> But what is our hope
>   As with ostentatious rightness
> These gratuitous sounds like water and light
>   Bless the Republic? Do they sponsor
> In us the mornes and motted mammelons,
>   The sharp streams and sottering springs of
> A commuter's wish, where each frescade rings
>   With melodious booing and hooing . . . ?
> (*N*, p. 64)

Auden never again equals the ingenuous audacity of that last nonsensical question, but elsewhere his speakers, in mock innocence, plunge gleefully forward through brief comical patches of foggy meaning. "On the mountain," we are earnestly informed in "Under Sirius," "the baltering torrent

[has] / Shrunk to a soodling thread" (N, p. 39). "Serenade" opens with the bold statement that

> On and on and on
> The forthright catadoup
> Shouts at the stone-deaf stone. . . .
>   (N, p. 16)

In *Nones* and later volumes poems are liberally sprinkled with words like "faffling," "dedolent," "moskered," "mornes," "motted," "deasil," "widdershins," "fermatas," "connurbation," "routiers," "ubity," "dowly," "cloop," "depatical," and "olamic." In his Austrian house, Auden tells us, are "the very / best [dictionaries] money can buy" (AH, p. 8). From the more esoteric of their entries have come some of the least used words ever to appear in poetry—or anywhere else. Set alongside their most used brethren these odd terms exhibit Auden's complete mastery of his comic medium. He has sailed to every corner of the usage world and brought back specimens from the antipodes.

In context, the practices isolated above generally overlap or operate simultaneously, and their variety is far greater than rough classifications can hope to indicate. Examination of a few longer passages, therefore, may help to show everything working at once. "Mundus et Infans" contains a particularly nice display of incongruous diction from specialized usage areas:

> Kicking his mother until she let go of his soul
> Has given him a healthy appetite: clearly, her rôle
>   In the New Order must be
> To supply and deliver his raw materials free;
>   Should there be any shortage,
> She will be held responsible; she also promises
> To show him all such attentions as befit his age.
>   Having dictated peace,
>
> With one fist clenched behind his head, heel drawn up to thigh,
> The cocky little ogre dozes off, ready,
>   Though, to take on the rest
> Of the world at the drop of a hat. . . .
>   (CP, pp. 72–73)

The basic incongruity here is between the infant subject and the adult language used to describe him. But smaller incongruities flourish endlessly in the diction. The most important words in the infant-description come from widely scattered special-usage contexts, and vary considerably in solemnity level:

> soul (theology, highly solemn)
>
> healthy appetite (here a parental cliché, used almost exclusively for bragging about robust children; usually mock-solemn, solemn for bores only)
>
> rôle (social psychology, solemn; descended to upper-middle-class cliché, also solemn)
>
> New Order (national politics or political journalism and public relations, solemn)
>
> Supply and deliver raw materials (economics, solemn)
>
> shortage (economics, journalism; solemn)
>
> held responsible (middle-class cliché, solemn)
>
> all such attentions as befit his age (eighteenth-century stilted, or twentieth-century imitation legal, idiom; very solemn)
>
> dictated peace (military, journalism; solemn)
>
> cocky little ogre (parental colloquialism; mock distaste, affectionate joking)
>
> take on the rest of the world (slang, humorous banter)
>
> drop of a hat (very tired middle-brow cliché, now probably always humorous).

My crude notations indicate only the most obvious usage features at work in the poem, but the sampling is representative. Each piece of special jargon, wrenched from its normal community of discourse, becomes assertively pretentious and absurd. Crowded together with alien subjects, each earnestly solemn usage turns mock-solemn, and its potential ludicrousness stands forth in relief. More damaging still, the neat insertion of specialized unsolemn locutions—the homey slang and breakfast table cliché, purposely banal—defeat whatever dignity is left in the normally staid usages, turning everything to comic mockery.

"In Praise of Limestone," one of Auden's comic masterpieces, is an even more complex collection of incongruities, many of them subtle and delicate and unobtrusive in this mildly funny poem:

> If it form the one landscape that we the inconstant ones
>   Are consistently homesick for, this is chiefly
> Because it dissolves in water. Mark these rounded slopes

With their surface fragrance of thyme and beneath
A secret system of caves and conduits; hear these springs
   That spurt out everywhere with a chuckle
Each filling a private pool for its fish and carving
   Its own little ravine whose cliffs entertain
The butterfly and the lizard; examine this region
   Of short distances and definite places:
What could be more like Mother or a fitter background
   For her son, for the nude young male who lounges
Against a rock displaying his dildo, never doubting
   That for all his faults he is loved, whose works are but
Extensions of his power to charm? From weathered outcrop
   To hill-top temple, from appearing waters to
Conspicuous fountains, from a wild to a formal vineyard,
   Are ingenious but short steps that a child's wish
To receive more attention than his brothers, whether
   By pleasing or teasing, can easily take.

Watch, then, the band of rivals as they climb up and down
   Their steep stone gennels in twos and threes, sometimes
Arm in arm, but never, thank God, in step; or engaged
   On the shady side of a square at midday in
Voluable discourse, knowing each other too well to think
   There are any important secrets, unable
To conceive a god whose temper-tantrums are moral
   And not to be pacified by a clever line
Or a good lay: for, accustomed to a stone that responds,
   They have never had to veil their faces in awe
Of a crater whose blazing fury could not be fixed;
   Adjusted to the local needs of valleys
Where everything can be touched or reached by walking,
   Their eyes have never looked into infinite space
Through the lattice-work of a nomad's comb; born lucky,
   Their legs have never encountered the fungi
And insects of the jungle, the monstrous forms and lives
   With which we have nothing, we like to hope, in common.
So, when one of them goes to the bad, the way his mind works
   Remains comprehensible: to become a pimp
Or deal in fake jewellery or ruin a fine tenor voice
   For effects that bring down the house could happen to all
But the best and the worst of us . . .
                      That is why, I suppose,

> The best and worst never stayed here long but sought
> Immoderate soils where the beauty was not so external,
> The light less public and the meaning of life
> Something more than a mad camp.
> (*N*, pp. 11, 12)

Formal, oratorical syntax and pastoral subject may lead the new reader innocently forward for as much as half a dozen lines here before the spoof becomes apparent. But the correct nicety of the subjunctive opening ("If it *form*"), the old-fashioned gentility of "*Mark* these rounded slopes," the pleasant "fragrance of thyme" from the world of Cuddy and Hobbinall: all this becomes highly suspect with the unlikely appearance of "spurt" and "chuckle." In this green and proper verbal landscape springs might decorously "flow," "bubble," or even "laugh," but hardly "spurt," or "chuckle." Though a species of flowing, "spurt" belongs to a usage world of awkward ejaculations, fingers on nozzles, severed arteries, and "chuckle" (though a kind of laughter), belongs in a usage neighborhood of nonpastoral heartiness, coarse pleasures, comic evils, salacious leers, crude delight. From here on, of course, the mild suspicion of purposeful usage dissonance becomes a fact. The genteel form, style, and subject turn mock beneath the coarse subjects ("displaying his dildo") and Rabelesian style ("a clever line / Or a good lay"). As the poem unfolds, the texture of incongruities becomes particularly complex and skillful:

thank God (informal, conversational; mock-solemn)

shady side (half-slang pun, never solemn)

temper-tantrums (parental conversation about offspring, either solemn or not)

clever line (mildly sexual slang, humorous)

good lay (pun: half sexual slang, half art form definition; the latter solemn, the former not)

blazing fury (fine-writing, literary cliché; solemn intention)

fixed (pun: half slang [bribe], either solemn or humorous; half technical term [accurately placed], solemn, formal)

adjusted to the local needs (psychology, economics, journalistic cliché; solemn)

infinite space (popular astronomy, physics; solemn)

goes to the bad (slang, humorous)

fake jewellery (colloquial, seldom solemn)

bring down the house (colloquial idiom, never solemn)

mad camp (three-way pun: mad cap [slang, humorous]; encamp-
    ment, solemn; camp [originally homosexual slang meaning exces-
    sively feminine, precious]).

Whatever their original soberness, jumbled together in "In Praise of
Limestone" all the unlike usages become mildly absurd, and they are the
very verbal stuff of the entire poem. There is a constant, persistent,
inveterate leap from level to level in nearly every line. The result is a
ceaseless expectation upset—the verbal liveliness that gives the charge to
this poetry.

Comedy is mild in "In Praise of Limestone," where most dissimilar
usages are not violently unexpected. At the other extreme, as though Poet
and Antipoet were wildly unlike, yet trapped in a single mad persona, is
"Dame Kind," with a verbal slapstick made up of extreme
incongruities:

> Steatopygous, sow-dugged
>   and owl-headed,
> To Whom—Whom else?—the first innocent blood
>   was formally shed
> By a chinned mammal that hard times
>   had turned carnivore,
> From Whom his first promiscuous orgy
>   begged a downpour
> To speed the body-building cereals
>   of a warmer age:
> Now who put *us,* we should like to know,
>   in *Her* manage?
>   (*HC,* p. 53)

Here of course, in a mocking ode to evolution, the "Dame Kind" sobri-
quet immediately sets the tone. "Dame," though a title of honor in some
quarters, reduces a gigantic cosmic force to the rather ignominious stature
of an elderly woman. Along with this goes the mild absurdity Americans
attach to honorific British titles, and the hint of unsolemn irreverence
"dame" carries from its colloquial usage. Diction clashes with itself,
syntax with syntax, syntax with diction, and every stylistic trick with
subject. The opening old-fashioned invocation, with its high-flown ornate
syntax, flounders preposterously in the awkward colloquial modernity of

its first prepositional phrase. "Whom else," a common twentieth-century colloquial idiom, is made purposely ludicrous by the uncolloquial attention to case ending. "Promiscuous orgy" deflates religion by mismatching manner and subject—the euphemistic high diction absurdly stilted, the sexual subject disastrously undignified. Even more incongruous, "steatopygous" clashes within itself. An esoteric discovery of the dictionary-haunting zealot, its own awkward sound and low subject destroy its solemn Greek etymology—and of course these clash with everything else as well, with the grave subject (Dame Kind) and with the formal syntax and diction. "Sow-dugged" further turns Mother Nature into a slatternly drab, and shares no linguistic locale, ordinarily, with such a near-technical term as "carnivore." And both words are equally far removed from the homey colloquialism of "downpour," or the linguistic world of Wonder Bread and Wheaties from which "body-building cereals" comes. This is Auden at his high comic pitch, and though "Dame Kind" is not his most philosophically profound performance, its linguistic exuberance is the sort that makes all the comic poems crackle.

"Pleasure Island," with a larger vision of life, is made out of the same linguistic stuff:

> As bosom, backside, crotch
> Or other sacred trophy is borne in triumph
>   Past his adoring by
> Souls he does not try to like; then, getting
>   Up, gives all to the wet
> Clasps of the sea or surrenders his scruples
>   To some great gross braying group
> That will be dumb till Fall.
>   (*N*, p. 25)

High style goes against low subject: "sacred trophy is borne in triumph" against "bosom, backside, crotch"; "gives all to the wet / Clasps of the sea" against an unspirited swim by some feckless writer, typewriter now abandoned to the irresistible attraction of enervating beach and frivolous party. Diction and syntax belong to the world of heroes and their mighty actions, trophies for mammoth triumphs of holy intent, epic srugles with the sea, monumental drinking bouts. But the subject is weak-willed modern man, succumbing to seductions of the ordinary.

Linked with strong feelings of love, similar incongruous usage creates the mockery in "Streams," an ode that praises water by parodying nature poetry (the procedure of all the "Bucolics"). The opening stanza waggishly celebrates water (dashing and loitering), fastidiously separates it from its less charming companion elements ("Air is boastful at times, earth slovenly, fire rude"), and isolates its list of attributes for praising. One of these shows the prevailing comic practice:

> How could we love the absent one if you did not keep
> Coming from a distance, or quite directly assist,
>   As when past Iseult's tower you floated
> The willow pash-notes of wanted Tristram?
>
> *(SA,* p. 29)

The mock solemnity of the exclamatory question, the epic heroes turned billet-doux writers, the awkwardly formal syntax, the mild euphemisms ("absent one," "wanted Tristram") all clash with each other and with that single piece of diction from a completely anomalous usage world, "pash-notes." But the speaker in "Streams" genuinely admires streams, and his love clearly shows. When love becomes stronger yet, comedy diminishes, but even at its comic mildest, as in "Ischia," Auden's verbal texture is fashioned from the same sort of incongruities that riot in "Dame Kind":

> . . . how gently you train us to see
>   Things and men in perspective
>
> . . . .
>
> Noble are the plans of the shirt-sleeved engineer,
> . . . What design could have washed
>   With such delicate yellows
> And pinks and greens your fishing ports
>
> That lean against ample Epomeo, holding on
> To the rigid folds of her skirts? The boiling springs
>   Which betray her secret fever
> Make limber the gout-stiffened joint
> And improve the venereal act. . . .
>
> *(N,* p. 21).

Irony just barely keeps the love from becoming sentimental here. Manner and matter differ only enough to make the thing loved slightly absurd. The formal rhetorical question ends incongruously in an image of female dress, "ample Epomeo" makes a thick-tongued funny sound, the mundane "shirt-sleeved engineer" is not quite at home in this linguistic world of literary diction and Italian subject, despite his "noble" plans. The island is genuinely lovely, the speaker is saying, but slightly preposterous too:

> Suddenly there, Vesuvius,
>   Looming across the bright bland bay
>
> Like a massive family pudding. . . .
>   (N, p. 22)

As the travel folder prose goes ineptly awry in the midst of its best literary effusions, the speaker's cry of affectionate delight is properly tempered by his own absurdity, and by that of his world, and with this masterful control Auden makes one of his best comic poems.

One final point about comic style: the sounding voice is everything in these comic poems, for certain pitches and pauses, certain knowing stresses, are by themselves comic gestures, regardless of what words these tones give shape to. If incongruity can arise from a clash between manner and matter, it can arise also from the distance between either and the sounding voice. Recited one way the lines of Lear and Hamlet, anguished and meditative, can exalt us to tears, but recited differently, without a word altered, the same lines can crumple us with laughter. Once the mocking voice begins, nothing can stand solemnly before it. In the silence of print we need some preliminary hints and a few subsequent jogs to make us hear the right voice and sustain it. But the signal given, by rhythms, diction, subject—or whatever—the comic voice begins, and after that the writer's task is easier. Everything will be made comic by that voice. The speaker need only pause with fastidious distaste on such harmless locutions as "healthy appetite" or "co-operate," as he does in "Mundus et Infans," and at once these innocents stand exposed as embarrassing clichés or vogue banalities. We blush to recall our own naïve use of them. Let the reader examine the voice he hears in the opening stanza of "Grub First, Then Ethics":

> Should the shade of Plato
>   visit us, anxious to know
> how *anthropos* is, we could say to him: "Well,
>   we can read to ourselves, our use
> of holy numbers would shock you, and a poet
>   may lament—where is Telford

whose bridged canals are still a Shropshire glory,
   where Muir who on a Douglas spruce
rode out a storm and called an earthquake noble. . . .

                        (*AH*, p. 23)

Note how important is the *pronunciation* of "Well"—a key word that sets off the right voice for the rest of the poem. Note too the melody and tone color demanded by the clause "we can read to ourselves." The sound of the voice alone means mock matter-of-fact innocence. The mock-portentous pause after "may lament" announces the forthcoming absurd examples, their trivial irrelevance to be pointedly missed by the sounding voice, delivering them in the earnest tones of a naïve respondent eager to inform and celebrate. *Sounds* have appropriate usage contexts, as do subjects, diction, syntax, and the like. The voice sounds in Auden's comic poems, clashing with the voice sounds ordinarily associated with the manner and matter at hand, turn all to comedy. As in all poetry, voice sounds and silent print lift each other by the bootstraps. Print creates voice; voice gives meaning to print.

IV

Whatever value posterity assigns to the skills examined in this chapter, Auden's success in making comic poems out of usage specialties is unsurpassed. But if these skills may be judged an important innovation in the future, as I have suggested, they have a serious genetic weakness that puts their future in doubt. They may literally fade from sight before posterity arrives to judge them. The danger is that usage associations are the most ephemeral of all language properties. This is the main reason why Pound could scarcely find a case of logopoeia before LaForgue. A hundred years from now, when usage contexts have inevitably changed, some of Auden's most dazzling skills will surely have vanished like the bright colors of Renaissance painting. What will then remain? An honest answer is not very heartening. If he could purposely aim at survival, a poet would surely do well to make art out of the most stable language resources available. Frost's idiom, for instance, is made up of frequently used words employed by all groups and types of people. Special usage associations make up a very small part of their meaning. (This is probably much less true of his syntax.) His language, then, will probably affect our descendants much as it does us. The songs of Blake and much of Herrick seem to have this kind of durability too. At the other extreme, the grand manner has also been a stable usage, if an exclusively literary one. Having survived for at least four hundred years, the traditional elevated idiom of English poetry, despite its unfashionableness in some quarters today, may well remain a common language for centuries to come, if future readers and writers continue to grow up amid the literary heritage stretching now from Shakespeare at least through Yeats. But the work of past masters of logopoeia (Pope, for instance?) who relied heavily on usage subtleties in their art is considerably dimmed today. Much of their skill and verbal liveliness, and therefore message, goes almost unrecognized except by antiquarians who have learned to live vicariously in their verbal world. The schoolboy a hundred years from now may have to consult a footnoted gloss to find out how to react to "a clever line / Or a good lay" (N, p. 11). What will he make of a far more subtle passage such as this?

> . . . laid out in exquisite splodges
> Like a Chinese poem, while, near enough, a real darling
> Is cooking a delicious lunch. . . .
> (SA, p. 19)

Will he respond as we do to the delicately handled usage complexities in "exquisite," "splodges," "real darling," "delicious lunch"? Can he know that the commas around "near enough" signal us to pronounce those ordinarily innocuous words in a mimicking voice that *today* denotes comic mockery? The prognosis is rather gloomy. And these lines from "Mountains" are not one of Auden's minor efforts but from one of his very best poems, and they are typical of the language in all his finest work. The reader two hundred years from now may wonder, as we do of Cowley, where all the brightness once lay. But such speculations do not confirm the evaluations of Auden's contemporary detractors, or in fact imply anything about value judgments. Fond folk wisdom notwithstanding, time is really not that allegedly sensitive critic, separating the trivial from the great. Shapeless igneous lumps last longest, while Phidias' famous ivories, Callimachus' handiwork, and even golden birds soon turn to dust. No magical fate protects "the best." An author can perish amid the trivial social hazards of a smoldering Carthage library, just as the recent departure of classical education—another mundane accident—will soon send all the seemingly immortal Greek and Latin writers to the dust bin. Auden brings to a very high perfection a verbal art made from the most fragile property of language. If Yeats and Frost carve their poems from more durable material, that is their luck, not a measure of relative worth. And mutability is a chancy thing at best. In our computer age, with mathematical language proliferating and "communications" only beginning its dizzy cultural revolution, some cataclysmic and unforseen linguistic change may suddenly make Frost's common usages as queer as Skelton's and Yeats' grandiloquence as archaic as Spenser's—or turn the printed word into a silent sign for the eye alone and end poetry altogether.

Meanwhile, Auden's comic poems remain, and, with a sampling of their verbal machinery completed, I will conclude by looking briefly at two poems in their entirety, to indicate how the whole poem produces its meaning, manner and matter working together to carry the same message. First, "The Willow-Wren and the Stare," one of Auden's finest and most moving comic poems. Travestied and genuine pastoral tradition join here as Auden surrounds wooing swain and fair maiden with the rustic innocence of pliant Nature—and all under the scrutiny of her murky-minded offspring, the willow-wren. Incongruously silhouetted against this antique poetic drop scene, Auden's lover stands out as conspicuously modern, muddle-headed, and absurd. His bewildering failure to understand his own mixed motives and half-grasped insights contrasts with the observant and perspicacious stare, wiser than he by far. Auden's control is flawless. As the poem begins, a parodied love song displays the smitten wooer's fatuous love:

> "Dearest of my dear,
> More lively than these waters chortling
>   As they leap the dam,
> My sweetest duck, my precious goose,
>   My white lascivious lamb."

The lover's absurdly mixed usage reflects the befuddled silliness of human nature. Never certain of what they are or mean, men stumble solemnly forward, their foggy insights tumbling forth in foolish speech, always comic, never more so than when they are in love. Beginning with his unapt "chortling," the lover sinks further beneath a helpless accretion of comic confusion. Appropriate only in a verbal milieu of raucous gusto, "chortling" falls a ludicrous misfit into the unsullied language environment of pastoral innocence. Worse yet, "lascivious lamb" soils completely the purity of its companion endearments, and as usage from the carnal world invades that of the tenderly innocent, the contradictory style itself shows men inept and fumbling, taking a wrong step every time. The person who utters these stylistic mixtures is as contradictory as his idiom. Without knowing it he is driven by both carnal desire and innocent love. Manner and matter join to carry the same meaning.

Floundering indecisively, but successfully forward, Auden's lover next rises to gloriously ludicrous heights by announcing the time for physical love in the pompous idiom of a long-gone pastoral tradition, complete with euphemistic circumlocution, periodic sentence, and perhaps even Renaissance sexual slang in "Wild Robin":

> "Hark! Wild Robin winds his horn
>   And as his notes require,
> Now our laughter-loving spirits
>   Must in awe retire
> And let their kinder partners,
>   Speechless with desire,
> Go in their holy selfishness,
>   Unfunny to the fire."

Man, speech-making animal to the end, must compulsively verbalize all his flapping confusion. Thus, recovered from his sexual trance, the lover once more mounts his podium to blunder forward in his most human act, speaking. Explaining, analyzing, describing, he sets off to thank his beloved and tell what love means to him. He rises at once to the very grandest high oratorical manner, then plunges equally fast into a fumbling mixture of high and low, solemn and silly. And as he sinks into this morass of incompatible verbiage, Auden ends the floundering incoherence with a rhythmical collapse:

> "I have heard the high good noises,
>   Promoted for an instant,
> Stood upon the shining outskirts
>   Of that Joy I thank
> For you, my dog and every goody."

Throughout, the willow-wren plays questioning straight man, while the enigmatic stare supplies riddling answers that are themselves models of Auden's art:

> *What does he want?* said the willow-wren;
> *Much too much,* said the stare.

Did he know what he meant? said the willow-wren
God only knows, said the stare.
(*SA*, pp. 41–42)

These lines provide explicit comment on the message implicit in the speaker's style. Motives are mixed, love impure, humans imperfect, and all this is good; life is a blessing. In commenting tersely on all this, the stare manages to make the paradoxes of his manner and his matter nearly identical. Men want "much too much," the stare says. The *matter* of this refers to the comic vision illustrated by the lover's action. Men are at once in two worlds, engaged in the solemn, baffling business of struggling along in the midst of life—loving, suffering, disappointed, filled with joy, confused. But at the same time they can stand off at a distance, watching themselves from the aspect of eternity. The incongruity between these two visions makes divided man a comic creature, just as does the incongruity of his speech, when it comes from two equally disparate usage worlds. Men want "much too much": man's reach exceeds his grasp. The *manner* is just as incongruous as its matter. While the lover watches himself from two different worlds, one near, the other far, his language comes from equally distant worlds. In a philosophical usage environment "much too much" carries the sober gravity appropriate to weighty intellectual comment on man's attempt to understand himself and his cosmos. But in its slang world "much too much" carries with it the salacious humor of this slang reference to seduction. The comic incongruities in both matter and manner ultimately mean the same thing. They carry, or more accurately *are*, Auden's comic vision. The second pair of lines works the same way. What does life mean? From one angle the answer is colloquial. "God only knows." This usage means "Who knows?"—an answer always funny, an unthinking shrug of mock weariness at incomprehensible life. In a solemn, philosophical usage situation, the line has a different meaning: "God only [alone] knows." From this angle, though still incomprehensible and uncertain, life is serious, but God alone knows what it is all about. Since he does know, we cannot entirely laugh off its meaning and cease trying to straighten out the puzzle of our self and our world. Life is funny and unimportant, serious and important.

"Mountains" is, if anything, an even finer poem, one of Auden's comic masterpieces, a work without a linguistic slip anywhere in a verbal performance of the most difficult sort. In "Mountains," as in all the "Bucolics," Auden writes ostensibly of nature, but never of nature as a sensuous thing. He describes not the three-dimensional affective object, or even his emotive reaction to that object, but his response to *ideas* about physical nature. The ideas produce an emotional reaction, however—love. Sometimes faint, it is nevertheless there, love for the *concept* of nature. Just as many people can genuinely love mankind (suffering, guilty, human) but feel indifferent about most individuals, so Auden (who also loves mankind in this way) can love Nature and be indifferent or even partly hostile to some specific manifestation of it. "Woods" may be warmly celebrated, but as for those actual, leafy, rough-barked vegetables, Auden approaches them like his eighteenth-century ancestors picnicking among the vernal spinneys and copses laid out by William Kent or Capability Brown. Safely munching a precooked repast served from silver cannisters resplendent on a lawn of white linen, they could gaze beyond indispensible servants at their opposite numbers, those charming rustics lucky to live every day among the unspoiled gratuities of Fond Nature. Auden differs from these faded elegants only in being completely aware of the artificiality of his indulgent Romanticism. He can therefore indulge and mock his indulgence at the same time. Occasionally, as in "Mountains," his mocking admiration of Nature remains a background while in the foreground he displays fastidious distaste for some special land form. The speaker pretends to hide his distaste. If it shows, he implies, we must forgive him for being just slightly inept at the panegyric skills. But this planned ineptness is intended to be transparent, an even more skillful and devastating exhibition. We are meant to note his imperfectly suppressed distaste, so that beneath the genteel pretense of celebration we can watch the speaker's gleeful and mischievous attack on mountains and their earnest devotees. Yet, in addition to all this, the mirthful destruction and personal dislike is at the same time laughed off as a private aberration of the speaker. His final judgment, beneath all these attitudinal layers, is that a mountain is an unruly, suspiciously unpleasant child of Old Mother Nature, who must be loved anyhow for its obstreperous self, but kept a sharp eye on too. The ode to mountains then is a teasing, mocking sort, expressing mostly a fake alarm, intended to show the speaker's willingness to love (but never to turn his back on) even this progeny of Gaea.

Organized about a list of attributes, the poem throughout assembles its affectionate mockery around a definition that makes mountains an allegorical feature in a moral landscape—"a wall / Between worse and better."

All the way through, mountains are playfully assumed to be abnormal—gauche and suspiciously sinister deviations from the tasteful, civilized decorum of normal landscapes. And the people who like them or (heaven forbid) actually *live* among the crags are certain therefore to be either quietly or outrageously monstrous. Normal civil men ("the Masters," "Madam," the "normal eye") shun mountains as they would the Holy Family sculpted from beer cans. In one sense, then, the entire poem is a good-natured spoofing attack on Romanticism, by a speaker who partly feigns and partly *is* the persona of an overly fastidious, civilized, eighteenth-century, urban man. He eschews enthusiasm, a taste for raw nature, and earnestness as the mark of crude Romantic bores, and his sly attack begins at once: "I know a retired dentist who only paints mountains." *That* for the romantic pretenses of mountains and their gawking celebrants, he implies. That dentists are somehow notoriously comic subjects, and those with artistic aspirations flatly ludicrous, is a matter Auden depends on our accepting. Similar reliances on other contemporary usage contexts are everywhere in the poem. As always, the speaker's diction throughout carries its heavy burden of logopoeia. The arch phrases, mock-portentous revelations, the jesting questions, and purposely mundane verbal borrowings all separate the rather elegant speaker from his subject. He holds mountains at arm's length, examining their curious oddity with a finicky intellectual analysis, as though they were slugs or dissected toads. When compelled to get down to cases and explain their properties and virtues, the speaker adopts, for mocking purposes, the manner of an Augustan city man, clearing his throat to begin definition and discussion. "Yes, yes—h'm—mountains," he says in effect, "a swollen topographical distortion; inhabited by peculiar races; and admired for their splendor, I am told, by poets of doubtful stability, questionable manners, and earnest enthusiasm." That is the ostensible substance of the speaker's pronouncement. Tongue in cheek he describes one sort of excessive mountain lover, the climbers, as

> . . . unsmiling parties,
> Clumping off at dawn in the gear of their mystery
>   For points up. . . .

The absurd usage incongruities in the speaker's report—the slang of "parties," "clumping," and "points up" clashing with the refined poesy of "dawn" and "mystery"—destroys the dignity of climbing. These climbing types, surely, "are a bit alarming," he ventures, careful to use a familiar colloquial idiom, whose understatement always is meant to be humorous and slighting. Mountain lovers disposed of as low-brow vulgarians, sadistic ogres ("beheading daisies with a stick"), or solemn clumpers, the speaker turns again to the land form itself. Perhaps mountains are "Another bourgeois invention like the piano," he speculates in a fake question, designed maliciously to abuse even while he denies the validity of such a conjecture. The landscape is described: "Red farms disappear" as though surreptitiously done away with, "Cows become sheep" (the work of witches?), a culture emerges with preposterous songs, hints of violence, exiled monsters, genetically suspicious natives—and so on. The whole masterly performance, with its range and complexity of devices, reaches without once faltering the comic heights of its climactic last stanza:

> To be sitting in privacy, like a cat
>   On the warm roof of a loft,
> Where the high-spirited son of some gloomy tarn
>   Comes sprinting down through a green croft,
>   Bright with flowers laid out in exquisite splodges
> Like a Chinese poem, while, near enough, a real darling
> Is cooking a delicious lunch, would keep me happy for
>   What? Five minutes? For an uncatlike
>   Creature who has gone wrong,
> Five minutes on even the nicest mountain
>   Is awfully long.
>   (*SA*, pp. 17–19)

"High-spirited son," "gloomy tarn," "sprinting," and all the rest of the flawlessly managed usage incongruities and absurdities demolish at once those enthusiastic and awful low-brows whose mountain-loving banalities are everywhere mimicked. At the same time, while the comic speech turns mountains into a foolish anomaly, it turns mockery on the speaker himself too. His whole preposterous performance, after all, unites him with mountains, climbers, and all the rest of Nature's absurdities. So the mockery of mountains and climbers and Nature is in reality fake. Come let us mock mockers, too, the speaker implies. And the whole poem becomes, as it was from the beginning, good-natured and affectionate—

love expressed indirectly through teasing, jibes, pretended distaste, wit, horseplay, and persiflage. Seen from a distance all existence appears absurd, benign, and blessed, something to be loved.

Both poems seem to me overflowing with things Auden has often been criticized for lacking. Humility is everywhere in both. Emotions flood everything—powerful good-natured love, coupled with a healthy delight in amiable foolishness. Both poems are "profound" enough to satisfy the most cheerless moral arbiter. Auden presents a large and sweeping vision of life seen from up close and afar at the same time. And in "Mountains," and in many others like it, there is a personal identity, a sincerity—whatever this illusive quality should be called. Most of these comic poems contain exactly what Joseph Warren Beach could not seem to find in an earlier Auden—"Auden" himself, not necessarily the real man without his poetic robes, the commuter between New York and Austria (no poetry shows us that sort of figure). But there is a familiar identity, a style—everything included in the terms "manner" and "matter." All these create the image of a Grand Persona that persists from poem to poem. His voice is a mimicking, parodying, comic voice, playing with a dozen voices, but it is all his as well, absolutely unmistakable, unique, consistent, unified, and it helps create the comic vision that persists equally from poem to poem, even when their quality varies as it must. This mercurial and elusive figure of the poet, pursuing for years a philosophical model of human existence he could accept, divided by his own temperamental predilections, disguised behind the facade of a score of different speakers—the figure of this poet surely comes forth in the comic poems as clearly as any poet does in his work. The intellectual search, the temperamental affinities, and the skills of his craft unite in a person we can easily call Auden.

Index